NEWSLETTERS FROM THE DESKTOP

NEWSLETTERS FROM THE DESKTOP

Designing Effective Publications with Your Computer

Roger C. Parker

VENTANA
PRESS

Newsletters from the Desktop: Designing Effective Publications with Your Computer

Copyright © 1990 Ventana Press

Library of Congress Cataloging-in-Publication Data

Parker, Roger C.
    Newsletters from the desktop: designing effective publications with
    your computer / by Roger C. Parker. — 1st ed.
       p.   cm.
    Includes bibliographical references
    ISBN: 0-940087-40-5
    1. Newsletters—Publishing—Data processing. 2. Desktop publishing. I. Title.
Z286.N46P37 1990
686.2'2544536   89-25071

Cover design: Southern Media Design & Production, Chapel Hill, NC

Book design: Karen Wysocki, Ventana Press

Desktop publishing: Pixel Plus, Chapel Hill, NC

Linotronic output: Azalea Typography, Durham, NC

Editorial Staff: Marion Laird, Terry Patrickis, Elizabeth Shoemaker

First Edition, First Printing

Printed in the United States of America

Ventana Press, Inc.
P.O. Box 2468
Chapel Hill, NC 27515
919/942-0220
919/942-1140 Fax

Limits of Liability and Disclaimer

ABOUT THE AUTHOR

Roger C. Parker is author of the highly acclaimed *Looking Good in Print: A Guide to Basic Design for Desktop Publishing*, *Desktop Publishing with WordPerfect*, and *The Makeover Book: 101 Design Solutions for Desktop Publishing*, published by Ventana Press. He has conducted numerous seminars and workshops on desktop publishing design, makeovers and newsletters. He is president of The Write Word, Inc., an advertising and marketing consulting firm based in Dover, NH.

The author may be reached at
The Write Word
466 Central Ave., Suite 3
Dover, NH 03820
603/742-9673

TRADEMARKS

DEDICATION

Newsletters from the Desktop is dedicated to conscientious newsletter editors everywhere who struggle to produce great publications in spite of limited resources and impossible, never-ending deadlines.

CONTENTS

INTRODUCTION

Of all the publishing formats, I've found the newsletter to be the most satisfying way for people who share common interests to exchange news and ideas.

Communicating information has become a vital part of our personal and professional lives. And newsletters play a major role in that process.

Desktop publishing technology makes newsletter production easier and faster than ever before. Formats can be as simple or complex as necessary. Circulation can be as low as 100 or as high as 1,000,000. Regardless of their shape, size or color, all newsletters are designed to serve their audience—allowing Persian cat fanciers to communicate with each other, small stereo stores to expand their markets, associations to grow, and corporations to build and maintain employee (and shareholder) morale.

The desktop publishing revolution started in the mid-1980s when the original Hewlett-Packard and Apple laser printers appeared on the scene, promising freedom from the frustrations and expense of conventional newsletter typesetting and paste-up. For the first time, an entire page of text and graphics could be quickly, economically and automatically created on the computer screen.

The revolution continued, with the appearance of Aldus Pagemaker for the Macintosh and Xerox Ventura Publisher for the IBM PC. In the years since, enthusiasm for newsletters has grown by leaps and bounds, as hardware and software have become more sophisticated, easier to use and less expensive.

The purpose of *Newsletters from the Desktop* is to help you make the most of your desktop publishing hardware and software. The power is already there, just waiting to be tapped. This book shows you how to use it to build an effective, attractive, readable newsletter.

The suggestions and examples offered aren't precise formulas you must follow. Rather, they present a range of options to choose from in planning and producing your newsletter. Successful newsletters don't materialize from a magic recipe; they're built through a process of trial and error, experimentation and refinement, using tried-and-true design principles and tools adapted to your particular publication.

Who Needs This Book?

You may be launching your association's first newsletter, or you may have been told that your mission—should you agree to accept it, of course—is to "spruce up" an existing newsletter. (Improving the appearance of an existing newsletter and at the same time preserving its original spirit and identity can be an enormous challenge.) In either case, this book is for you.

Newsletters from the Desktop is also for you if you're new to computers and are looking for a survey of the basics of desktop publishing and advanced word processing. The book doesn't focus on the specifics of operating desktop publishing programs, but instead shows what the tools can produce. However, you'll find a wealth of information to help you choose the right computer hardware and software.

What's Inside?

Chapters 1 through 8 describe the six main components of your newsletter design or redesign. You'll see how size, shape, position and color can work together to achieve unity, contrast, consistency and readability.

Planning and identifying your goals and limitations are addressed in Chapter 2. The six building blocks of newsletter design—grids, nameplates, body copy, reader cues, visuals and graphic accents—are covered in Chapters 3 through 8.

In Chapter 9, you'll learn how to pull it all together to successfully integrate your newsletter's design with the specific text and visuals that comprise each issue.

Chapter 10 translates theory into reality, with case-study examinations of the design process—analyzing, choosing and refining. In Chapter 10, you can look over the graphic artists' shoulders as they design a newsletter and produce the first issue.

"The Newsletter Gallery" in Chapter 11 showcases some well-designed newsletters. They illustrate the importance of planning and integrating all the design components.

In Appendices A, B and C, you'll take a closer look at hardware and software equipment options, including Macintosh versus IBM, various combinations and high-resolution phototypesetting.

The glossary provides concise definitions of typographic and design terms mentioned throughout the book, and the bibliography lists many sources for books, magazines and seminars for your continuing self-education.

My overall goal in writing *Newsletters from the Desktop* was not only to show how important good design is to a newsletter's success, but also to demystify the sometimes-intimidating aspects of design. This book shows you that designing or redesigning a newsletter can be a creative and fulfilling process.

Roger Parker
Dover, New Hampshire

CHAPTER ONE

WHAT'S INVOLVED

Newsletter publishers are one of the primary beneficiaries of the exciting desktop publishing revolution. Desktop-published newsletters are cost-effective and timely, unencumbered by many of the expenses, delays and frustrations faced in traditional newsletter publishing.

Work that used to take weeks now can be done in days. No more trips to the typesetter. No more hours hunched over a light table pasting up copy.

Relying on relatively inexpensive inkjet and laser printers, desktop publishing simplifies and expedites the production process. In short, it gives the newsletter publisher more time and resources to do other things, such as improving editorial quality or starting another newsletter!

Here's an example of why I'm so enthusiastic about desktop-published newsletters. One of my first newsletter projects involved preparing a four-page bimonthly publication to describe new stereo components on display in a retail store.

Accordingly, the newsletter's design was based on photographs supported by headlines and subheads and set off by Scotch rules (parallel thick and thin lines).

Although attractive when printed, this design was a nightmare when last-minute changes were required (and, as newsletter editors know, last-minute changes are *always* needed). In the past whenever a sentence or paragraph on page 1 needed to be changed, all the headlines, subheads and body copy that followed had to be rearranged, then all the rules masked with white-out and new rules created. Changing a single sentence on page 1 necessitated hours of work.

What was a design nightmare in 1983 is simple and practical today, and promises to be even easier in the future. With most desktop publishing and word processing programs, pages 2, 3 and 4 automatically readjust to accommodate any changes on page 1. With many programs, text and graphic accents on pages 3 and 4 automatically move up or down in each column—or across to the next column—to compensate for changes made on earlier pages.

Page 1 changes can still cause damage on the following pages, but repairing this damage on the computer screen is far easier than manually moving blocks of text and redrawing rules in each column.

A MIXED BLESSING

In spite of all its contributions to speed and efficiency, desktop publishing isn't a cure-all. While this new technology has eliminated some of the hassles of traditional typesetting, it has created some new concerns.

Assembling electronic pages looks so simple when demonstrated by an experienced salesperson at a computer store or a trade show. The initial burst of enthusiasm is often followed by disappointment and frustration when the canned demonstration is over and you must actually do the work.

Desktop publishing is a tool, not a magic solution. Just as automatic transmissions simplify driving but don't replace the need for an alert, trained driver, desktop publishing alone does not an effective newsletter make. The hardware and software have to be properly put to work.

WHO'S AT THE CONTROLS?

Who should do the work? Instead of reducing the work of the editorial staff, desktop publishing sometimes adds new areas of responsibility. When tasks previously done by typesetters and paste-up artists are added to an editor's workload, it's important to be realistic about the amount of time those tasks take, even with the speed of desktop publishing. Editorial burnout can result unless job descriptions are shifted to reflect the added demands.

NO INSTANT GRATIFICATION

The first issue of your newsletter is the hardest to produce. After you've mastered the technology and have published the first issue, time and money savings quickly multiply. But initially there's a significant financial investment and training period to deal with. You must buy the right computer hardware and software and allow time for a learning curve that's usually directly proportional to the capabilities of the hardware and software.

Complicating this first step is the fact that computer stores sometimes undersell you on the hardware and software needed to do the job right. Salespeople have to be familiar with a wide range of products. Therefore, in-depth knowledge of a particular area such as desktop publishing tends to be sacrificed for generalized knowledge of a lot of areas—including accounting, games and financial modeling.

In the absence of expert guidance, your search for the best desktop publishing hardware and software can be a challenging quest. Try to find a computer store with a desktop publishing specialist who understands your needs and can make informed recommendations. Or get to know desktop publishers at local user support groups.

THE BIG SQUEEZE

Finally, newsletters don't design themselves. In fact, they can be surprisingly complicated. Most newsletters are a complex mixture of articles that can include everything from long stories to short calendar listings. In addition, most newsletters must accommodate a potpourri of photographs, illustrations and other graphic elements. All must be woven into an integrated whole, often under strict deadline conditions.

Successful newsletters are designed to accommodate change—to squeeze each issue's varying amount of text and graphics gracefully into a previously defined format. A strong, capable editor, who's present throughout the production phase, and a design that allows flexibility will preserve the newsletter's editorial and design integrity. This kind of management will also mean fewer headaches for those operating the desktop publishing system.

ALL SHAPES, SIZES AND FREQUENCIES

Newsletters offer a tremendous range of production alternatives. They can be as long or as short, as simple or as complex as needed to communicate the desired message.

8 1/2" x 11" Simple Newsletter ▲

9" x 14" Complex Newsletter ▶

A newsletter can be as simple as a single sheet of paper printed on both sides or as complex as a four-color, 24-page, saddle-stitched publication. Newsletters range in size from 5 1/2 by 8 inches to full-size tabloid pages; the most popular size is a single 11- by 17-inch sheet folded to form four 8 1/2- by 11-inch pages.

Newsletter frequency can range from weekly to quarterly. It can be printed in one (black and white), two, or even four colors, on inexpensive newsprint or on glossy, coated stock.

THE EXTENDED FAMILY OF NEWSLETTERS

If you're a newsletter editor, you're in good company. In the United States alone, more than one million newsletters are published every year, estimates Howard Penn Hudson, publisher of the *Newsletter on Newsletters.*

For example, corporate internal newsletters (often called "house organs") help motivate employees by instilling a sense of pride and teamwork, rewarding outstanding achievement and maintaining goodwill. They also communicate news of general interest.

Corporate external newsletters sell former customers new services or products, attract new customers, promote products, and build support among such groups as government regulators, the media or stock-market analysts.

Association newsletters try to maintain enthusiasm among existing contributors, members and supporters. They're also intended to attract new contributors, members and supporters, and influence important constituencies such as voters, the media or politicians.

In-House Newsletter

Subscription newsletters communicate specialized information not available elsewhere. They interpret and simplify data and opinions and provide a new perspective on the events of the day, helping subscribers make sense of over-communicated, under-analyzed information.

These are just a few types of newsletters, and each type requires a different design. The design for a newsletter targeted for a local hair-styling salon wouldn't work for one whose readership is Wall Street stock analysts. A college alumni newsletter design would be substantially different from one whose goal is to keep neurosurgeons up-to-date on the latest advances in laser surgery.

ANATOMY OF A NEWSLETTER

Although newsletters come in a variety of sizes and shapes, ranging from a single side of an 8 1/2- by 11-inch page to 24 (or more) pages, all newsletters are based on the same basic parts. Pick up a typical newsletter and you'll likely find most or all of the elements that follow.

Subscription Newsletter

Nameplate
The nameplate, or banner, consists of the newsletter's title. It's usually set in a large, distinctive typeface at the top of the front page, although variations are possible (for example, running the title vertically up the side of the front page.)

Because nameplates typically remain unchanged from issue to issue and year to year, it pays to devote a lot of care to their design. Newsletter nameplates can be created with specialized software drawing programs, such as Adobe Illustrator, Aldus Freehand or Corel Draw. These programs give you a lot more control over type size and placement than do most word processing or page layout programs.

Nameplate Subtitle
The nameplate is often reinforced by a subtitle that emphasizes the editorial focus or intended audience.

Folio
Often listed with the nameplate and subtitle is the folio, or dateline, which lists the volume and issue numbers and the current date.

Seals and Logos
In many cases, the front page contains the logo, or seal, of the association or firm publishing the newsletter. Like nameplates, logos and seals can be created using specialized drawing programs and saved as electronic files so they can be easily added to future issues.

Table of Contents
A table of contents on the front cover increases readership by drawing attention to articles on inside pages.

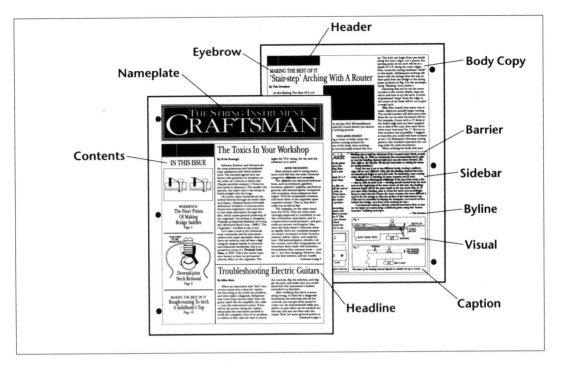

Masthead   The masthead of a newsletter is usually found on page 2. Mastheads typically include the address, copyright information, subscription rates and telephone number, as well as a list of the names and positions of everyone associated with the publication of the newsletter.

Headers   Often, the newsletter's title, or subtitle, is repeated at the top of every inside page, along with issue number and date. This helps reinforce the newsletter's identity.

Footers   Alternately, page numbers and sometimes the newsletter's title are printed at the bottom of each inside page.

Eyebrows   Eyebrows are department heads that help readers identify the category an article falls under.

Headlines   Headlines invite the reader into the copy that follows. The ideal headline is short enough to be set in large type, yet long enough to attract the reader's attention.

Subtitles   Subtitles, sometimes called decks or blurbs, summarize the importance or the editorial focus of the article that follows.

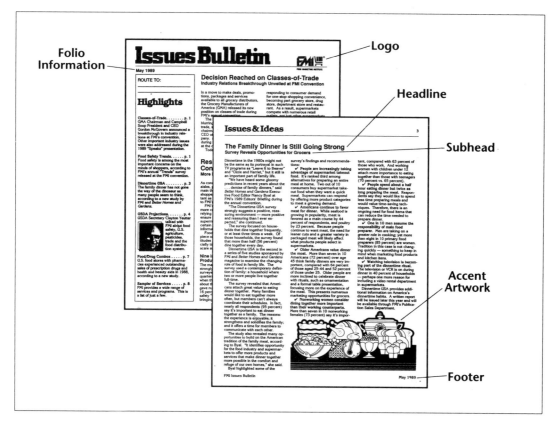

Subheads   Subheads, placed within long articles, perform two functions. First, they maintain the reader's momentum by breaking long blocks of copy into manageable, bite-sized chunks. Second, they provide an opportunity for readers skimming a page to find out what's in an article.

Bylines   The byline, or author identification, can be placed at the start or end of an article.

Body Copy   Body copy, or text, provides the core of a newsletter. Articles are placed in one or more adjacent columns. Most word processing and desktop publishing programs can produce multicolumn formats.

Jumplines   Jumplines help readers locate articles continued on different pages or identify where an article began.

Pull-Quotes   Pull-quotes—short phrases that summarize important points in an article—give a preview of an article's contents.

Author's Biography

Often, an author's background credentials are spelled out at the end of a story. Information about the author's department or location can also be included.

Sidebars

A sidebar is an "article within an article" that supplements the longer article it's set adjacent to. Sidebars often provide added detail or perspective to topics discussed in feature articles.

Primary Visuals

Articles are sometimes accompanied by photographs, illustrations or charts and diagrams. The size of these visuals should reflect their importance. With desktop publishing, you can scan photographs and artwork, and manipulate and resize them on your computer screen so you can preview how they'll fit on the finished page.

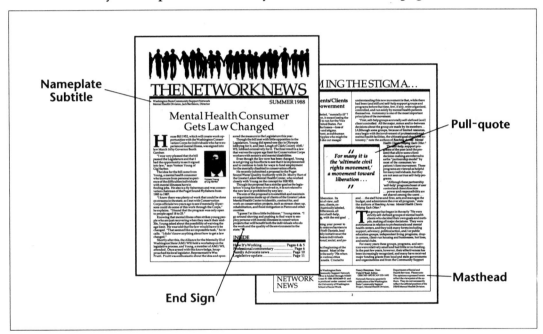

Nameplate
Subtitle

Pull-quote

End Sign

Masthead

Captions

Captions describe photographs and artwork. Many desktop publishing and word processing programs let you link a photo or illustration with its caption, so they'll remain locked together even if you edit surrounding text.

Accent Artwork

Often, nonrepresentational illustrations can enhance the mood of a newsletter. Vast libraries of clip art (pre-drawn illustrations) are available on diskette.

Mug Shots   What a horrible term, but how else can you describe short photos that accompany new arrivals, recent promotions and members of the Twenty Year Club? When grouping them together, be sure head sizes are nearly equal and that the individuals face the reader or into a page (instead of staring over the reader's shoulder!).

Calendars   Calendars provide information-at-a-glance about upcoming events that will be of interest to your readers.

End Signs   End signs, symbols that indicate the end of an article, can be found in the extended character sets of many typefaces. In addition, some typefaces consist entirely of symbols, like the Adobe Zapf Dingbats collection. Ideally, the symbol should relate to the theme of the newsletter (e.g., a small, open book for a library newsletter or a fish for an aquarium newsletter).

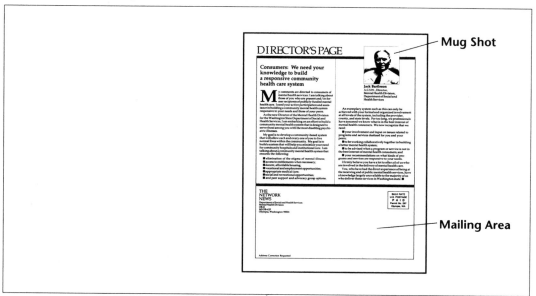

Mailing Area   If your newsletter is a self-mailer (sent via mail without being enclosed in an envelope), the back page will contain space for the address label, as well as return address information. Often, a pre-printed postmark is included.

Barriers   Barriers are rules and boxes used to separate adjacent articles. With some software programs, barriers can be linked to adjacent text so they'll "float" with the article they belong to when the article is edited.

MOVING ON

If the thought of designing or redesigning a newsletter seems overwhelming, you can approach it systematically. Think of it as a seven-step process:

1. Plan your newsletter.
2. Design a nameplate.
3. Choose an appropriate grid.
4. Format the body copy.
5. Add road signs.
6. Integrate visuals.
7. Add detail with graphic accents.

The following seven chapters address each of these points.

Newsletters are often designed and produced "on the fly." The contents are forced into an existing framework, and the primary goal is simply to fill the available space. This approach rarely produces a satisfactory newsletter. However, with the capabilities available with desktop publishing, newsletters can easily combine design harmony and issue-to-issue consistency. As you'll learn in Chapter 2, forethought can help you establish a working partnership between design and content.

CHAPTER TWO

PLANNING YOUR NEWSLETTER

Behind every effective, well-designed newsletter are plans, plans and more plans. Planning and producing a newsletter is essentially a four-step process. Note that of the following four steps only the last one involves turning on your computer:

➤ Defining goals and limitations

➤ Collecting ideas

➤ Preparing rough sketches

➤ Translating and refining

Let's take a closer look at each of these steps.

DEFINING GOALS AND LIMITATIONS

At this stage you need to establish the overall look you want to create and consider any restrictions that will limit your choices.

Among the decisions you'll want to make is what you will call your newsletter. By giving the newsletter a title early on, you can decide which words of the title to emphasize. If the name's too long, you can shorten it.

After settling on a name, reflect on the overall purpose of the newsletter. Is it to maintain current customers or supporters, or to attract new ones? Is it to communicate information or praise employee efforts? If you add a statement of purpose to the title, people will immediately know what your newsletter's about and who it's for.

A short, concise title followed by a strong statement of purpose often looks better and communicates more efficiently than a wordy title.

Mixing Text and Graphics

Begin planning your newsletter by taking an inventory of the text and graphics that would appear in a typical issue. Start by listing the major articles likely to be included in each issue. Will your newsletter consist of one or two major articles or many small articles? Upcoming events and recent promotions, plus several longer articles? Then list the major visuals you have available. Can you get photos? If not, you can compensate by using white space, oversized initial caps or other text elements that add visual interest.

Conforming to Corporate Identity Standards

If you're designing a newsletter for a large corporation, you may need to use predetermined typefaces, colors and column layout. Find out if you must include your association or firm's logo or seal.

Newsletter Distribution

The method of distribution you choose will affect the design. Will it be a self-mailer (folded, addressed and stamped on the back page)? If your newsletter will be mailed in an envelope, the front page becomes extremely important. However, if it's to be self-mailed, you should devote more time to the back page.

Because a self-mailer is usually folded in half or in thirds, it requires a different set of design priorities. Readers will encounter your address-label panel first. It's important to provide some teasers—a few catchy phrases describing what's inside—next to the address panel to draw the reader inside.

Another distribution issue is whether your newsletter will be three-hole punched. If it will, you'll need to allow extra space so that the holes don't interfere with text or graphics.

Scrutinize Your Competition

The widespread use of word processing and desktop publishing programs makes it increasingly important to distinguish your newsletter from competitive publications. This is especially true since most desktop software programs offer the same typefaces.

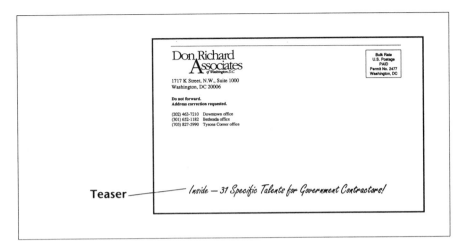

Take a close look at your competition's design so that your newsletter will emerge with a visual identity all its own.

Newsletter Size

This is again a function of budget resources. Most newsletters tend to be printed on vertical 8 1/2- by 11-inch pages. But this size isn't cast in stone: you can consider using a different newsletter format.

You might, for example, plan your newsletter to be in a vertical, legal-size format. This will stand out and is especially suitable for newsletters that contain long articles.

Or consider a horizontal format, which is ideal for showcasing a few important articles.

Tabloid publications can be exciting. They give you a lot of space to work with, especially if they open up into a broadside.

Tabloids let you place large, attention-getting headlines on the inside spreads along with generous amounts of copy and white space. They're ideal for long, information-filled newsletters as well as for those whose main points can be read at a glance.

Two-Color Printing

Will you use conventional black ink on white paper, or can you add a second highlight color? If you have the money for color, can you afford to use custom-mixed colors, or will you use standard, out-of-the-can (process) colors?

Restrained use of a second color ink can make a major contribution to your newsletter design, but be sure that you have the budget for it.

One alternative is pre-printing a second color ink. Portions of your newsletter's nameplate and consistent accent colors used as borders or standing dividers can reduce the cost of printing a second color. Simply print up enough blank sheets of paper with the second color added to your title or used in screens. Subsequently, each printing job becomes a one-color press run, even though readers will receive a two-color publication.

Or, instead of black ink, use very dark gray. This can look original and distinctive, especially when combined with off-white paper.

Using Bleeds

Bleeds (graphics that extend to the edge of the page) can be extremely effective in adding interest to a page, but they significantly increase printing costs. Bleeds are also harder to produce with laser printers, since most laser printers can't cover a full 8 1/2- by 11-inch page.

The Quality Alternative

Most newsletters are published using artwork produced on 300-dot-per-inch laser printers. In most cases, 300-dot-per-inch laser-produced output is sufficient. Some newsletter publishers, however, go a step further and—after producing their work on laser printers—proofing camera-ready artwork on high-resolution phototypesetters. Few newsletter publishers own their own phototypesetters, because of the cost. Instead, they rent time on them at service bureaus.

High-resolution phototypesetting increases the crispness of the letters and makes background shades appear smooth. It also makes it easier to include bleeds. (See Appendix A for more on printer alternatives.) Whether you opt for high-resolution output depends on your budget and the type of laser printer you're using. If you use a PostScript printer, such as Apple LaserWriter NT or NTX, you can easily send your newsletter files to a service bureau for high-resolution output.

You should decide early on about this because it will influence design decisions. For example, if you're limited to 300-dot-per-inch laser printing, you'll probably want to avoid gray screened backgrounds or screened letters. Screens don't reproduce well on a laser printer and often appear mottled. Limit screened backgrounds and letters to newsletters that can be printed with a phototypesetter.

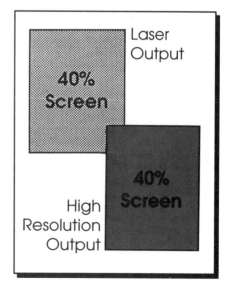

Choosing Paper

The typeface and type sizes you choose will influence your selection of paper to print your newsletter on. Some papers are more absorbent than others, and this can contribute to the visual clarity of the print. When using absorbent paper, try to avoid small, intricate typefaces, because their characters tend to blur. Other papers—such as coated stocks—are so reflective they also require larger, simpler letters.

Establishing Production Schedules

If you're preparing a weekly newsletter, you'll want to adopt a simple, easy-to-produce layout, since a more complex layout would be too time-consuming to deal with each week.

Fine detailing—elaborate initial caps, lined-up column bottoms and sophisticated wraparounds—require a lot of time, both for the initial design and for fine-tuning.

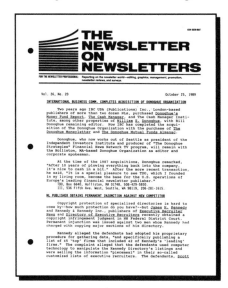

Simple layout

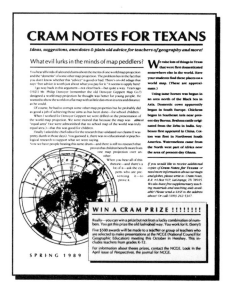

Complex layout

Inventory Newsletter Purpose and Content

The following Inventory Sheet may help you formalize your newsletter's purpose and content, and choose an appropriate nameplate and page layout.

INVENTORY SHEET

The purpose of my newsletter is to:

(Check all that apply)

☐ Inform members about upcoming events.

☐ Showcase recent firm or association activities.

☐ Recognize individual employee or member achievement.

☐ Analyze and interpret recent events in-depth.

☐ Create and maintain enthusiasm for association or firm goals.

The following articles or features are likely to be included in each issue:

☐ Single, major interpretive article (12 or more paragraphs).

☐ Two or more focus articles (8 or more paragraphs).

☐ Several short "updates" (2 or 3 paragraphs).

☐ Calendar of upcoming events (1 or 2 line entries).

☐ Recognition of employee or member achievement (single paragraphs).

Copy will be based on:

☐ Interviewing participants.

☐ Analyzing and rewriting existing information.

☐ Writing articles from scratch.

Visuals will consist of:

☐ Charts and graphs that interpret numbers.

☐ Existing photographs.

☐ Photographs that must be specially taken.

☐ Clip art on hand (itemize).

COLLECTING IDEAS

As you consider design, look around for inspiration. Other newsletters can generate ideas and suggest techniques that you might be able to use, too. Pay special attention to newsletters whose looks reflect the atmosphere of the newsletter you want to create. The goal isn't to steal ideas, but to borrow techniques that might work well with your own publication.

A good way to start is to build a file of newsletters you admire. (See Chapter 11 for examples of well-designed newsletters and the bibliography for additional sources of inspiration.)

Newsstands are another source of inspiration. Visit a large newsstand and notice the magazines that have their own unique personalities.

Chances are that by the time you've adapted an idea to your own newsletter, there will be little resemblance to the original—but it will have influenced your creative process.

PREPARING ROUGH SKETCHES

Desktop publishing and word processing programs are tremendously powerful production tools, but they can be inhibiting as far as creating new ideas. Just because you can try out various page layouts on a computer screen doesn't necessarily mean that you should always have your computer turned on when designing your newsletter. You'll probably find that your ideas flow much faster when you turn off your computer and simply sketch them with a pencil and paper.

Making rough sketches lets you try out different ideas and instantly discard those that don't work. You can quickly make headlines larger or smaller, try out different column arrangements and test alternative ways of placing visuals on a page.

TRANSLATING AND REFINING

After you've defined your goals and sketched and refined your design ideas, the final step is to develop actual column measurements, create templates for your newsletter and produce a sample issue.

Once you have pencil sketches for the front cover and inside pages that reflect the purpose, audience and content of your newsletter, you can translate your drawings to a computer. When you're satisfied with your design, you can create templates—electronic files that provide the structure for each individual issue of your newsletter. Often, this is best accomplished by first increasing your rough sketches to actual size and setting up a grid that reflects the margins and column spacing you've decided to use. Then, fill in this initial on-screen layout with dummy copy and headlines.

Remember, this is a trial-and-error stage. You'll probably find that some ideas don't transfer successfully from rough drawings to actual page layout. But it's better to find out now, rather than at deadline time!

UNITY AND CONTRAST

Good design establishes a balance between unity and contrast. Effective newsletters have page-to-page and issue-to-issue unity. This manifests itself in such ways as consistent graphic treatment of headlines, department heads, subheads, pull-quotes, body copy, column widths, borders and visuals.

Yet, contrast is also necessary. Each of the various elements of newsletter page architecture should contrast with each other to avoid gray pages that lack visual interest. That contrast can be reflected in the hierarchy of importance. Headlines clearly stand apart from subheads and body copy, for example. At a glance, readers can separate the important from the supportive.

As you design, or redesign, your newsletter, it's important to balance unity and contrast to give your newsletter visual appeal and call attention to selected text and graphics.

MOVING ON

To wrap up your preliminary planning phase, use the following checklist to determine if you've laid a solid foundation for your project.

- ✔ I've created thumbnail sketches and experimented with various layouts before deciding on a layout.

- ✔ The proposed layout reflects the mixture of text, graphics and repeating elements likely to be included in each issue.

- ✔ I've analyzed competing newsletters.

- ✔ My layout is practical, considering my production schedule.

- ✔ The layout is appropriate for its method of distribution.

- ✔ I've considered alternative page sizes, two-color printing and bleeds.

- ✔ I've considered high-resolution typesetting.

Today's desktop publishing and word processing hardware and software offer tremendous design flexibility. But this power has to be focused. By taking the time to plan your layout, you can tailor your design to suit your goals, budget and overall editorial balance.

In Chapter 3, you'll survey various grid options and learn about the column formats most often used in newsletter design. You'll see how grids help you build unity and contrast into your layout by organizing the placement of text and graphics. By observing the strengths and limitations of each format, you'll be able to choose the one best suited to your own newsletter.

CHAPTER THREE

CHOOSING A GRID

Just as a skyscraper is supported by an internal core of steel beams hidden from view behind the exterior, an effective newsletter is built on a grid. This structure of invisible lines guides the placement of text and graphics. In this chapter, you'll explore the strengths and limitations of the most common grid formats, how to integrate a new grid step-by-step into an existing newsletter and how to refine your grid once you've developed it.

Because they provide a unifying structure, grids are the foundation of your newsletter's design. They consist of a matrix of unprinted horizontal and vertical lines that provide the basic framework upon which your newsletter is assembled.

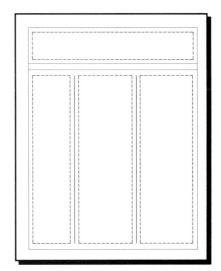

If every page of a newsletter were based on a different grid—columns of different widths, beginning and ending at different points on each page—chaos would reign. Grids are essential for providing page-to-page and issue-to-issue consistency.

Grids also make it easy to introduce the unexpected into your publication. Once you've created a grid, you can add visual interest by varying the way you arrange the text or visual elements.

When creating and using a grid, consider the following tips:

Select a grid that's appropriate to the content of your newsletter. Your grid should reflect the overall look you're trying to achieve, in addition to accommodating the articles and visuals that will appear in each issue.

Establish page margins. Be sure to provide sufficient "thumb area" for readers to hold your publication. Then define the upper and lower edges of text columns.

Create grid sheets for planning purposes. You can quickly get an idea of how each issue of your newsletter will look by using a previously printed grid sheet.

As you work on your grid, you can refine it as you go. For example, you'll probably want to modify the distance between adjacent columns of type once you've chosen a typeface and type size.

GRIDS AND WHITE SPACE

One common design pitfall is placing too much type on a page. A well-designed grid leaves enough white space at the top, bottom and sides of your publication. Grids also establish consistency, and thus a recognition factor. You can achieve page-to-page consistency by creating a sink or drop—a horizontal band of white space at the top or bottom of a page.

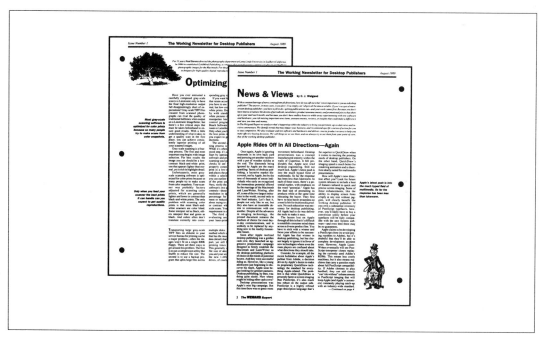

Vertical white space also enhances a page. You can leave a certain amount of blank space on each side of a page, or you can use part of the space for subheads, table of contents, pull-quotes and other reader cues (as described later in this chapter).

Page Margins

Grids can define the margins of a page—how close text and graphics will come to the edges.

Margins are an important element in page design. Narrow margins with wide, text-filled columns create darker pages with a horizontal orientation. Wide margins with narrower columns of type create a more vertically oriented page.

In most cases, the "live area" of a page—the area where text and graphics are placed—is considerably smaller than the trim size of a publication (the size of the finished product).

However, you can allow an occasional photo or graphic element to "bleed" to the edge of the page. This technique can be very effective when used with restraint.

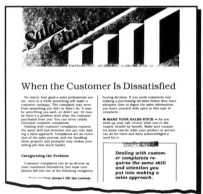

COLUMNS

It's important to remember that the number of columns in a grid doesn't necessarily correspond to the number of *text* columns on a page. For example, a five-column grid doesn't translate into five narrow columns of type.

This example shows two double columns of text with a narrow margin that can be used for reader cues and photos.

When articles are short, they can be contained in double columns of type, set in two adjacent columns. This lets the reader quickly scan articles on one page.

Another alternative is placing a double and triple column of text next to each other.

Alternating Column Widths

As the number of columns used in a grid increases, it's possible to build some contrast into your newsletter without destroying page-to-page continuity.

Switching from two to three columns of type on facing pages of a newsletter can disorient a reader, destroying continuity.

However, if you're using a five- or seven-column grid, you can switch between different column formats without disruption. Even though the grid's underlying theme remains hidden, its unifying presence will be evident in the page layouts.

Single-Column Grids

Single-column grid formats perhaps identify a newsletter as a "letter about news." They communicate the immediacy of a late-breaking story.

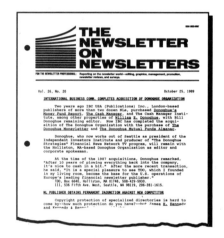

Single-column formats are easy to design and produce at the last minute. They're an ideal choice for daily or weekly newsletters and are often used for newsletters produced at conventions or trade shows. Their lack of graphic complexity implies that their message is extremely important.

Although single-column grids can create newsletters that look like they are hot off the press, single-column formats can be too rigid.

For one thing, you're limited to a narrow range of typefaces and type sizes, since wide columns of text require a large type size. And extra space must be added between the lines to enhance readability.

In addition, it's difficult to place visuals on a wide measure of text. If you place a square illustration on a page, you must increase its size to cover the full width of the page—which often makes the visual disproportionately high. Placing it in the middle of the page, surrounded by white space, wastes a lot of space. Aligning it with the left- or right-hand margin means that you have to fit text around it. None of these options are ideal.

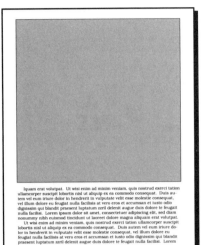 

Two-Column Grids

Many successful newsletter designs use two-column grids. You can easily prepare a two-column grid with most desktop publishing and word processing programs.

Two-column newsletter formats have a "classic" look. Perhaps that's because we associate two-column formats with textbooks and other formal communications. However, they have some limitations.

A major problem is that two-column pages often suffer from too much balance and the design can be boring. Readers looking at a spread are presented with four parallel columns of text, with insufficient white space to open up the page.

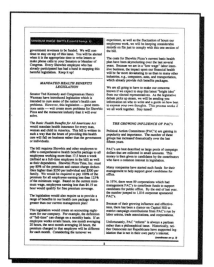
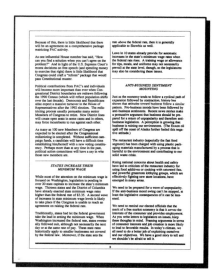

Two-column grids also limit your choice of type size; because of their width, you must still use a rather large type size.

The use of reader cues or graphics is restricted as well. Headlines can span either one or two columns. And it's difficult to incorporate subheads and pull-quotes without interfering with the reader's eye-tracking.

In this example, the reader cues must be placed within the column, which means they must be set so large they block eye movement.

It's also hard to incorporate photographs into two-column grids, especially in square and vertical rectangle shapes. They must extend the full width of a column, unless they're going to be adjacent to short lines of text or trapped white space—which can be distracting. If they're enlarged to conform to the column width, they can become so tall they take over the page.

Because of these limitations, a straight two-column grid works best when your newsletter consists of a combination of a few visuals and a few relatively long articles.

There are ways to get around these problems. Consider trimming a little space from each column and placing the two columns off-center on the page. You might move the columns to the right on left-hand pages and to the left on right-hand pages. This simple technique builds a band of white space into the outside borders of each spread and breaks up the symmetry presented by two equal-width columns.

This technique can also be used to add emphasis to headlines and visuals that can expand beyond the column width into the white space.

Two-column formats are often chosen out of habit, without regard to their limitations. Although you can create an attractive newsletter on a two-column grid, its relatively wide columns and lack of opportunities to build in visual excitement can inhibit your design. If you decide on two columns, be aware of the format's limitations and spend extra time experimenting with ways to add typographic color and avoid excessive balance.

Three-Column Grids

Three-column formats offer more typographic flexibility, as well as more opportunities to use visuals and reader cues. Because three-column formats have narrower text columns than two-column formats, it's easier to choose a type size that's large enough to easily read but doesn't dominate the page. Headlines can extend across two, or more, columns, amplified by subheads and pull-quotes just one column wide.

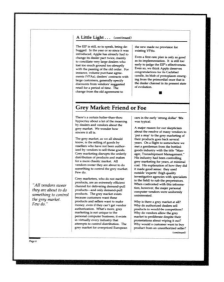

Three-column formats also offer more opportunities for placing and sizing visuals. Charts and photographs can extend across one, two or three columns. Vertical photographs placed in single columns are large enough for impact, yet don't overwhelm the page.

Although popular and relatively easy to produce with most desktop publishing and word processing programs, three-column formats share many of the limitations of two-column formats. These include exaggerated symmetry and the difficulties of integrating reader cues and visuals into the body copy.

Headlines are limited to one-, two- or three-column spans. Reader cues must usually be placed within the columns, where they can interrupt the reader's eye movement unless care is taken. Be sure three-column headlines don't inadvertently dominate the page.

Opportunities for using visuals are still rather limited. Photographs must be one, two or three columns wide. Reduced to a single-column width, horizontal photographs can lose their effectiveness; when they fill two or three columns, they can become so large they dominate the page.

Symmetry can be a problem with three-column formats if readers facing a two-page spread are presented with six equal-weight columns of text.

However, you can add interest and build shape into the three-column format. For example, you may want to include photographs that spill slightly into adjacent columns, with shorter lines of type wrapped around them. (Try to avoid extending them more than a quarter of the width of the adjacent column.)

Sidebars offer yet another opportunity for breaking monotonous symmetry. Because they're boxed and often appear against a shaded background (called a screen), sidebars create a different dynamic on a page.

They also can fill either one or two columns in a three-column grid. However, if you include a sidebar that extends over two columns, be sure to adjust type size and leading (see Chapter 5). Otherwise, the sidebar won't stand out from the body copy and will be confusing and difficult to read.

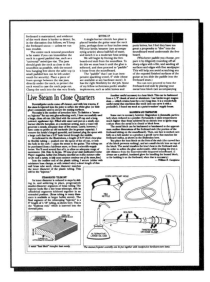

Still another technique that can add interest to three-column formats is to reserve the outside columns on each two-page spread for white space. That space can be used to emphasize reader cues, such as headlines, eyebrows, subheads and pull-quotes.

Photographs and illustrations positioned in the middle columns can also break into the outside columns. This allows visuals to be the right proportion rather than restricting their width to a single column or expanding it to fill two or three columns.

Many variations on the "empty column" format are possible. For instance, you can create mirror-image pages, with the empty columns placed at the outside of each page, or you can just as easily place them on the left-hand side of each page.

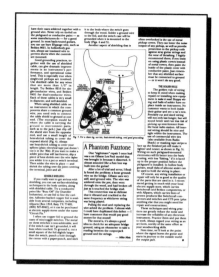

Another variation is to use the three-column format but make the two text columns slightly wider than the empty column. This increases word density (the number of words on a page), yet provides visual interest.

In the example above, notice how the masthead and publisher's information are placed in the empty column on the front cover and pull-quotes are placed in the empty columns. This technique works particularly well with newsletters that contain a few long articles.

Four-Column Grids

Four-column grids offer a lot of design flexibility, but careful attention must be devoted to typography when four columns are used for 8 1/2-by 11-inch newsletters. Narrow columns must be compensated for by using a relatively small type size. Because of the tendency of type to lose definition and detail at small sizes, these formats work best when output with high-resolution phototypesetting and printed on a coated paper stock.

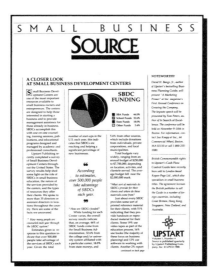 

However, sidebars, illustrations and photographs can be used to break up the pronounced vertical orientation of four-column newsletters. Notice how a box spanning three of the four columns in the above example does just that. Box- and frame-oriented desktop publishing programs such as Ventura Publisher and Quark XPress make this an easy effect to achieve.

The four-column format works well when used for single-page, two-sided newsletters containing short, four- or five-paragraph articles.

But you probably wouldn't want to read a multipage newsletter with four columns of straight text. Just think how tiring it would be to face *eight* narrow columns of type set on a two-page spread!

But, notice how effective the format is when each page contains an empty column of white space containing occasional illustrations, pull-quotes or subheads.

Notice the visual interest created by running the introductory paragraphs of articles across three of the columns. Notice also how the concentrated white space defines the articles on each page and frames the illustrations and subheads.

Five-Column Grids

The five-column format is one of the most flexible formats available. It can accommodate newsletters containing a variety of both long and short articles.

Five-column grids based on two double columns of type and a single, narrow empty column offer a lot of flexibility in using reader cues and visuals. The narrow column of white space is usually placed on the left side of a left-hand page and on the right side of a right-hand page, where it frames each two-page spread. White space can be consistently placed on the left side of each page, but this interferes slightly with articles continued from page to page.

Headlines can gain impact by beginning in the white space adjacent to the columns of type they introduce. Subheads can be placed adjacent to their topics, rather than inside the columns, where they might interfere with the reader's eye-tracking. Pull-quotes and the table of contents can be placed in the narrow columns. This technique works particularly well with tabloid-size newsletters.

If all five columns of type were filled, as in the following example, the tabloid newsletter would be far too dense.

Five-column formats offer many options for placing visuals. For example, you can place vertical charts and photographs in the narrow column adjacent to the text. Just be sure to align them flush-left or flush-right, so they're linked to the body copy they support.

You can also add visual interest to a page by placing rectangular and square visuals within columns of text and extending them into the adjacent white space.

The *Change* newsletter illustrates the way an underlying five-column grid can hold together pages which, on the surface, appear to be very different.

On page 2, for example, a text block three columns wide, set extra large with extra line spacing, contrasts with a two-column-wide visual.

On page 3, the article is also set in two comfortably wide columns, with a recipe set in a narrow column.

Page 4 maintains the five-column grid by placing another recipe in the narrow left-hand column and uses the second and third columns for the body copy. A large illustration that extends across the last two columns on page 4 and the first column of page 5 unifies the spread.

Body copy runs across three of the columns on page 5, and a conversational "hint" defines the right-most column on the spread.

Five narrow columns of text on a page could be difficult to read, but not when balanced by a large headline occupying almost a third of the left-hand page and a narrow, tinted column to the right containing still another recipe.

This spread illustrates yet another way to use the five-column grid. The page is anchored by a large vertical photograph that extends across three of the five columns on the left-hand page. Breathing room is provided in each of the remaining columns by white space below the text. The bottom of the page is defined by the line art that continues from column to column. Text columns are unified by consistent headlines and background shading. A narrow frame of white space helps the photograph stand out against the background.

The last two-page spread in the newsletter illustrates even more of the flexibility offered by the five-column grid. The spread begins with a three-column-wide headline and introduction set in white type against a dark background. Text is grouped within the next three pairs of columns. "Helpful hints" are placed in the remaining fifth column to the right.

Six-Column Grids

Six-column newsletters can accommodate a lot of reader cues that, in turn, can introduce numerous short features. They're also good for long feature articles with frequent subheads or pull-quotes. This is particularly attractive if you base your grid around alternating narrow and wide columns. Here, flush-right headlines in the narrow columns introduce one-paragraph stories in the wide columns.

Let's say that you have a single-page, 8 1/2- by 11-inch newsletter printed on both sides, that contains numerous short two- and three-paragraph articles. You can center double columns of type and place the reader cues in the outside columns. As always, you must choose a typeface and size that's as legible as possible (see Chapter 5).

Seven-Column Grids

Like newsletters built on a five-column grid, seven-column newsletters avoid the problem of excessive symmetry. They can accommodate a mixture of long and short articles plus visuals of various sizes.

 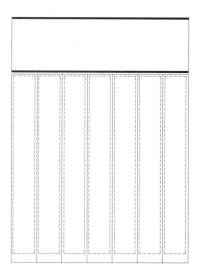

Seven-column newsletters can provide the reader with three comfortable, easy-to-read columns of text, flanked by an accent column used either for breathing room or to emphasize important headlines, visuals and reader cues, such as pull-quotes. This accent column can be on the right or left edge of each page or can "float" between columns.

Defining White Space

When using white space to build contrast into a newsletter, it's important that you provide some scale to define the white space. This is especially important when using asymmetrical five- and seven-column grids. Otherwise, your pages might look unfinished, or dwarfed by the size of the page. When you add an appropriate border, however, the white space does a better job of framing the page and emphasizing any reader cues contained in it (see Chapter 8).

White space can also be defined by repeating visuals, such as a reduced size of the nameplate on each page, or by adding graphic accents, such as short horizontal rules or page numbers.

The same is true for sinks. Without some definition, the white space can look like something has been omitted from each page. Adding a border to the top of the page solves that problem.

GRID SHEETS

One of the best ways to put grids to work is to create your own grid sheets with your desktop publishing or word processing program. These let you sketch out variations on your newsletter's column format and experiment with different ways of adding interest to your layouts.

If you use a desktop publishing program, locate the command used to establish multicolumn formats and create several files, each with a different number of columns. In most cases, you'll probably notice a series of light or dashed lines to indicate column positions.

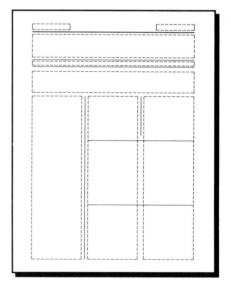

Next, use your program's box-drawing tool to outline the various columns. Use dashed lines. If your program has a master page or default page feature, you have to do this only once, since the outlined boxes will automatically be repeated on each of the following pages.

If you're designing a new newsletter, you might want to make a variety of dashed-line box grids, using from two to seven columns.

If, however, you're redesigning an existing newsletter, you may want to prepare only the grids you're most likely to use.

Using your program's line-drawing tools, you can include horizontal rules to indicate the top and bottom limits of columns of body copy.

Many word processing programs let you create your own grid sheets. Use your program's box-and line-drawing tools. Specify dashed lines instead of the default solid lines. Experiment with different line thicknesses until you find the one that works best.

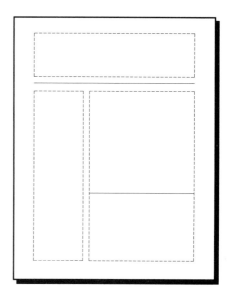

Some desktop publishing programs let you create boxes shaded with parallel horizontal lines. These can be used to indicate lines of type. Start by eliminating the line around each box, by clicking on "none," and click on the option that will shade your box with parallel horizontal lines.

Before you print your final grid sheets, you might consider adding visual elements that will remain constant from issue to issue. For example, by creating gray screened boxes, you can reserve space for your publication's nameplate, masthead and address-label area. If your newsletter's a self-mailer, you can indicate the address panel.

MOVING ON

Your grid is likely to go through many refinements between the rough drawing and final production stages.

For example, as you'll see in Chapter 9, gutters (the space between columns) should be adjusted to compensate for different text type sizes and alignments (flush-left, flush-right or justified).

Before finalizing your grid sheets, you may want to review the checklist below:

☑ The grid I've chosen leaves sufficient white space at the top, bottom and sides of each page of the newsletter.

☑ My grid reflects the mixture of text and graphics I'm going to include in my publication.

☑ My grid is flexible enough to incorporate text and graphics of various sizes.

☑ My grid lets me use white space to emphasize text and graphics.

☑ My grid successfully uses borders, page numbers or text to define the white space that frames each page.

☑ My grid combines columns for sidebars and articles of special interest.

☑ I avoided a format that is so symmetrical it becomes monotonous.

☑ My grid allows for enough variation without destroying the underlying unity of the newsletter.

In Chapter 4, you'll examine the nameplate, the distinctive way the title of your newsletter appears on the front page. You'll look at the various ways to design and place one that will add a special touch to your newsletter and emphasize its message and market.

CHAPTER FOUR

CREATING A NAMEPLATE

The nameplate, or banner, on the front of your newsletter is second only to grids in importance as a unifying element. It's the first thing that captures your reader's eye and provides immediate visual identification of your newsletter. It sets the tone of your publication and differentiates it from other newsletters.

Typically, the nameplate includes the newsletter's title and a subtitle that elaborates on the title or identifies the publisher. Or a subtitle can identify the newsletter's intended market or editorial focus. (In these cases, the subtitle becomes almost a motto.) The nameplate can also include publication information (called folio), such as the issue date, volume and number.

Nameplates provide issue-to-issue unity for your newsletter. Their size, shape, position and color remain constant, even though the text and visuals on the front cover change with each issue.

A nameplate can provide further unity when a variation of its design is used as a header on the inside pages. This is an especially useful technique if you feel people are likely to copy and distribute articles to friends and co-workers.

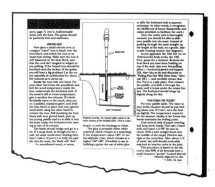

The elements you'll need to consider in creating (or redesigning) a nameplate for your newsletter include typeface, type size, type style, alignment, background, graphic accents and color, as well as artwork such as a logo or symbol associated with your firm or group.

Because you want to design the nameplate only once, it's worth taking the time to get exactly what you feel is the most appropriate and effective one possible. A good nameplate can provide years, even decades, of reader familiarity. For example, the title of *Newsletter on Newsletters*, published by the Newsletter Clearing House, has remained the same for over ten years.

As you begin your nameplate design, consider the following:

➤ Choose the right title and subtitle.

➤ Isolate important words.

➤ Choose the right typography for the most prominent word (or words).

➤ Use secondary words to add graphic contrast and supplement the editorial message of the title.

➤ Consider adding color, bleeds or framing.

➤ Carefully select a size and position.

THE TITLE AND SUBTITLE

The title you choose will influence the appearance of your newsletter. Ideally, the title should have strong symbolic value. It should convey the content to the targeted audience.

The length of the words you choose will have a lot of influence on your design. A title consisting of long words requires smaller type than a title made up of short words.

Short titles with only a single short word or two can have far more impact than a title like *The Proceedings of the American Perennial Association*. The longer title would require smaller type, which can be enhanced by surrounding the nameplate with plenty of white space. Nonetheless, shorter is usually better when it comes to titles.

Try to edit out unnecessary or empty words from your title (e.g., *newsletter, the*, etc.). The best titles use summary or action words, such as Advisor, Advocate, Digest, Investigator, Update or Report.

Remember that the nuances of typeface design become more obvious when type is large. Differences in typefaces that aren't visible at small sizes are very visible at large sizes.

TYPOGRAPHY

One of your most important decisions in designing a nameplate is selecting a typeface. Thousands of typefaces are available to desktop publishers, and each has a unique set of characteristics.

The first decision you'll want to make is whether to use a serif or sans-serif typeface. Let's look at the characteristics of each.

Serif and Sans-Serif Type

Serifs are small strokes, or feet, at the ends of letters. Used in a newsletter's body copy, serifs can enhance readability by providing letter-to-letter transition that helps your reader's eyes move from word to word. When used for large sizes, serifs play a more decorative role.

Serif typefaces often give a nameplate a dignified appearance.

Goudy Old Style, for example, gives a title a scholarly or classical feeling, whereas Palatino has an elegant, refined look.

Slab typefaces like ITC's Lubalin Graph or Memphis can communicate an architectural or engineering feeling.

The tradition of Goudy Old Style

The style of Palatino

The structure of Lubalin Graph

Type without serifs, called sans-serif, offers a clean, contemporary look. Many options are available within sans-serif typefaces. These include Helvetica, which is simple and straightforward; Futura—with its slanted sides—which is more playful; Avant Garde, with wider letters, which projects an ambience of richness.

The frankness of Helvetica

The fun of Futura

The fullness of Avant Garde

Script and Decorative Faces

Elaborate typefaces that might be unreadable if used for text can work very well in nameplates.

Script typefaces can be safely used in one- or two-word titles, especially when you're trying to communicate an upscale, elegant feeling.

Gourmet Chocolates

Decorative typefaces, such as Brush, Hobo or Art Deco, can create distinctive nameplates. Indeed, the attention-getting qualities that preclude their use for body copy make them ideal for nameplates. In some cases, they might also be appropriately used inside your newsletter for department headings.

Wallpaper Distributors

Type Weight

Another way of adding interest to a two- or three-word title is to set part of it in the light version of a typeface, the rest in the heavy version—like the treatment used for the title of *Practical Supervision*.

Many typefaces used for desktop publishing applications are available in more than one weight. Light and dark variations that can add color to your nameplate are often available. You might consider light typefaces for nameplates with long words and dark, or heavy, versions for short titles.

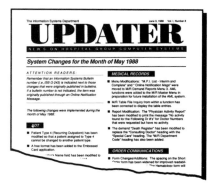

Condensed versions of many typefaces are also available, further expanding your creative opportunities.

Typeface Messages

Spend some time becoming familiar with the various typeface options available as downloadable fonts. Note your reactions to the various typefaces. These reactions stem from your emotional responses and associations. American Typewriter has a last-minute, newsy feel to it.

Late-Breaking News

The gentle curves of Souvenir impart a relaxed, friendly feeling.

Home Gardener

DESIGN TIPS AND TRICKS

All letters in a title don't have to be the same size. One useful technique is to frame the newsletter's title by increasing the size of the first and last letters.

Or, to add position contrast, the inside letters in a title can be vertically centered between oversized first letters for each word. The inside letters can be aligned with the tops or bottoms of the beginning and ending letters. This technique also influences the color contrast of your nameplate, by placing more white space above or below the inside letters.

Another option is to reduce your newsletter's title to an acronym. This works best, of course, if there's a harmony, or flow, between the letters. ZQT doesn't work as well as ABA.

Adding Style Contrast

Style options for your nameplate include the use of all uppercase, small capitals, lowercase and outline type. Nameplates set in all uppercase type are useful when you want formality or when the title of the newsletter includes several long words. Since uppercase type has no descenders (the stems of letters such as g, p and q that extend below the baseline), the lines of a title can be spaced closely together.

"Small caps" offer another option. The first letter in each word can be set in standard uppercase type, the remainder in small caps (smaller versions of a typeface's uppercase). Again, this lets you reduce line spacing. Small caps also work well with an oversized initial cap.

Another advantage in using small caps is that their expanded width can help spread a short word across the top of a newsletter without losing legibility.

SMALL CAPS NEWSLETTER

Short words can also work well in lowercase type, especially when they're combined with longer, more descriptive words. Lowercase nameplates are particularly appropriate for informal newsletters.

Outline type can be used to emphasize one word of a title.

Emphasizing Words

Decide on the most important words within the title you've chosen. The best-looking nameplates are often built around words of different sizes. They emphasize essential words, giving them clarity and impact.

A good way to emphasize words is to use an acronym set in large type, with the words it represents set in smaller type. It's easier to design an effective nameplate using ABA than American Backscratchers' Association, with each letter given equal weight.

Another alternative is to set one word inside another one.

Secondary Words

Once you've chosen your title and isolated the most important words, you might want to use supporting words to add contrast and interest to your nameplate.

You can use type size to emphasize the primary words and de-emphasize supporting words.

Or you can emphasize words by using both serif and sans-serif type in the title. If you use a serif typeface for your primary title, you might want to use a contrasting sans-serif type for secondary words.

If the primary word in your title is set in a sans-serif typeface, you can set supporting words or a subtitle in a serif typeface.

Or you may want to combine roman, bold and/or italic styles within your nameplate.

You can add contrast by manipulating the horizontal or vertical alignment of the secondary words relative to the primary words.

You can add interest to your nameplate by setting primary words in a heavier type weight than secondary words.

Finally, you can add color to your nameplate by shading or outlining some, but not all, of the words.

ADDING COLOR

The most legible combination for a nameplate consists of black type against a white background. But a number of alternatives are available.

For added contrast, the words in a nameplate can be *reversed*—white type against a black background.

The background itself doesn't have to be completely black, of course. It can be *screened* a shade of gray.

Or, if you're using two-color printing for your newsletter, the background can be printed in the second color. This secondary, highlight color may be repeated elsewhere on the page (e.g., as page borders or horizontal rules separating adjacent articles).

You might want to repeat a background color by using it behind boxed features such as the masthead, table of contents or a sidebar.

Multicolor Printing

A good way to add interest to your nameplate is to set it in a second color. This color can be preprinted. You can preprint the second-color nameplate, plus borders, for six months' or a year's worth of newsletters. Then each time you print your newsletter, you'll have to pay only for one-color printing, yet the cumulative effect is a two-color print job. You'll save money on each issue, plus you might be able to buy a larger amount of paper at special savings.

Bleeds

If your printing budget allows, you might accentuate the background of your nameplate by bleeding it to the sides or top edge of the page.

Newsletters containing bleeds are more expensive to print, but the effect is often worth it. The cost is higher because oversized paper has to be used and then trimmed to final size. (Ink cannot be placed where the gripper edges of the printing press pull the paper through the press.) Or standard-size paper can be used and later trimmed down to a smaller publication size.

Another reason bleeds are harder to produce is that laser-printer output doesn't cover an entire 8 1/2- by 11-inch page. Usually, a half-inch margin of white space surrounds the "live," or printable, area of the page. If you have a PostScript printer, such as an Apple LaserWriter series or the equivalent, you can get around this limitation by making proofs of your pages at 95 percent actual size and instructing your commercial printer to increase the laser-prepared pages by 5 percent. Note that this limitation doesn't apply to phototypesetting, which can cover 13- or 15-inch image areas—or even larger, depending on the model used.

FRAMING WITH RULES

Another solution is to use your desktop publishing or word processing program's box-drawing tool to frame your nameplate with rules of equal thickness. The thickness of the rules can either complement or contrast with the thickness of the type used for the title.

```
┌─────────────────────────────┐
│                             │
│        NAMEPLATE            │
│                             │
└─────────────────────────────┘
```

For a more classic effect, you can use a pair of rules, one thicker than the other. The sharpness of the box's four corners can provide contrast to the rounded letters within your newsletter's title.

```
┌─────────────────────────────┐
│ ┌─────────────────────────┐ │
│ │       NAMEPLATE         │ │
│ └─────────────────────────┘ │
└─────────────────────────────┘
```

Or, for a friendlier, less formal approach, you can use your software program's rounded-corner box-drawing tool for a softer look.

You might choose to frame only the top and bottom of the nameplate, or include a pair of horizontal rules to highlight the subtitle. When horizontal rules are used in a nameplate, it's important to make sure that the thickness of the rules is appropriate for the size and weight of the typeface.

PLACEMENT AND ALIGNMENT

In planning your design, you must decide on the alignment of type for the nameplate and the page.

Nameplates, like other elements, can be flush-left, flush-right or centered on the page.

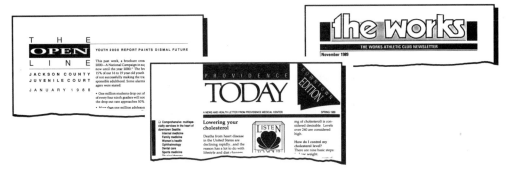

You can also align words within the nameplate itself. For instance, some words can be flush-left within a centered nameplate, or flush-left within a nameplate placed flush-right on the page.

Off-center alignment can be very powerful. Centering the nameplate places equal space to the left and right. Flush-right or flush-left alignment creates a lot of white space on one side of the page.

It's important to note that alignment doesn't have to follow page alignment, as long as it's based on the underlying column grid structure. In other words, the nameplate can be aligned—flush-left or flush-right—with just one of the columns forming the underlying grid of your newsletter.

For example, in a five-column grid, the nameplate can be aligned to the second column. This emphasizes the white space in the empty first column.

Another option is to align the nameplate with only two of the three columns on a page.

Although most nameplates run horizontally across the top of the first page, they can also run vertically up the left-hand side of a newsletter. This option eliminates the possibility of the nameplate conflicting with headlines.

PRODUCTION OPTIONS

Although you'll be using desktop publishing or word processing software to produce your newsletter, you may choose to prepare the nameplate using conventional technology.

Paste-ups

You might, for example, have a graphic artist or phototypesetter prepare your nameplate as a piece of camera-ready art that you or your commercial printer can attach with rubber cement to the artwork prepared with your laser printer or a service-bureau phototypesetter.

Or, you might prepare your nameplate with press-on lettering and have a photostat (high-contrast photograph) made of it for placement in each issue.

Drawing and Font-Manipulation Programs

In order to gain more control over the creative process, and to avoid the extra step described above, you might find that a separate graphics program will provide you with the flexibility you need to create your newsletter's nameplate.

This is a two-step process. The first step is to create a nameplate file, using a drawing or paint-type program. The second step is to import the file as a graphic into your newsletter.

Graphics programs offer far more typographic capability than even the best word processing or desktop publishing programs. Most graphics programs let you

➤ Set type larger.

➤ Have more precise control over letter spacing.

➤ Rotate type, set it at an angle or set it to follow a curved line.

➤ Slant, stretch or compress type.

➤ Set type in shades of gray.

➤ Add fountain effects (smooth transitions from light to dark) to either the type or the background behind it.

➤ Overlap letters or add ornamentation to certain letters.

➤ Manipulate typefaces to create new and unique type designs.

You can strive for very creative effects when manipulating the type in the nameplate because, after readers encounter it for the first time, your nameplate becomes a visual symbol and a graphic element rather than a means of communication.

Nameplates offer a rare opportunity to safely distort type by stretching or compressing it, or to experiment with overlapping letters.

Typical graphics programs let you group numerous individual elements—text, visuals (e.g., logos or association seals) and graphic accents—into one file that can be placed as a single unit on the front of your newsletter and then, if desired, repeated at reduced size on the inside pages.

Image Scanners

Although primarily viewed as a way of incorporating photographs into newsletters, image scanners can play a role in designing a nameplate. A scanned image of a word—or association logo—can also be used in the nameplate.

For example, where an informal look is desired, the starting point for creating a nameplate might be taking a handwritten word, and then scanning, tracing and manipulating it with a drawing program before placing it in a nameplate file.

OCTOBER 1989

A NEWSLETTER FOR PARENTS & KIDS

Likewise, an image scanner and a graphics program can let you make an electronic file out of a logo or association seal that's to be used in a nameplate. If this is done with a graphics program that can prepare encapsulated PostScript files, the logo or seal can then be increased or decreased in size without loss of quality.

Freelance Graphic Designers

It's not necessary to master an advanced illustration or drawing program just to prepare your newsletter's nameplate. It's usually easy to hire a qualified person to design it for you and provide you with a ready-to-place file. Both freelancers and established graphic design studios can help you produce a sophisticated nameplate.

You can often find a skilled freelancer by attending meetings of your local computer user group or by looking for computer graphic artists' advertisements in user-group newsletters. Another source of contacts might be local advertising or a communications club.

POTENTIAL PITFALLS OF NAMEPLATE DESIGN

Some common design mistakes made in creating newsletter nameplates include

- ▼ A lack of contrast between the nameplate and the rest of the newsletter—in particular, between the nameplate and the headlines that follow.

- ▼ Undersized nameplates or large ones that overwhelm the front page.

▼ A lack of contrast between the elements. Symptoms include a lack of white space, all title words given equal emphasis or insufficient contrast between the subtitle and the rest of the type on the page.

▼ Complex and "busy" nameplates that contain too many elements, too much information, too much background and an overabundance of graphic accents.

By avoiding these pitfalls, you can create a more effective, more appealing nameplate.

MOVING ON

As one of the newsletter's most important features, the nameplate not only identifies your newsletter and reinforces its purpose, it should provide important issue-to-issue unity.

Your ability to create a distinctive nameplate is being enhanced by a new generation of drawing programs that make it easy to manipulate text in ways that were never before possible.

To ensure that you've created the best nameplate for your publication, review the following checklist:

- ☑ The nameplate emphasizes the most important word, or words, of my newsletter's title.

- ☑ I've eliminated unnecessary words from the nameplate and reduced the size of supporting words.

- ☑ The typeface reflects my newsletter's intended audience, message and editorial focus.

- ☑ I've reinforced my newsletter's identity by repeating the nameplate at a reduced size on inside pages.

- ☑ My nameplate has been properly aligned with the underlying page grid.

- ☑ I've explored the use of screened backgrounds, two-color printing and bleeds to emphasize the nameplate.

By evaluating your nameplate as it develops, you can make it a highly effective, powerful communication tool.

Regardless of the type of newsletter you're producing, the essence of your message will be contained in the editorial content. In Chapter 5, you'll examine the process of choosing the typeface, type size and line spacing most appropriate for the text of your newsletter. You'll also look at the various ways body copy can be styled—or manipulated—for maximum effectiveness.

CHAPTER FIVE

WORKING WITH BODY COPY

After creating an appropriate grid for your newsletter and creating a nameplate, the next step is to choose the typeface, type size, line spacing, alignment and other specifications for the body copy that will communicate your message.

THE RIGHT TYPEFACE

Your goal in choosing a body-copy typeface should be to find one that's easy to read. It should also contain enough letter-to-letter variations to enhance legibility without calling attention to itself or creating visual clutter. Many typefaces that work well for display purposes—in a nameplate or headline, for example—aren't appropriate for body copy. Even when set in small sizes, display type calls too much attention to itself, slowing readers down and creating visually distracting patterns, or texture, on the page.

Serifs

Before you consider typeface options, decide whether you want to use serif or sans-serif type or both. Serifs are small strokes at the ends of characters that help readers make letter-to-letter transitions. Serif type is more conventional, and sans-serif type (with no serifs), more contemporary. Although the trend seems to be moving toward sans-serif type for body copy, this is sometimes at the expense of readability.

Typefaces that are well suited for body copy are often characterized by moderate stress created by smooth, relatively even strokes, visible but not ostentatious serifs, a moderate x-height (defined below) and a comfortable width.

In most cases, the most useful serif faces are called Transitional. Typical examples include Caslon, Century Old Style, Times Roman and Stone Serif (a contemporary typeface created along classic lines). Transitional typefaces avoid the excesses of many Old Style or Modern serif faces.

For example, Old Style typefaces, like Goudy or Garamond, are characterized by less stress than Transitional faces, which can contribute to grayer looking pages.

Modern typefaces, like Bodoni or New Century School, have pronounced stress, which can make a page look busy.

Caslon is a Transitional favorite. Like Times Roman, Caslon characters are visually distinct enough to aid readability, without being so busy they distract from the text.

Proportions

Another factor to take into account when choosing a typeface for body copy is the x-height of the letters. Before going any further, however, let's become familiar with three important terms.

➤ Ascender—the tall vertical stroke of lowercase letters such as h and t.

➤ Descender—the stroke (as in g and p) that extends below the line of type.

➤ Baseline—the line that the type rests on.

X-Height

The x-height refers to the height of lowercase letters (for example, x, e, i, a, w and o) from baseline to top of the character. The x-height does not include ascenders and descenders.

Some serif typefaces, such as Bookman, have a high x-height. Others, like Times Roman, have a low x-height.

Times   Bookman

X-height affects word density per line, per page and per newsletter. Letters with high x-heights occupy more horizontal space than letters with low x-heights.

> We observed the brownish fox
> jumping happily around the
> sleeping puppy. We observed the
> brownish fox jumping happily

> We observed the brownish
> fox jumping happily around
> the sleeping puppy. We
> observed the brownish fox

High-x-height letters not only require more horizontal space, they also need additional leading (space between lines of type). Compare the two examples above. Notice how the moderate x-height of Times Roman leaves a significant sliver of space between the x-height of its lowercase letters and the ascenders of letters such as b, d, f, l and t. Likewise, notice the significant amount of space between the baseline and the descenders of letters like g, p and y. This space helps separate a line of text from the line above and below it.

However, high-x-height typefaces, such as Bookman, leave less space between lowercase letters and the tops of ascenders and, likewise, between the baseline and the descenders.

Because of their very low x-height and high descenders, typefaces such as Berthold Modern (an extreme example) often give a noticeable vertical orientation to the page. So if you use them, you'll need to compensate for this effect in your layout.

This typeface is Bernhard Modern. The ascenders are very tall, more than twice the x-height.
This typeface is Bernhard Modern. The ascenders are very tall, more than twice the x-height.
This typeface is Bernhard Modern. The ascenders are very tall, more than twice the x-height.

For maximum readability, it's a good idea to add extra leading when working with very high- or very low-x-height typefaces.

And—also for readability—you will probably want to add extra leading when using sans-serif typefaces.

Stress

Typefaces with a pronounced stress (wide variation in weight between thick and thin strokes of each letter) often cause problems in body copy. They can create visual confusion.

This paragraph is set in the typeface called Bodoni. This paragraph is set in the typeface called Bodoni. This paragraph is set in the typeface called

With typefaces with extreme stress, the fine strokes of characters tend to get lost, and the heavy strokes become prominent.

So be careful with typefaces such as *Bodoni* as a body-copy typeface. For example, Bodoni's extreme stress creates too much action on a page, especially if it's printed on a glossy paper.

Counters and Bowls

Other typeface characteristics that affect readability are called *counters* and *bowls*. Counters are partially enclosed areas, found in c or s. Bowls are totally enclosed areas like the eye of e or the center of g.

If the open spaces within these letters aren't wide enough to be clearly defined, the letters lose their definition and are harder to identify. If they're too wide, they can be distracting, which is why long blocks of boldface or heavy-weight type is often difficult to read.

TYPE SIZE AND LINE SPACING

Type is measured in points and picas. There are 12 points to the pica, 6 picas (or 72 points) to an inch. Often there's little correlation between type size and apparent height of the type. The point size of type is determined by measuring from the top of the ascenders to the bottom of the descenders. So different typefaces, set the same size, can appear dramatically different in size. That's because one typeface might have a low x-height while the other might have a high one.

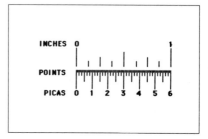

16 pt. Helvetica   16 pt. Times Roman

The vertical distance between lines of type is called *leading.* The term is a carryover from the early days of printing when strips of lead were inserted between the lines of type. Leading typically is measured from the baseline of one line to the baseline of the next line.

This is 10 point type
set with 12 point leading.
This is 10 point type
set with 12 point leading.
This is 10 point type
set with 12 point leading.

This is 10 point type

set with 15 point leading.

This is 10 point type

set with 15 point leading.

This is 10 point type

set with 15 point leading.

Relationships

There's an intimate relationship between typeface, type size, line spacing and line length. If you change one element, you should probably change at least one or more of the other elements.

For example, if you increase type size without changing line length, you may need to increase leading so that readers won't reread the same line of text.

If you reduce the column width, you should probably reduce the type size. Large type in a narrow column looks disproportionate and it slows down readers and forces too many words to be hyphenated. With justified text, it can also force unnaturally wide word spacing.

Likewise, as shown previously, if you change from a low- to a high-x-height typeface or from a serif to a sans-serif typeface, you may need

This is 14 pt. type with 16 pt. leading set on a 24 pica column width. This is 14 pt. type with 16 pt. leading set on a 24 pica column width.

This is the same size type set on a 12 pica column width. This is the same

to increase line spacing. The extra white space helps isolate each line of type, making it easier to read one line at a time.

Type Specimen Samples

To help you decide on the combination of typeface, type size and line spacing most suitable for your newsletter, you can create a type specimen file. This way, you can try out different combinations set to the column widths you've specified in your grid.

For example, if you're going to set type in columns 23 picas wide, try out alternative typeface, type size and leading choices.

Start by printing out a sample of 12-point type with 11-point leading. Then experiment. For example, change the leading to 13 or 14 points. Each time you change face, size or spacing, print out your sample and clearly label the specs for each sample.

When creating type specimen sheets, you might find it useful to experiment with the following alternatives:

One column:
Range of type size alternatives: 11 to 15 points
Leading alternatives: 13 to 17 points

Two columns (each column):
Range of type size alternatives: 9 to 13 points
Leading alternatives: 11 to 15 points

Three columns (each column):
Range of type size alternatives: 8 to 13 points
Range of possible leadings: 11 to 15 points

(double-wide columns for editorials, sidebars, etc.):
Range of type size alternatives: 10 to 13 points
Range of possible leadings: 11 to 14 points

Four columns (each column):
Range of type size alternatives: 9 to 13 points
Range of possible leadings: 11 to 15 points

Five columns (double-wide text columns):
Range of type size alternatives: 9 to 12 points
Range of possible leadings: 10 to 14 points

You'll soon notice that some samples are far more readable than others. Some are too dense, while others look too open. By creating your own type specimen samples, sized to the width of your columns, you'll be able to narrow down your specifications to those that are most appropriate for your newsletter.

In addition, you're likely to be surprised by how much a relatively small change in the x-height of letters affects word count per column inch.

ALIGNMENT

Another major decision involves alignment—whether to set type flush-left/ragged-right or justified. Alignment affects both the appearance and the readability of your newsletter.

In justified copy all lines are of equal length. The first and last letters in each line are aligned with the first and last letters in the lines above and below them. Justification is made possible by the automatic adjustment of letter and/or word spacing within the lines. In the following example, notice how word spacing in the second line is different from word spacing in the third line.

Flush-left/ragged-right copy is characterized by equal word spacing within each line. Since word spacing is the same, and lines composed

> We observed the brownish fox jumping happily around the sleeping puppy. We observed the brownish fox jumping happily

of different words (containing different letters) are usually different lengths, it's rare for two or more lines to be the same length.

> We observed the brownish fox jumping happily around the sleeping puppy. We observed the brownish fox jumping happily around the sleeping puppy.

Culturally, we're accustomed to seeing "serious" communications set in justified type. This is probably a carry-over from years of reading newspapers and news magazines where text density is a necessity.

Studies have shown that flush-left/ragged-right type is more readable because the equal word spacing helps readers move quickly through the body copy. More important, however, is that in flush-left/ragged-right copy, word spacing is tighter, leaving less white space between words and more white space at the ends of lines. The resulting larger areas of white space produce a stronger effect and greater impact as a design element.

TYPE STYLES

After you have decided on the typeface, type size, line spacing and alignment, you can selectively emphasize certain words, sentences and paragraphs by varying type styles.

Most body copy is set in roman (regular upright, unslanted) type. Other styles—used for emphasis or variety—include boldface type, italics, bold italics, underlining and small capitals.

Boldface • *Italics* • ***Bold Italics*** <u>Underlining</u> • Small Caps

Boldface and italic type should be used in small doses within body copy. Boldface type can draw attention to names within columns, but it can also make it harder to read adjacent words.

When more than a few words are set in boldface type, the text block tends to dominate the page.

Italics should also be used with discretion. The slant of italicized type slows reading down and makes it harder to correct typographical errors. This is because the slanted type on your computer screen often overlaps the spaces between words.

Bold italics darken a page and take up even more space.

This line is set in Times Roman type.

This line is set in Times Italic type.

This line is set in Times Bold Italic type.

Underlining should generally be avoided in desktop publishing. It reduces readability by obscuring the descenders of lowercase letters. Underlining is useful for typewritten copy; in fact, it's one of the few ways you can add emphasis with a typewriter. For desktop-published documents, however, boldface and italic type are much better choices.

Small caps (approximately 80 percent of the height of uppercase letters) can add emphasis to a few words—perhaps the title of a book—without darkening the page the way boldface type does. Small caps within a paragraph can call attention to a few words without competing with the uppercase letters that introduce sentences and proper nouns.

FINE-TUNE SPACING AND LINE ENDINGS

After you've set your type in columns, you can make refinements in its appearance in several ways.

Tracking

Most advanced word processing and desktop publishing programs let you alter letter spacing. Often, just a slight reduction in letter spacing can significantly increase word density and allow you to fit more words into a given space.

Yo-Yo   WAVE
Yo-Yo   WAVE

Properly used, this technique can make the newsletter look more professional.

Again, you can experiment with various tracking percentages by doing "before" and "after" samples of the typeface, type size and line spacing you've chosen.

Start by printing your sample using your program's normal (default) setting for letter and word spacing. Then, highlight your sample text block and change the letter and word spacing. Print out a sample at each setting. This will show you how changing the tracking quickly translates into a darker or lighter publication. Increasing tracking can also make your newsletter more readable for older or vision-impaired subscribers.

Word Spacing

Most desktop publishing and word processing programs let you assign minimum, maximum and desired word spacing to control the look of your body copy.

Reducing maximum allowable word spacing can eliminate large, unsightly holes that sometimes occur in lines of justified text. However, more words will be hyphenated when word spacing is reduced.

sleeping puppy. We observed the brownish fox jumping happily around the sleeping puppy. We observed the brownish fox jumping happily around the

around the sleeping puppy. We observed the brownish fox jumping happily around the sleeping puppy. We observed the brownish fox jumping happily around the

Reducing space can also darken columns of justified copy.

Most desktop publishing and word processing programs allow you to specify desired or optimum word spacing, which lets you tighten or expand word spacing in both flush-left/ragged-right and justified copy.

Letter- and word-spacing commands can be combined. For example, with a large-x-height typeface set in a small size in narrow columns, you might want to simultaneously tighten letter spacing (to increase word density) and open up word spacing (to help separate each word from its neighbors).

Hyphenation and Justification

Hyphenation works hand-in-hand with justification. With most word processing and desktop publishing programs, you can adjust default settings for hyphenation and enter discretionary hyphens (a specific location where you want a word to break if hyphenation is needed). You can also specify words that should not be hyphenated, such as proper nouns.

Remember that some words, such as proj'•ect (noun) and pro•ject' (verb), are often hyphenated differently when used as verbs or nouns.

You can also adjust the hyphenation zone of your text. Decreasing the hyphenation zone increases the number of words that must be hyphenated, and vice versa.

Column Endings

A final decision for multicolumn newsletters is whether to align the ends of columns at the bottom of a page.

Aligned column endings create a more formal tone, but they take more time to prepare.

ALIGNED COLUMNS

We observed the brownish fox jumping happily around the sleeping puppy. We observed the brownish fox jumping happily around the sleeping puppy. We observed the brownish fox jumping happily around the sleeping puppy. We observed the brownish fox jumping happily around the sleeping puppy. We observed the brownish fox jumping happily around the sleeping puppy. We observed the brownish fox jumping happily around the sleeping puppy. We observed the brownish fox jumping happily around the sleeping puppy. We observed the brownish fox jumping happily around the sleeping puppy. We observed the brownish fox jumping happily around the sleeping puppy. We observed the brownish fox jumping happily around the sleeping puppy. We observed the brownish fox jumping happily around the sleeping puppy. We observed the brownish fox jumping happily around the sleeping puppy. We observed the brownish fox jumping happily around the sleeping puppy.

IRREGULAR COLUMNS

We observed the brownish fox jumping happily around the sleeping puppy. We observed the brownish fox jumping happily around the sleeping puppy. We observed the brownish fox jumping happily around the sleeping puppy. We observed the brownish fox jumping happily around the sleeping puppy. We observed the brownish fox jumping happily around the sleeping puppy. We observed the brownish fox jumping happily around the sleeping puppy. We observed the brownish fox jumping happily around the sleeping puppy. We observed the brownish fox jumping happily around the sleeping puppy. We observed the brownish fox jumping happily around the sleeping puppy. We observed the brownish fox jumping happily around the sleeping puppy.

Irregular column endings lighten up and add contrast to a layout by creating varying amounts of white space at the bottom of each page.

They also speed up production, since no one has to labor over lining up column endings.

PARAGRAPH FORMATTING

Another decision to make is how to start new paragraphs. You have the option of indenting the first line of each paragraph, or adding extra line space for separation, with no indent. If you choose to indent, you must determine how deep you want the indent to be.

Extra space between paragraphs can impart a dignified, formal atmosphere, especially when used with justified type.

Indented paragraphs are often considered more intimate and conversational and are often the preferred choice for flush-left/ragged-right type.

paper. Some, however, cannot transmit information that runs from edge to edge. In other words, the scanner must have margins.

Unattended Operation

Virtually all machines can receive and print a fax automatically without the intervention of an operator.

However, if your machine shares a line with a telephone and doesn't have an auto voice/data switch, the fax machine won't be able to receive messages unattended during those periods of the day when the telephone must be accessible.

Transmission Time

Because it affects your telephone charges for fax transmissions, transmission time (the length of time it takes a document to get from here to there) is a key feature and selling point. It also may affect your administrative costs associated with fax. Consequently, manufacturers often present impressive numbers to prospective buyers to convince them that their machine is the fastest. Unfortunately, the machine's performance in the workplace may not match the manufacturer's performance claim.

Your actual transmission time is influenced by several factors. Consider, for instance, the speed, or baud rate, of the modem (the device that actually sends the information over the telephone lines). As mentioned earlier, Group 3 fax machines send information at a minimum of 2,400 characters

If you indent the first line of each paragraph, be sure the depth of the indention is proportionate to both the type size and the column width you've chosen. Your program's default paragraph indent may be too deep for narrow columns.

A safe choice is to base indention on an em space (a space equal to the width of the uppercase M in the point size of the typeface you're using in your text).

How much wood would a woodchuck chuck if a woodchuck could chuck wood?

Adding paragraph spacing equal to a little less than half of your normal line space is more pleasing than the exaggerated paragraph spacing created by double-spacing. The lines are far enough apart to indicate the start of a new paragraph, yet not so far apart that unnatural horizontal bands of white space appear on your page.

happily the sleeping puppy. We observed the brownish fox jumping happily around the sleeping puppy. We observed the brownish fox jumping happily around the sleeping puppy.

We observed the brownish fox jumping happily around the sleeping puppy. We observed the brownish fox jumping happily around the

happily the sleeping puppy. We observed the brownish fox jumping happily around the sleeping puppy. We observed the brownish fox jumping happily around the sleeping puppy.

We observed the brownish fox jumping happily around the sleeping puppy. We observed the brownish fox jumping happily around the

Most desktop publishing or word processing programs let you control the amounts of white space before and after paragraphs. This allows you to choose a more precise amount of space than you'd get by simply double-spacing with the RETURN key.

Indents Add Contrast

Most desktop publishing and word processing programs allow you to indent all the lines in a paragraph from the left. This is a useful technique for formatting a list without darkening the page. The narrow band of white space next to the paragraph adds visual interest to the page and calls attention to the emphasized words without destroying the unity of the list.

Sentence Spacing

In high-school typing class, you were probably taught to press the space bar twice after the period at the end of each sentence. This was good advice when you were using monospaced type. The extra space was necessary to accentuate the end of each sentence.

Now that you're using proportionally spaced type, this is bad advice. With word processing and desktop publishing, two spaces after each period create unnaturally large "holes" between sentences, especially in justified columns.

The extra space between sentences can be eliminated in two ways. One is to train yourself, and those who prepare word-processed manuscripts for you, to press the space bar only once after each period. However, many people find it difficult to break habits ingrained over many years.

An easier alternative is to use your software program's Search and Replace or Change feature to find all occurrences of two spaces and replace them with a single space. This takes only a few seconds. Using this feature should become second nature to you. (I went so far as to create a macro—or keyboard shortcut—to speed-up executing the command.)

You'll be surprised at how much this simple change will improve the appearance of your newsletter. In addition, eliminating the extra space often shortens paragraphs and can prevent *widows* (single words or syllables that sit alone on the last line of a paragraph or page).

COPYFITTING

Paying attention to copyfitting can save you a lot of time, which you can use to further refine your newsletter. Copyfitting helps you write more efficiently and gives your writers parameters so they can prepare the right amount of copy to fit available space.

Determine Word Count Per Column Inch

The first step in counting words is to ascertain the number of words that will fit in a six-inch text column set in the typeface, size and leading you've chosen.

Today's word processing and desktop publishing programs include a word-count feature, typically associated with the spell-checker. To determine the word count, you may want to follow these steps:

➤ Create a column, the same width as your body-copy columns, six inches high.

➤ Prepare a word-processed file consisting of sentences and paragraphs that simulate the content of your newsletter.

➤ Place this file in your previously created column and format it the same as your body copy (i.e., using the same typeface, type size, type style, letter spacing and word spacing).

If you're using a system with a built-in spell-check program, highlight the words in the column of text and activate the spell-check or word-count feature.

Next, divide this total by six—the number of inches in the column. The resulting figure will be the number of words per column inch. (As you'll see in Chapter 9, you can use this figure to guide your own writing or when assigning articles to others.)

If your page layout program lacks a word-count feature, simply export the column of text to a word processing program and let the spell-check or word-count feature compute the words per column inch.

STYLES

Most desktop publishing and word processing programs make it easy to quickly and consistently format the body copy in your document. You can create electronic files—called styles—that store all the specifications for the types of body copy you're likely to use. These files can be instantly recalled and their attributes applied as you place the copy, or afterwards.

Styles can be created from scratch, or you can "style by example" by highlighting a previously formatted passage and giving it a name. From that point on, you can apply that style to any body copy.

Style options let you quickly select

➤ Typeface

➤ Type size

➤ Line spacing

➤ Alignment

➤ Left- and right-hand margins

➤ Paragraph indent

➤ Letter spacing

➤ Word spacing

➤ Modified hyphenation defaults

➤ Shading and color

Styles also play an important role in formatting paragraphs. You can specify the depth of the first-line indent as well as desired space above and below each paragraph.

You'll quickly grow to appreciate this feature, because it lets you assign different styles for the first paragraph (typically not indented) as well as the last paragraph in an article (which usually has more space following it than other paragraphs).

Styles not only expedite body-copy formatting and make it easy to maintain consistency; they also allow rapid reformatting. If you decide to use a different typeface, type size, line spacing or alignment, instead of reformatting each paragraph or text block, you can simply edit your style definition and all the text will be reformatted. This is much easier than having to change these specifications in each article.

A style definition can also be created for indented lists, which will specify the position of asterisks, bullets or numbers. For added emphasis and contrast with adjacent paragraphs, lists can be indented from both the left- and right-hand margins.

By adjusting the tab indent feature, you can control the amount of space between the asterisk, bullet or number and the copy. Entering a negative number into your software program's first-line paragraph indent improves the appearance and readability of the list by lining up the second and following lines of each entry below the first line rather than beneath the asterisk, bullet or number.

■ Let the square bullet stand alone
   for greater emphasis.

■ Let this bullet stand alone, too.

You can also use your styles feature to provide right- and left-hand indents for body copy used in sidebars. Sidebars should be indented an equal amount of space on each side so the text will contrast with the surrounding box.

If the sidebar text isn't indented, there won't be enough contrast with adjacent text, and the box surrounding it will look crowded.

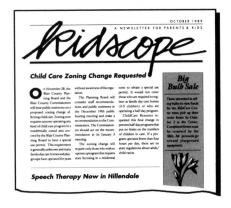

If you're indenting the first line of each paragraph, you'll probably want to create a special "first paragraph" style without an indent, since first paragraphs of stories typically aren't indented.

Likewise, you might want to create a style that specifies extra space after a paragraph that precedes a subhead or concludes an article.

REFINEMENTS

When working with body copy, be aware of the eye's tendency to create relationships where none exist. For example, concentrated space in adjacent lines of type—caused by exaggerated word spacing in large, justified text set in narrow columns—can cause "rivers" of white space running diagonally through your body copy. These rivers can be very distracting, since they draw the reader's eye like a magnet.

feugait nulla facilisi. Lorem ipsum dolor sit amet, consectetuer adipiscing elit, sed diam nonummy nibh   euismod tincidunt ut laoreet dolore magna aliquam erat volutpat. Ut wisi enim ad minim veniam, quis nostrud exerci tation   ullamcorper suscipit lobortis nisl ut aliquip ex ea commodo consequat.

When working with justified type, large type in narrow columns, or a narrow hyphenation zone, it's possible to end up with several consecutive hyphenated lines. Excessive hyphenation is distracting and slows down readership. Adjust the hyphenation zone and use discretionary hyphens and non-breaking words to eliminate the problem.

Remember to always be courteous, attentive, responsive and knowledgeable about your own product. Remember to always be courteous, attentive, responsive, and knowledge-

Widows and *orphans* are another frequently encountered problem area. Although some desktop publishing and word processing programs help eliminate them, they still require attention. A widow is a fragment of a line (a word, portion of a word, or less than a third of a line) left at the bottom of a page or column of type. An orphan is a word, portion of a word, or less than a third of a line left alone at the top of a page or column of text.

Equally distracting are single-line paragraphs or single lines of a paragraph isolated by themselves at the top or bottom of a page.

Widows and orphans can usually be eliminated by editing. Transposing a few words earlier in the paragraph often eliminates the problem.

Character Substitutions

A final body-copy refinement involves utilizing the extra punctuation marks and symbols desktop publishing makes available. Although some combinations of computers and software programs automatically use such characters, sometimes you must specify the characters.

Desktop publishing and word processing software used with laser printers, for example, allow you to use either an en dash or an em dash. Because of their more proportional length, these options make for better-looking body copy than single or double hyphens.

Another refinement replaces standard up-and-down quotation marks with differentiated open and closed quotes—commonly referred to as *curly quotes*. These do a better job of framing the quotation.

MOVING ON

As you now can see, there's far more to typography than text flow. Selecting the right type involves taking a close look at typeface design and making choices that add visual interest to your page as well as enhancing readability. It also involves positioning, manipulating and refining the type elements.

To evaluate the typography in your newsletter, refer to the following checklist:

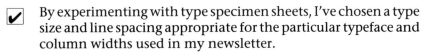 By experimenting with type specimen sheets, I've chosen a type size and line spacing appropriate for the particular typeface and column widths used in my newsletter.

 I've considered overall content and design in choosing the proper alignment.

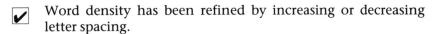 Word density has been refined by increasing or decreasing letter spacing.

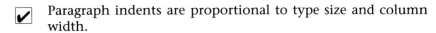 Paragraph indents are proportional to type size and column width.

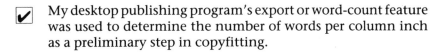 My desktop publishing program's export or word-count feature was used to determine the number of words per column inch as a preliminary step in copyfitting.

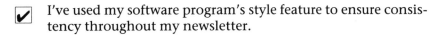 I've used my software program's style feature to ensure consistency throughout my newsletter.

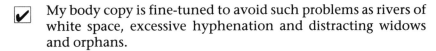 My body copy is fine-tuned to avoid such problems as rivers of white space, excessive hyphenation and distracting widows and orphans.

Long, unbroken expanses of body copy create gray-looking newsletters that discourage readership. In the next chapter, you'll look at ways of adding visual interest to a page with reader cues, such as headlines and pull-quotes. They provide "hooks" to attract readers who are skimming your newsletter, encouraging them to read on.

CHAPTER SIX

A DDING READER CUES

Reader cues—headlines, subheads, tables of contents, continuation heads, jumplines, pull-quotes, department heads and other markers—act as road signs on the reader's journey through the text. They give direction and highlight key information and points of interest. They also add visual relief and color to a page. If your signals are clear, your readers can quickly see what's most important and what they want to read.

In fact, the entire front page of a newsletter should be considered a reader cue. You can use it to attract readers inside by carefully choosing text and graphics and including a table of contents.

Each reader cue functions as a hook, or magnet, that can lure people who might just be scanning your publication into actually reading it. By breaking up long blocks of text into bite-sized chunks, reader cues add white space, visual variety and readability.

A unified design can be reinforced by using the same typeface, type size, spacing and alignment for each type of cue—headline, subhead, pull-quote, etc. Consistent treatment avoids the chaos that can result when a reader cue is treated in a different way each time it's used.

Be sure to give the same emphasis to equally important items throughout your publication. For example, all "Level One" headlines should have the same type treatment, all "Level Two" subheads should be treated the same, etc. Readers should be able to determine an item's importance at a glance.

Contrast is important, too. Reader cues should be different from the body copy. And they should contrast somewhat with each other, so readers don't misread headlines as subheads, or subheads as pull-quotes or body copy.

STYLE SHEETS

As you design your reader cues, you can use your software program's style sheets to store your selections of typeface, type size, alignment, spacing and graphic enhancements. Style sheets help you maintain consistency, so that you treat the headlines, subheads, pull-quotes and initial caps on page 5 the same way you do on page 1.

MARK YOUR TEXT

To get started, return to your planning sheets and identify the information categories likely to be repeated in each issue of your newsletter. Then analyze your word-processed files to find key words, phrases and points where new ideas are introduced.

Highlight phrases or sentences that introduce important ideas or summarize the surrounding body copy, then draw lines to mark these paragraphs. This will help you locate appropriate places to insert pull-quotes, subheads and initial capital letters.

HEADLINES

Well-written, well-presented headlines can do more to increase the readership of your newsletter than any other element. Readers often base their decision to read on headlines. A good headline can lure a reader into a poorly written article, but a bad headline can torpedo even the best text.

Consequently, headlines must stand out. Consider the following design tools when choosing a headline style (or other reader cue):

SIZE ■ As a rule, the greater the size difference between headline and body copy, the better.

TYPEFACE ■ Sans-serif headlines and serif body copy work well together.

WEIGHT ■ Size and typeface contrast can be enhanced by using different stroke weights: heavy weights are particularly effective.

STYLE ■ Boldface, as well as italics and boldface italics used sparingly, adds motion and gives voice to your headlines.

CASE ■ A combination of upper- and lowercase type provides contrast and readability.

ALIGNMENT ■ Reader cues can be set flush-left, flush-right or centered. (Centered type can slow down reading.)

SPACING ■ Unusual letter spacing transforms letters into visual icons (useful for repeating elements such as department heads).

SHADING AND COLOR ■ To distinguish headlines from the body copy they introduce, reader cues can be printed in shades of gray or (with restraint) in a second color. This works particularly well with department heads.

BACKGROUNDS ■ Like nameplates, reader cues can be placed against a reversed, screened or colored background.

GRAPHIC ACCENTS ■ Graphic accents, such as rules or boxes—as on this page—make reader cues stand out.

Adding Emphasis to Headlines

Headlines succeed when they contrast with, and at the same time complement, the body copy. In general, they're set noticeably larger than the body copy, but not large enough to overwhelm.

A frequent design mistake is setting headlines too small. Notice how much better the right-hand example looks with larger headlines.

It may be worth editing your headlines down to a few words so you can set them in larger type. Remember, the fewer the words, the larger and more eye-catching the headline.

Choosing the Right Typeface

Blocks of text are easier to read in serif typefaces, while headlines and other reader cues are usually more effective in contrasting sans-serif faces. And because it takes longer for the eye to form words from the stark shapes of sans-serif letters, the reader has more time to absorb the message of your headline.

Compare the totally different headline treatments in the examples above. The left-hand page is more formal than the right page, which uses contrasting typeface families for headlines and body copy.

When deciding whether to use different typeface families as well as sizes to create contrast between headlines and body copy, consider the amount of drama or impact you want. When you use different type families as well as sizes, you create a bolder, more assertive newsletter.

Typographic Options

You can improve your headlines by using different weights, or stroke thicknesses, of your chosen typefaces. Notice how much stronger the right-hand headline is than the left example. The heavier Helvetica Black has more impact than the standard boldface version.

Most familiar sans-serif typefaces (Stone Sans, Futura, Helvetica, Swiss, Univers, etc.) are available in more than one weight. The heavier weights are wider than the standard roman typefaces that come with your desktop publishing or word processing program.

This is Stone Sans.
This is Stone Sans Demi-bold.
This is Stone Sans Bold.

When a lot of words must fit in a short space, try using the light and dark *condensed* versions of the most popular typefaces.

Likewise, most of the familiar sans-serif typefaces are available in condensed light and dark versions. Condensed typefaces are narrower, letting you fit more words on a line.

They were the best of friends.

They were the best of friends.

Often, one of the best investments you can make for your typeface library is to purchase additional weights of the sans-serif typefaces you already have. These will add visual variety to your documents without introducing the "ransom note" effect that can occur when too many typefaces are used on one page.

Use italics when you want to phrase your headline in a questioning tone. Italics often represent or imply conversation. Thus, a question has more impact when presented in this style.

Uppercase Headlines

Unfortunately, using uppercase type to add emphasis to important headlines can produce the opposite effect.

Headlines set in all uppercase letters can actually weaken your page design. This might force you to use a smaller typeface or reduce surrounding white space, since uppercase type occupies about one-third more space than lowercase type.

The main problem with uppercase type is that it's hard to read. Lowercase ascenders and descenders help the reader identify the letters and recognize words, whereas uppercase shapes blend together into uniform rectangles.

Uppercase headlines can work, however, if they're limited to one or two high-impact words. Because uppercase type lacks descenders, you'll probably need to reduce line spacing to draw the lines together.

Headline Alignment

Newsletter headlines can be centered; however, that often can lead to serious problems.

Extending the headline, "From Sea to Shining Sea" without leaving enough white space to frame it, can seriously weaken the appearance of the page and keep the headline from emerging as a strong visual unit.

When centered headlines are set in large type in narrow columns, readers tend to read across the column and into the next one.

Finally, centered headlines, especially when they're more than one line in length, make the reader work harder. The eyes must search for the start of each line of the headline, then move to the left to find the beginning of the body copy. For this reason, centered headlines work best when they're short.

Flush-left alignment, on the other hand, makes the transition quicker and smoother from headline to body copy.

Flush-right alignment can be quite effective for short headlines.

You can also use a mixture of flush-left and flush-right headlines. If used with a lot of discretion, this technique can be used to balance the left- and right-hand sides of a page.

Headline Refinements

Next to your nameplate, headlines are the largest and most dynamic feature of your newsletter, so it's important to design them carefully. You'll need to pay particular attention to kerning (adjusting the space between letters) and line spacing.

VARY YOUR HABITS

VARY YOUR HABITS

It's a good idea to get in the habit of kerning all headlines set larger than 24 points. Kerning is the process of manually reducing letter spacing between selected pairs of letters. Virtually all desktop publishing and word processing programs let you eliminate or reduce white space between individual letters.

The larger your type size, the more important it is to refine letter spacing. Kerning accomplishes two things: the words come into clearer focus, and white space increases around the headline.

Likewise, it's important to eliminate extra white space between the lines of a headline. Unless instructed differently, most word processing and desktop publishing programs automatically space lines at approximately 120 percent of the type size chosen. Although an extra 20 percent of space is acceptable—even desirable—with small type sizes, the extra space becomes very noticeable at large type sizes, contributing another unfortunate example to the "Interstate Highway" school of design. Instead of emerging as a unit, headlines appear as a series of isolated lines.

Just as you can improve the appearance of your headlines by adjusting white space between letters and lines, you can frame headlines with extra space above and below them.

Always leave more space above a headline than between the headline and the body copy it introduces. This makes it clear that the headline and body copy belong together.

In the left-hand example, the relationship between the headline and body copy is less obvious. The headline, centered between two articles, conceivably could relate to the article above; or in a long article, it could be mistaken for a pull-quote.

One pitfall to avoid, however, is inadvertently creating a tombstone effect. This occurs when short headlines run parallel to one another in adjacent columns. When that happens, readers tend to read across the columns, instead of seeing each headline as a self-contained entity.

When two headlines have to be set next to each other in adjacent columns, you can reduce the tombstone effect by setting both headlines flush-left or by using a condensed typeface to force more white space to the right of each headline. You can also set one headline in a slightly larger type size or a different type style—perhaps italics.

Whenever possible, avoid "floating" headlines that have no clear connection to adjacent visuals or text blocks. Floating headlines not only display a lack of attention to detail, they slow the reader down. Readers will be confused by the headline's placement, neither centered nor aligned with the visual.

In addition, floating headlines weaken design by dissipating white space above and below the headline, rather than using it as a significant design element to deliberately emphasize the headline from above.

Continuation Heads

It's important to give your readers clear and accurate cues for articles continued on the inside pages. How often have you searched desperately for an article that was supposed to continue on page 5, but apparently didn't?

Continuation headlines should not compete with headlines introducing articles on inside pages. They should always be smaller than article headlines. In addition, they should contain at least some of the same words found in the article's headline. Don't make readers play a guessing game of locating the article they want to continue reading.

JUMPLINES

Jumplines identify where an article continues or where it's continued from. Like other reader cues, jumplines need separation and contrasting size and style so they won't be accidentally read as part of the body copy or a continuation headline. They're usually set in small italic type.

EYEBROWS AND SUBTITLES

You can enhance organization and continuity in your newsletter by introducing articles with *eyebrows* or department headings that categorize their content.

Because eyebrows and department headings are *recognized* more than they're *read*, you can legitimately use such design techniques as exaggerated letter spacing and reversed or screened backgrounds to make them stand out. Readability can take a back seat to visual impact.

Thus, you might want to pick up your nameplate design or use a script or specially modified typeface created with a drawing program.

Eyebrows and subtitles can also be explanatory sentences, supporting a headline. Called *decks* or *blurbs*, these sentences summarize the headline and help attract the reader to the article.

SUBHEADS

The same techniques that make headlines effective also work with subheads. Placed throughout an article to introduce a break in the editorial flow, subheads should contrast with body copy in type size, style, alignment, white space and graphic accents.

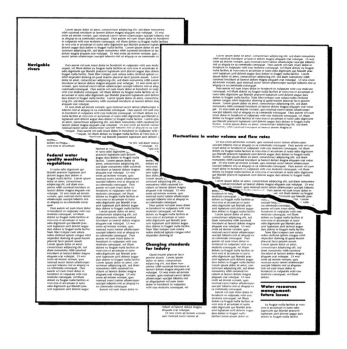

When there's insufficient contrast, subheads tend to blend into the body copy, failing to give readers a sneak preview of the content.

Larger and bolder subheads, in a contrasting typeface, communicate more effectively and add visual interest to the page.

Subhead Placement

When possible, subheads should be placed adjacent to the body copy they introduce. This is easy to do when you're using newsletter grids that have both wide and narrow columns.

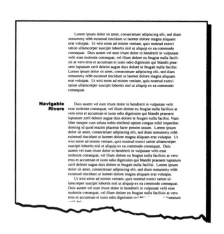

Avoid using centered, uppercase subheads, which often look like mini-headlines and can be distracting barriers. Like centered headlines, centered subheads fill white space and force readers to search for the first line of text.

Instead, use flush-left subheads set in upper- and lowercase type. These provide more space to the right and make it easier to find the first line of text.

For a different effect, a flush-right subhead located in a column to the left of the body copy forces white space to the left, locking the subhead to the body copy it introduces.

Avoiding Buried Subheads

Don't leave a subhead alone at the bottom of a column. Follow it with at least three lines of text before a column or page break.

PULL-QUOTES

Using pull-quotes is one of the best ways to entice readers into a newsletter article.

Design consistency is as important for pull-quotes as it is for other reader cues. Use your desktop publishing or word processing program's style feature to maintain consistent typography and spacing.

Pull-quotes can be set in another version of the same typeface used for headlines and subheads. Or you can use a larger, lighter version of a different typeface.

You could also choose a larger, italicized version of the body-copy typeface.

Condensed typefaces that allow more words to fit into a given space are often a good choice for pull-quotes placed in narrow five- or seven-column grids.

Placement

It's important to place pull-quotes within paragraphs, rather than between them. Otherwise, they could be mistaken for subheads.

Lorem ipsum dolor sit amet, consectetuer adipiscing elit, sed diambortis nisl ut aliquip ex ea

Pull-quotes are good for highlighting important information.

Commodo consequat. Duis autem vel eum iriure t my nibh euismod aliquam erat volutpat. Ut wisi veniam, quis nostrud exerci

Lorem ipsum dolor sit amet, consectetuer adipiscing elit, sed diambortis nisl ut aliquip ex ea

Pull-quotes are good for highlighting important information.

commodo consequat. Duis autem vel eum iriure t my nibh euismod aliquam erat volutpat. Ut wisi ip ea commodo consequveniam, quis

As for placing pull-quotes on a page, you have a lot of leeway. But avoid placing a pull-quote too close to the text from which it's extracted. Readers might be confused by reading the same thing twice. Use space and type treatment to distinguish the pull-quote from the body copy.

Pull-quotes can be confined to single columns, or extend across two or more columns in a multicolumn format.

Horizontal or vertical rules, boxes or screened backgrounds can be used to isolate pull-quotes from adjacent body copy.

INITIAL CAPS

Initial caps—large capital letters introducing the first word of an article or paragraph—are important as reader cues. Initial caps can also provide welcome visual breaks in long articles.

The three types of initial caps are dropped, raised and adjacent.

Consequat. Duis autem veleum iriure dolor in hendrerit in

Consequat. Duis autem vel eum iriure dolor in hendrerit in vulputate

Consequat. Duis autem vel eum iriure dolor in hendrerit in vulputate velit esse

The most distinctive, and easiest to create, is the raised initial cap. It strengthens your newsletter design by forcing white space between the paragraph it introduces and the preceding one.

Raised initial caps can be placed flush to the left margin of a column, or can be deeply indented—surrounding the paragraph introduction with white space both to the left and above it.

Dropped initial caps are a bit more difficult to create, although some desktop publishing programs can automatically produce them. Because dropped caps don't occupy as much vertical space, they don't decrease word density very much. Unlike raised caps, they don't break up copy by adding space between paragraphs.

For grids that combine narrow and wide columns, adjacent initial caps can be placed to the left of the paragraphs they introduce. They're easy to produce. However, readers sometimes have difficulty relating them to the copy they introduce.

Initial Cap Placement

It's important to link the initial cap with the remaining letters of the first word. You'll need to carefully adjust the letter space, to avoid an awkward gap.

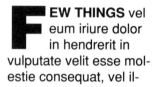

To smooth the transition between an initial cap and the paragraph it introduces, you can emphasize the first few words or the entire first line with larger or boldface type, or with small caps.

Typographic Options

Numerous typeface variations are available for initial caps. You can use a larger size of either the headline or body-copy typeface. Or you might select the same typeface used in the nameplate or department heads.

Another option is using a drawing program to create a special, stylized alphabet that can be imported as graphics files.

You might choose to use decorative letters available as clip-art files.

Regardless of which technique you use, the baseline of the initial cap must align with the baseline of one line of body copy. Otherwise, the initial cap will "float" instead of being integrated into the paragraph.

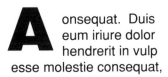 

The first letter in a headline or pull-quote is often enlarged, too. In pull-quotes, you can use oversized initial quotation marks in conjunction with initial caps. These quotation marks don't have to be the same size as the initial cap; they can be smaller than the initial cap and larger than the body copy.

Regardless of how you use initial caps, they need to be large enough to contrast with the body copy. Otherwise, they can be confusing. They might look like capitals with a case of the mumps!

Fine-Tuning Your Initial Caps

Initial caps generally look best when most of them are placed on the top one-third of a page. When they're grouped at the bottom, they can make a page look weighted down.

Finally, always double-check your work to make sure that your initial caps don't inadvertently spell an embarrassing word!

THE FRONT PAGE

It's important that you include more than one article on the front cover of your newsletter. By beginning two or three articles on the first page and continuing them inside, you increase the likelihood of readers opening to the inside pages. Otherwise, you may lose a lot of readers who never bother to turn the page because they're not interested in the article on the cover.

Also, you can run a "teaser" photograph on the cover that introduces an article inside. Augment the photograph with a headline, brief sentence and jumpline directing readers inside.

TABLE OF CONTENTS

Another way of increasing readership is to place a well-designed table of contents on the front page. It should list the titles and page numbers of articles that begin inside. Don't bury it or make it hard to read. If it's going to attract readers, it must stand out prominently.

In other cases, the table of contents can be placed horizontally above the nameplate—a spot where it's sure to be noticed. If you put it there, it won't have to compete with article headlines and body copy.

In an asymmetrical, multicolumn newsletter, the table of contents can be placed in a narrow column to the left or right of the body-copy area.

It can also be centered at the bottom of the front page.

Including photographs in your table of contents can invite readership. Try grouping a series of photos or portions of photos that relate to inside articles. If you use this technique, be sure to edit article titles down to the fewest possible words.

Design Considerations

White space can be effective in your table of contents, but it must be used carefully.

You often see article titles placed flush-left, with page numbers set flush-right. However, this alignment scheme can create a chasm of white space between the article title and the corresponding page number. If dot leaders are inserted to bridge the gap, the contents box and the page itself may look too "horizontal," creating a new problem.

Good Design Made Great	**1**
Newsletters	**23**
Business	**61**

Instead, try placing page numbers flush-left, titles flush-right and use typographic contrast for separation. Type size, family and style can distinguish the various components from one another.

85	**Brochures & Flyers**
127	**Reports & Proposals**
143	**Advertisements**

Or, you can use oversized page numbers—perhaps placed against a reversed or screened background—to add visual impact to your table of contents.

155	**Miscellaneous Documents**
185	**Catalogs & Booklets**
215	**Charts & Graphs**

Using these techniques consistently in each issue of your newsletter will increase their overall effectiveness.

OTHER READER CUES

Author bylines are an important reader cue. Contrast is necessary to prevent bylines from merging into the body copy and losing their impact.

Instead of or in addition to providing a byline at the top of an article, you might consider rewarding the writer with a one- or two-line biography at the end of the piece. These biographies should be set in a smaller, contrasting typeface so they're not confused with the text. Italic type works well here.

Other possible reader cues include oversized numbers, used to organize information in lists. Compare the two samples. The small numbers in the left-hand example provide little visual interest and don't draw your eye through the list. In the example at right, however, the oversized numbers create an urge to glance at each paragraph.

1. Lorem ipsum dolor sit amet, consectetuer adipiscing

2. Laoreet dolore magna aliquam erat volutpat.

3. Lamcorper suscipit lobortis nisl ut aliquip ex ea com

1 Lorem ipsum dolor sit amet, consectetuer adipis

2 Laoreet dolore magna aliquam erat volutpat.

3 Lamcorper suscipit lobor tis nisl ut aliquip ex ea

MOVING ON

As you've seen in this chapter, reader cues perform a dual role. They improve the appearance of your publication by adding white space and enhancing readability.

Contrast and consistency are the keys to effective reader cues. To succeed, they must contrast with adjacent body copy. Consistency is equally important: typographic decisions made at the start of your newsletter should be maintained throughout.

To evaluate the reader cues in your newsletter, you may want to refer to the following checklist:

✔ Reader cues are consistent in style throughout the newsletter.

✔ On the front page, I've included sufficient reader cues (e.g., table of contents, teasers and jumplines) that invite readers to turn the page and look inside.

✔ I've created headlines that reflect the content of the articles.

✔ Department headings and other reader cues amplify a headline's meaning.

✔ Headline alignment avoids parallelism, which can confuse readers.

✔ I've broken up long blocks of body copy with subheads and initial caps.

✔ Initial caps are large enough to contrast with the body copy they introduce.

Charts, graphs, illustrations and—most important—photographs play a major role in most newsletters. In the next chapter, we'll examine the various ways visuals can be manipulated, resized and laid out. We'll also look at the importance of treating visuals consistently.

CHAPTER SEVEN

PLACING AND MANIPULATING VISUALS

Visuals are important ingredients in your newsletter design. The time and effort you put into choosing and arranging them can pay big dividends in attracting and increasing readership.

Use visuals to add interest to your pages, set the tone of your publication, prioritize and reinforce important ideas, and distinguish newsletter issues from one another.

Photographs and illustrations are the most popular visual forms. (A picture *is* worth a thousand words, after all.) Likewise, charts and graphs prepared with a page layout program or imported from a charting and graphing program can breathe life into numbers. Clip art, used with restraint, can serve your needs occasionally.

CHOOSING YOUR VISUALS CAREFULLY

Be ruthlessly critical in choosing your illustrations. Rarely, if ever, should all available photographs be used. Choose those with the most story-telling power.

Select the type of chart or graph that will be most effective in getting the point across.

For example, choose pie charts if you're interested in comparing amounts.

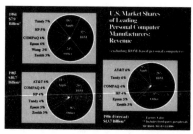

Use line graphs if you want to compare trends.

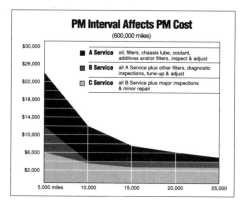

Use bar graphs to compare amounts.

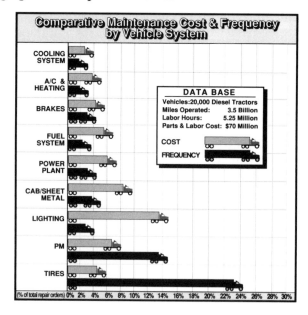

Be discriminating with clip art. Clip art works best when a few well-chosen pieces are used to add character to a publication.

Clip art loses its effectiveness when too many small pieces are used on a page.

Clip-art illustrations, such as maps, can take the place of expensive, time-consuming original artwork. Drawing programs let you manipulate clip art to disguise its "off-the-shelf" origins. Clip-art images can be enlarged, boxed and reshaped. In addition, paint-type drawing programs let you add different line borders and background patterns.

EMPHASIZING THE MOST IMPORTANT INFORMATION

Sometimes it's helpful to manipulate your photos to improve their communicating power.

For example, *cropping* a photo lets you trim unnecessary information off the top, bottom or sides to emphasize the important part.

Another technique, *silhouetting*, lets you drop out a distracting background from a photo, allowing the reader to focus on the most important element.

Silhouetting is particularly useful in association and employee newsletters, often characterized by photographs of employees taken in a work environment with cluttered backgrounds.

Silhouetting offers yet another advantage: it can change the shape of a photo from a square or rectangle into an irregular form that allows the text to wrap around it. This treatment is appropriately called a wraparound. Restraint with this technique is a virtue: one silhouette to a page or two-page spread is enough.

THE BEST SIZE AND SHAPE

Even the size of a photo communicates something to the reader. Important photos should be larger than detail, or supporting, ones.

Resizing

You can increase the communicating power of some photographs by resizing them. Using a variety of sizes and shapes improves page design and makes the status of each photo clear. Important photographs are large and supporting photographs smaller.

If you have access to an image scanner, you can experiment with various ways of cropping and sizing photographs to maximize their communicating power. (Scanner options are discussed later in this chapter.) On your computer screen, for example, you can see how just a portion of a photograph would look if dramatically increased in size and placed on a newsletter page.

Image scanners affect newsletter quality by improving communication with your commercial printer. You can show your printer exactly how you want the image to be cropped, sized and placed on the page.

Contrasting Sizes

One of the best ways to add interest to a page or spread is to use significantly different sizes of photographs. Whenever possible, try to avoid placing photos of equal, or near-equal, size on the same page or two-page spread. Photos of equal size tend to cancel each other out. The example below shows how photos of different sizes complement each other. You know at a glance which of the three is more important.

Likewise, you avoid excessive balance by not placing two photos at the same location on a spread. Otherwise, you would have mirror-image pages that compete with each other.

You're more likely to attract readers' attention if you present inter-dependent photographs in proper relationship to one another.

When resizing photographs for a page containing several head shots, like "Recent Promotions," it's important to keep heads the same size.

If some heads are larger than others, the unspoken message will be that these people are more important!

Contrasting Shapes

Another way to create lively pages is to use both vertical and horizontal photographs.

The left-hand example below lacks interest because both photos are the same shape, and the effect is too horizontal.

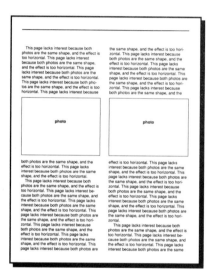 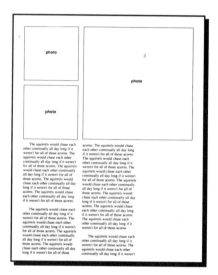

The design improves when the most important vertical element in one of the photos is emphasized, as in the right-hand example above.

Another way you can add contrast to photographs is to mix squares and rectangles. In the above example, the dominant photograph is a rectangle that extends into the white space adjacent to the body copy. The detail shots are squares, sized to fit the width of the column.

An attention-getting combination is a series of small square or rectangular photos contrasted with a large, silhouetted photo. The irregular circular shape of the silhouetted photo and wraparound type improve the page layout.

PROPER PLACEMENT

Placement of photographs is an important layout decision.

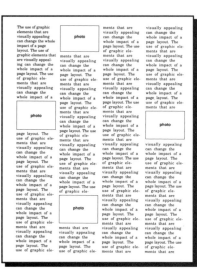 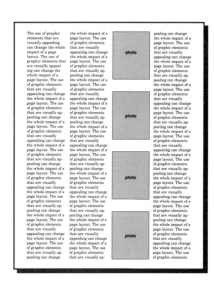

The left-hand example above is dull, because there's no dominant visual. Individual photos placed within text columns are so small, they seem to blend into the copy.

The right-hand page is more interesting. Grouped together vertically, the photos form a frieze that extends down the page and provides contrast with adjacent body copy and reader cues.

The photographs can also be grouped together vertically at the outer edge of a page.

Another choice is to group them into a grid, surrounded by white space.

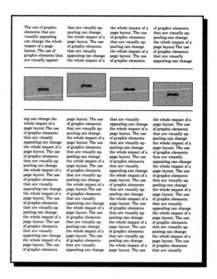

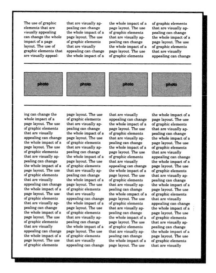

Or individual photographs can be placed along an artificial horizon. In the left-hand example, note how the photos are anchored above and below by horizontal rules that provide needed organization.

The horizontal space between photographs should be consistent across the page, and ideally the space above and below the photos will be the same. In the right-hand example, the space above and below varies widely across the grid. As a result, the page lacks the unity of the left-hand example.

Making one of the photographs in the grid significantly larger than the others adds variety.

Another alternative is to run one photo in one or more adjacent blocks of the grid.

Another approach is to have one photograph bleed to the edge of the page.

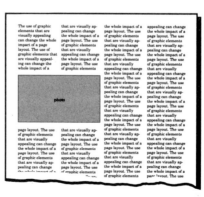

Always remember to have photographs of people facing into the page. People facing left should be placed on the right-hand side of a page; people looking to the right should be placed on the left-hand side. Reader's eyes will follow the direction of the eyes in the photograph. Likewise, your reader will want to see where speeding cars are headed.

FRAMES AND BACKGROUNDS

Visuals should both relate to and contrast with their environment. Charts, graphs, illustrations and photographs should be aligned with the edges of the underlying column grid. Otherwise, they'll look messy, disorganized and not properly related to adjacent body copy.

Photographs

Often, it helps to add thin rules to define the borders of a photograph that contains a large white area. Otherwise, it will bleed into the environment.

You can often enhance a photo by placing it against a reversed or screened background—a technique often used with photographs that relate to a sidebar. You might want to add a white border to the photograph to help separate it from the tinted background.

In other cases, you can use a white rule around the boundaries of a dark area of a photograph against a reversed background.

Sometimes, you can disguise clip art by setting it against a tinted background.

Bleeds

One of the best ways to enhance a photograph is to have it bleed off the edge of one or more sides of a page. Extending it to the edge makes a photograph look dramatically larger, partly because of the surprise factor created when you do the unexpected.

Bleeding a photograph off all four borders of a page is perhaps the most dramatic treatment. In this case, you might want to knock out a headline from a very dark or very light area of the photo.

Another option is to place text in a box within an uninteresting portion of a photo.

Charts and Graphs

Charts and graphs have specific requirements.

Always provide strong borders for them, and be sure they align properly with each other and the underlying column grid.

Also, introduce them with a headline and support them with a caption that explains their importance.

CAPTIONS

The features of a printed page most likely to be read are headlines and captions, in that order. Turning to a page or two-page spread, readers will normally look at headlines first, then at photos, then read captions.

Meaningful captions not only reinforce the intent of a photograph, but summarize the article they accompany.

Typography

Captions are effective only if they're readable and contrast with adjacent body copy. All too often, they aren't set in a sufficiently different style and are mistaken for part of the body copy.

Captions require careful typography. Frequently, important rules about line length and type size are forgotten. Captions should be set in a line length appropriate to the type size. Remember that long lines of small type under wide photographs are hard to read.

To avoid long captions under wide photographs, try indenting the captions. If you must use a long caption set in small type, be sure to add extra leading between the lines.

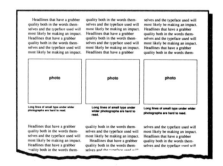

Alignment

Try to keep your captions as short as possible. Edit them carefully. For captions that require more than one line, flush-left/ragged-right alignment avoids unsightly hyphenation.

Placing a caption flush-right is a good way to lock it to the photograph.

When working with a grid of irregularly shaped photographs, consider grouping the captions together. If necessary, relate the photos to them with numbers and letters, or simply organize the captions in a clockwise direction, beginning with top left. Use an extra line of space to separate the captions.

Consistency

Consistency is important. Ideally, you should use the same typeface, size, style and placement of type throughout your newsletter. This is another area where the style capabilities of your word processing or desktop publishing program can help. Instead of entering the same format specifications for each caption, you can simply call up the style sheet that defines the specifications used for captions.

SCANNERS

As described above, image scanners are valuable newsletter design tools that let you create electronic files out of existing photographs. These files are easy to manipulate on your computer screen; you can crop, resize and silhouette photographs, then experiment with various layout schemes until you're satisfied with your page design.

Buy or Rent Time?

You don't have to purchase a scanner. Most phototypesetting service bureaus will scan your photograph for between $3 and $10. Many computer stores also offer this service. If you're a member of a local computer users' group, you might be able to find someone who'll scan your photos for you.

Whatever your source, you'll be pleased with the benefits of working with scanned images. Instead of being forced to imagine how page layouts will look, you can see the cropped and resized photographs on your computer screen.

Future Technologies

At present, the main role of scanned images is in layout planning, although this is a rapidly developing area. In most cases, you'll achieve the best results by using a scanned image as a layout tool, while continuing to submit glossy black-and-white photographs to your printer (who'll appreciate your guidance).

However, the advent of a new generation of affordable, 8-bit, black-and-white scanners, photo manipulation software and reproduction techniques may change all that. These new technologies let you store and reproduce more information about the original photograph. Instead of abrupt changes from light to dark, your scanned and reproduced photos can contain gradual transitions from light to dark.

Airbrushing and Grayscale Manipulation

Access to a scanner also lets you perform darkroom magic on your computer screen.

You can lighten dark areas and darken light areas, often transforming unusable photos into usable ones.

You can airbrush out distracting backgrounds and eliminate details, such as unsightly telephone poles. You can even add cobblestones to a paved road.

Recently introduced laser printer enhancements let you take advantage of the advances in scanner and image-manipulation technology. For example, the Intel Visual Edge dramatically improves the quality of photographs printed on Hewlett-Packard LaserJet printers.

Autofocus Cameras

An autofocus camera with a zoom lens is one of the most useful tools you can add to your production arsenal. These cameras, which have become more affordable in recent years, make it easy to include interesting photographs in your newsletter. Because they're totally automatic, you don't have to be an expert photographer to achieve acceptable results. You're virtually assured of sharp pictures. The built-in light meter automatically sets the right exposure. Built-in flash units automatically fire when light levels are low.

Most important, the zoom lens lets you frame as much or as little of the subject area as you want. You can use the wide-angle setting to include a lot of background details, or zoom in and achieve telephoto effects to focus on a face.

FRAME-GRABBERS

The day of the all-electronic newsletter isn't far off. Frame-grabbers let you adapt and manipulate visuals from videocassette recorders or electronic cameras.

Already, many newsletters are created electronically, without using conventional silver-based photography and film.

MOVING ON

Editing can improve the quality of your visuals by eliminating the unnecessary parts and emphasizing the important ones. Manipulation, resizing and proper page placement can often dramatically improve photographs and illustrations.

As you evaluate visuals in your newsletter, you may want to review the checklist below:

- ✔ I've chosen only the most important visuals, eliminating those that don't tell a story.

- ✔ Photos have been cropped and silhouetted, leaving only the essential elements.

- ✔ Visuals have been properly aligned with each other and with the underlying grid.

- ✔ When several photos appear on one page, one is significantly larger than the others to avoid too much parallelism.

- ✔ My captions reflect a consistent design.

- ✔ Visuals have been enhanced with proper backgrounds and frames.

- ✔ When possible, I've replaced lists of numbers with appropriate charts and graphs.

- ✔ I've used clip art creatively.

In the next chapter, you'll examine graphic accents. Today's desktop publishing and word processing programs offer a wealth of drawing tools, which can be used to create rules (horizontal and vertical lines of various thickness), boxes and tinted backgrounds. A variety of symbols are also available for everything from highlighting important information to marking the end of articles.

CHAPTER EIGHT

ADDING GRAPHIC ACCENTS

Rules, boxes, screens, symbols, logos and oversized letters and numbers are just some of the graphic accents that can add visual interest to your publication.

Rather than being "read," they communicate at a glance. Your firm's logo, affiliation seals and repeating elements found in each issue—such as masthead and address panel—are also graphic accents.

Using the same size, shape, position and color for graphic accents throughout your newsletter can unify the overall design. Consider how the design would be weakened if a different border treatment were used for each page. It would look chaotic, and people would be less likely to read through your newsletter.

The major categories of graphic accents are page borders, text dividers and backgrounds. In choosing the right graphic accents and placing them as effectively as possible, consider the following:

➤ Add appropriate page borders. Decide whether you want to box each page or provide extra emphasis to the top and bottom of each page.

➤ Create barriers between columns. The most appropriate barriers depend on typeface, type size and alignment.

➤ Add barriers within columns. Horizontal rules can be used to emphasize subheads and isolate items.

➤ Add necessary backgrounds. Heavy rules and background tints can darken your newsletter; thin rules and light backgrounds can open it up.

➤ Introduce appropriate symbols. Use them to call attention to important features or signal the end of an article.

➤ Emphasize repeating features, such as mastheads and mailing label areas.

PAGE BORDERS

Desktop publishing and word processing programs offer a variety of ways, including rule- and box-drawing tools, to enhance page borders. Rules are lines of varying weight. You can emphasize the top, bottom or sides of a newsletter with horizontal or vertical lines.

Alternately, you can box pages to create a more formal effect.

Your software program's rule- and box-drawing tools can be combined. For example, you can box your page with thin rules enhanced by an extra-thick rule extending across the top of the page.

White space itself can define page borders. When using it to define the edges of a page, scale it appropriately for the page density.

In the left-hand example, the text and graphics appear to "float" on the page. Instead of providing a luxurious background, excessive white space makes the text and graphics look like they were shrunk by mistake.

In the right-hand example, adding a few simple horizontal rules integrates the white space into the design. Instead of being "empty," the white space to the left of the text and graphics serves a purpose.

SEPARATORS AND DIVIDERS

Vertical downrules can be used to separate columns of text. They can be particularly useful with flush-left/ragged-right type, but they're also effective with justified text.

In general, it's a good idea to avoid using downrules with narrow justified columns. They can make the page hard to read.

Vertical dividers don't have to be limited to rules of varying thicknesses. Most desktop publishing and word processing programs let you create vertical dividers out of dots or other symbols, such as asterisks. If your desktop publishing program can't do this, you can create them with an auxiliary drawing program.

Rules can also separate different topics covered within columns. You can make these rules the same thickness as the top and bottom borders, or as thick or thin as you want.

Horizontal barriers can intersect with the vertical downrules or can be separated slightly by an indent at each edge.

Horizontal rules can be used to slow down eye movement, so that the reader is more likely to notice and digest the subheads within, or adjacent to, columns of text.

When used with exaggerated line spacing, horizontal rules can also emphasize long headlines set in relatively small type.

Be sure to choose rules of appropriate width. Thick downrules darken a page; thinner rules lighten it. In general, the narrower the gutter between columns, the lighter the rule.

BACKGROUNDS

Boxes can help subdivide a page and set off important information.

For example, you can use shaded boxes to emphasize sidebars or pull-quotes. Shaded boxes can also help draw attention to a table of contents or calendar listings.

Backgrounds can make photographs or illustrations stand out.

Use screened backgrounds with discretion if your newsletter is produced with a 300-dot-per-inch laser printer. Laser-produced tint screens often have a grainy texture. Screens work best with phototypesetter output or when added conventionally by the printer.

SYMBOLS

Clip-art libraries and certain typefaces, such as Zapf Dingbats, provide a wide variety of attention-getting graphic accents (e.g., pointing hands, bullets, empty or filled square boxes, etc.).

As always, appropriateness and restraint are key to using accents successfully. It's easy to get carried away and use too many graphic embellishments.

REPEATING FEATURES

Certain features appear in every issue of your newsletter—editorials, calendar listings, mastheads and mailing label areas, for example. Because the design and placement of these repeating features rarely change from issue to issue, they can become virtual icons, looked at without being read. Properly designed, they can enhance your newsletter instead of fading into oblivion.

Placement is important for repeating graphic elements. To emphasize them, run them in the same size and place in each issue.

Editorials

Many newsletters feature a lead article or editorial written by the person in charge—the president of the firm or the director of the association. When given standing department heads, repeating features can contribute to the familiarity of your newsletter.

One of the most common newsletter pitfalls is to introduce an editorial with a department head, such as "Letter from the President," instead of a headline related to the content. "Letter from the President" might make a good eyebrow. However, a headline identifying the most important idea discussed in the editorial (e.g., "Our Goal for 1990: 23% More Members") is a far more intriguing headline than "Letter from the President"!

To personalize your newsletter, you could run a photo or signature of the president or director as part of the standing artwork that introduces the editorial.

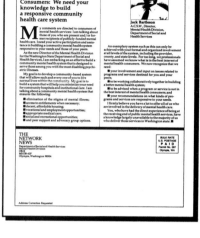

With an image scanner, you can take a photograph and enhance it by modifying the contrast—or range of black to white tones—by dropping out the grays or adding a special screen. For example, you can often create an interesting, stylized visual out of an otherwise-boring photo by posterizing it, creating a high-contrast black-and-white illustration.

Or with certain page layout programs, you can add an "etching," or line-drawing, effect by adding a pronounced diagonal-line screen.

Mastheads

Mastheads identify the people involved in preparing your newsletter, as well as addresses, phone numbers, subscription information and publication data (frequency, change-of-address information, etc.).

The same principles used in designing an effective table of contents apply to a masthead. Use space to frame the elements, not to separate them from each other. Flush-right type, for example, can be used to link names with titles in an adjacent column.

Alternately, you can stack positions in centered type above names.

A masthead is typically boxed, although you might put it in one column of a multicolumn grid.

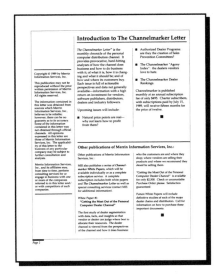

Another useful technique, often used in tabloid-size newsletters, is to reverse masthead information out of a vertical border.

Mailing Labels

Pay attention to postal requirements if your newsletter is a self-mailer. Postal permit numbers save time: you can print your bulk mail information on the address panel instead of stamping each newsletter.

Try to place "teasers" (brief statements written to lure readers into the newsletter) or a table of contents as close to the mailing label area as possible. That way, people will start reading your newsletter as soon as they pull it out of their mailbox, mailing label up.

Logos and association seals, usually repeated in each issue, can compete with your nameplate. If that's the case, you can place such an item in a different area of the newsletter (for example, a box by itself in the lower right-hand corner of the front page).

Affiliation seals can often be positioned in the masthead area.

Transitional Elements

Page numbers, header information and symbols form a transition between reader cues and graphic accents. Page numbers are reader cues, helping readers locate articles beginning, or continued, on the inside pages. However, because they form part of the visual background, they're also graphic accents.

Headers can repeat the nameplate at reduced size at the top of each page. Readers may not be actively aware of the title, yet its consistent placement forms an important part of your publication's identity.

Likewise, symbols or end signs placed at the bottom of a feature article both indicate where the article ends and enhance the visual identity of your publication.

MOVING ON

Your newsletter's effectiveness depends a lot on its design. Graphic accents, such as rules, boxes, tint screens and white space, are valuable design tools that can help you attract readers.

As always, restraint and appropriateness are the keys to success. Overuse of your desktop publishing or word processing program's drawing tools can result in gimmicky, cluttered newsletters.

To evaluate the graphic accents in your newsletter, review the following checklist:

- ✔ My page borders have been designed with the appropriate box or rules.

- ✔ The weight of downrules reflects gutter size.

- ✔ I've selected horizontal rules of the appropriate thickness to separate articles on a page.

- ✔ White space has been used to frame and emphasize text and graphics.

- ✔ I've avoided trapped white space.

- ✔ End signs indicate article endings.

Having looked at what's involved in planning and building your newsletter design, it's now time to look at some problems that might arise when all the elements are put together. In Chapter 9, you'll see how options that work well alone don't always work with other design elements. You'll also examine precautions to take so that production pressures don't weaken a fundamentally strong newsletter design.

CHAPTER NINE

PULLING IT ALL TOGETHER

The six building blocks of newsletter design—grids, nameplate, body copy, reader cues, visuals and graphic accents—must all work together harmoniously to accommodate each issue's mix of text and graphics. The harmony often comes during the last design phase, when you can fine-tune your page layouts to achieve the effect and overall quality you want.

The preceding chapters have shown you a variety of techniques that perhaps sparked your curiosity and enthusiasm for designing—or redesigning—your newsletter. As you've seen, the various elements of page architecture can be handled in many ways.

Now is the moment of truth when you put those ideas and techniques together. Instead of trying them out in isolation, you can assemble a sample newsletter containing the "best of" ideas from several chapters—perhaps a column layout idea from Chapter 3, a nameplate from Chapter 4, etc. To foster creativity and experimentation, use a pencil and paper and create thumbnail sketches. Your design skills will blossom with the help of pencil-and-paper, reduced-sized newsletter sketches. Consider them trial runs of what will become a life-size, well-designed newsletter.

LAYOUT CONSIDERATIONS

You may need to go back and adjust the size of your gutters (the vertical corridors between columns) in the grid you selected in Chapter 3 to properly accommodate your text and graphics. As you learned in Chapter 5, large type requires more space between columns than small type. Without the added separation, readers might read across the column breaks, rather than moving down to the next line.

Alignment decisions also affect gutter size. A larger gutter is required between columns of justified type than flush-left/ragged-right type. This is because the uneven line endings of ragged-right type provide more space between columns.

Downrules also should be taken into account when choosing appropriate column spacing. Less gutter space is needed when vertical rules separate columns.

Other simple and effective refinements can be used to achieve unity in your newsletter design.

Likewise, symbols and other graphic tools used in the body of your newsletter can echo elements of your nameplate. For example, bullets setting off items in a list can relate to a nameplate that's designed with round shapes and type. Boxed or bordered items can reinforce a nameplate designed with square serifs and heavy rules.

When used with discretion, clip art or highly stylized initial caps can support a seasonal theme or create an old-fashioned atmosphere for certain issues or selected features.

When it's time to produce an actual issue of your newsletter, establish a production sequence and use it for each issue. Here's a logical sequence to follow:

1. Establish a realistic production schedule.
2. Plan article size and placement.
3. Determine an approximate word count for each article.

4. Insert text and edit as needed.

5. Allow time for last-minute refinements.

PRODUCTION SCHEDULES

Everyone involved should know the deadlines. By sharing your production schedule with clients, co-workers and supervisors, you'll be more likely to elicit their cooperation in supplying information and submitting articles on time.

On the next page is a production scheduling worksheet that you can copy and adapt to your particular newsletter. Notice how the schedule works backward from the date targeted for readers to receive the newsletter in the mail.

It's extremely important that your client and co-workers or supervisors initial the Newsletter Deadline Planner. This documents their awareness of the deadlines and discourages last-minute changes.

ARTICLE SIZE AND PLACEMENT

As a starting point, list the items to be included in every issue.

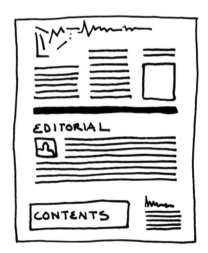

Then, once again, create small-scale drawings. These let you try out alternative positions for text and visuals. Experiment with article placement, different photograph sizes and shapes, and various headline options.

Start by working on small thumbnails and gradually work them into larger, more detailed drawings. Fill in departments and features repeated in each issue, such as an editorial, calendar of events or list of recent promotions and anniversaries.

Newsletter Deadline Planner

Prepared by _____   Today's date _____

Newsletter cover date _____ Volume _____ Issue _____

Schedule approved by _____

Planned arrival date in readers' hands _____

Necessary mailing date (First Class) _____ (Third Class) _____

Addressing/ZIP sorting/Delivery to Post Office _____

Delivery from printer _____ Approval of final printer's proofs _____

Delivery of camera-ready artwork to printer _____

Final internal approval of proofs (last opportunity for changes) _____

Page layout completed/Proof files circulated _____

Page layout begins _____

Receipt of camera-ready artwork from service bureau (if high-resolution phototypesetting is being used) _____

Delivery of files to service bureau (in the case of high-resolution phototypesetting)

_____

Deadline for articles and photographs _____

Final approval of issue content/Assignment of articles _____

Thumbnail sketches _____

Planning stage/Story planning meeting _____

Indicate the placement and anticipated length of your most important feature articles. Then, position secondary articles. Before you know it, you'll fill your entire newsletter.

To Jump or Not to Jump

A major decision you have to make in laying out each issue is whether to continue, or jump, articles from one page to another. This involves a trade-off, particularly on the front cover. On the one hand, by including more than one article on the first page, you're offering readers variety, and thus more opportunities to become involved in reading your newsletter. On the other hand, readership drops off each time you ask someone to continue reading on an inside page, especially noncontiguous inside pages (i.e., page 1 articles continued on page 4 or 5). Article readership doesn't drop off as dramatically on articles that continue on facing spreads.

Jumps can also destroy the flow of an article. Many readers won't turn the page when they encounter the jumpline. Instead, they wait and read the rest of the article when they get to the inside pages. This interrupts the rhythm of the writing and means that readers might forget some of the initial paragraphs.

So the decision to jump, or not to jump, should not be taken lightly.

Many of the best-looking newsletters limit an article to either a single page or two-page spread. This means that articles must be written to fill the space. In these situations, selectivity and copyfitting assume increasing importance. When space is tight, some articles will have to be postponed to later issues, while others will have to be heavily edited.

This, again, reinforces the fact that editing and designing cannot be separated; there's a close relationship between content and appearance. The design of an "omnibus" newsletter containing both long and short features must be totally different from a newsletter that gives in-depth treatment to a few important topics.

Horizontal versus Vertical Layouts

Another decision to make at the planning stage involves whether to adopt a vertical or horizontal orientation for your newsletter.

Vertically oriented newsletters are characterized by long columns of type—articles that begin at the top of a page and extend to the bottom.

Horizontally oriented newsletters are characterized by square or rectangular blocks of text in short adjacent columns.

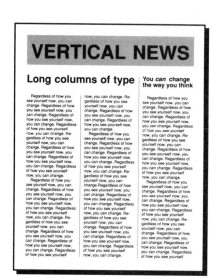

Because text flows down one column until it hits the bottom and then continues at the top of the next, vertically oriented newsletters are easier to produce. Horizontally oriented newsletters, however, often are easier to read, since the columns are shorter. (Most readers find it easier to read three parallel 2 1/2-inch columns than one 7 1/2-inch column.) But planning, copyfitting and production are more difficult.

Word Counts

Word counts measure the number of words per article, based on an average word count per line and per column inch. Typeface, size, line spacing and tracking all affect your count.

Below is a sample sheet you can copy and use for writing assignments, so that articles can be written to fit your space. Detailed pre-production roughs of each issue make copyfitting easier. If you're writing the articles yourself, you're more likely to write them to fit, rather than trying to shoehorn them into available space.

To determine the word count of each article, multiply the number of column inches devoted to each article in your layout by the number of words per column inch. (See the word count technique described in Chapter 5, page 78.)

Newsletter Assignment Sheet

Article _____ Photographs _____

Newsletter issue _____

Delivery deadline _____

Topic _____

Key points _____

_____

_____

Desired length _____

Desired format (e.g., word processing files, etc.) _____

Assigned by (editor) _____

Accepted by (writer or photographer) _____

Today's date _____

Everyone involved should receive copies of the assignment sheet: editor, illustrator, photographer and writer. You can use your office copier to reproduce them. To give them a more official look, use your word processing or page layout program to create better-looking sheets and have them printed on consecutively numbered, two-part carbonless forms. That way, everyone involved gets a numbered original.

EDITING TO FIT

This process calls for accommodation rather than compromise. Although it would be nice if everything fit together like a well-designed jigsaw puzzle, this rarely happens in real life. Usually, some articles are too long, others too short.

Freedom to edit is a necessity. Otherwise, your newsletter's design might be weakened.

For example, more often than not, assigned articles will be too long, or additional items will show up at the last minute, requiring you to make some adjustments.

At this point, rather than reducing type size or line spacing, you might want to review the principles of good writing. These principles will help you identify "empty" words that can be removed from articles. Also, you might have a second person read the articles to identify repetitious passages.

One useful technique is to structure articles the way newspaper reporters do: place the most important information in the first paragraphs, with each following paragraph containing less important information. Then you can easily edit from the bottom, if necessary, to fit available space without losing the most critical information.

If space shortages are a chronic problem, you might evaluate whether some articles can be run under one heading. For example, perhaps three separate items describing upcoming events can be included in a single "Upcoming Events" article or in a calendar.

Perhaps information concerning promotions and special recognitions can be grouped together into a "Milestones" page of listings, rather than a series of individual articles.

Sometimes, space can be located by cropping background or foreground details from a photograph.

If you're dealing with an isolated head shot, try silhouetting all or part of it, and wrapping text around it.

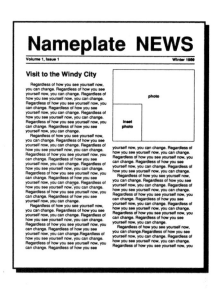

Sometimes, taking a fresh look at your newsletter will reveal photos that don't add much to the editorial content or layout. In those cases, you can gain valuable space by eliminating them. Or, you might place small "detail" photographs inside larger "establishing" ones.

If you have a deep sink at the top of the page, or wide margins, perhaps a photograph can extend into part of the white space.

If you've wrapped text around an illustration, you might try reducing the illustration's size, which will increase the line lengths of the wraparound.

If your article is still too long, take a look at the reader cues you're using. Consider eliminating a pull-quote, subhead or initial cap to provide some valuable breathing room.

Editing still remains the best technique for copyfitting. Even good articles can repeat themselves or contain more detail than necessary. Likewise, the best headlines can often be shortened. In addition, transposing words within a paragraph might eliminate a widow.

EXPANDING TO FIT

If articles end up too short, a simple way to fix the problem is to add some space around existing headlines, subheads and pull-quotes. A few points of white space, uniformly surrounding headlines, subheads and pull-quotes, might be enough to fill out a column without compromising the design of the rest of your newsletter.

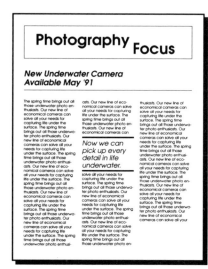 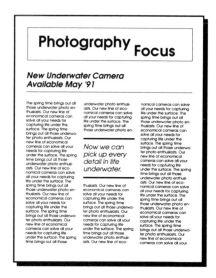

Another way to stretch articles is to add subheads or pull-quotes. Likewise, you might include an introductory subtitle, or blurb, between the headline and the beginning of the article.

If your article includes tightly cropped photographs, you might restore them to their original state, allowing more background (e.g., sky or ceiling) or foreground (e.g., desk, hands, speaker's podium) to show.

Another solution is to shorten body-copy columns.

Finally, you can edit an important headline and make it larger.

Vertical Justification

Some software programs offer a vertical justification feature, which automatically inserts small amounts of extra leading, or line spacing, to fill out a column of text. Although this can be a useful feature, be aware of its potential side effect—throwing off the alignment of text baselines in adjacent columns.

By designing your newsletter around columns of different lengths, you can build flexibility into your layouts. When articles are too long or too short, their length can be accommodated by varying the amount of white space at the bottom of each page. Newsletter designs with carefully aligned column bottoms require far more adjustment.

LAST-MINUTE REFINEMENTS

After you make individual refinements, take time to check for unity and contrast in your newsletter as a whole.

Be sure design decisions made early on are carried through the entire newsletter. Likewise, decisions made in later stages may require adjustments to preceding design and layout elements.

Check for an appropriate balance between similarity and contrast. Each page and two-page spread should present a different "look" yet maintain an underlying unity with the rest of your newsletter.

Make sure there's a reason for everything; apply the test of functionality. Can every typographic decision and graphic accent be defended on the basis of enhanced readability?

Check carefully to see if anything has been inadvertently left out. Good-looking newsletters are often compromised by "small" flaws such as missing vertical downrules or omitted department heads.

TYPICAL PITFALLS

Here's a summary of the most common newsletter pitfalls:

Insufficient Editing

The number-one cause of gray-looking newsletters, as well as burn-out among newsletter editors, is the "newsletter-as-container." In this scenario, newsletter editors lack the power or resolve to do what their title implies—*edit*—and newsletters become receptacles into which as many words and visuals as possible are put. For a newsletter to succeed, the editor must be able to rewrite headlines, transpose words and shorten articles. Format should never be sacrificed for copy or quality for expediency!

"Association President Robert V. Johnson Wants You to Take Part in Our Annual Spring Membership Drive"

"Sign Up Six New Members and Win a Free Dinner at the El Morocco"

"Brag and boast" headlines are another frequent example of insufficient editing. Newsletter contributors often write headlines from the writer's, not the reader's, viewpoint. It's the editor's responsibility to see that headlines have a reader orientation.

Lack of Contrast

A lack of contrast between text and graphic elements on a page results in gray, monotonous pages. Obvious examples are headlines, subheads and pull-quotes that aren't significantly larger than body copy, with insufficient type family, type style, alignment or color contrast.

Visuals that lack contrast can also lead to gray pages. Equal-weight photographs or illustrations tend to cancel each other out. This is particularly true when several small photographs appear on a page next to the articles they introduce, rather than being organized together.

No Dominant Visual

Every page and every two-page spread should be assembled around one, and only one, dominant visual. Ideally, this visual should reflect the primary message of the page or spread.

Unkerned Nameplate

The number-one cause for disappointing nameplates stems from a failure to kern, or manually reduce, letter spacing. Nothing spells "desktop published" as much as a large nameplate with exaggerated letter spacing. Kerning can make the difference between a nameplate consisting of isolated letters and one with character.

WAV ELY REVIEW

The above nameplate, with default letter spacing, lacks distinction. It simply looks like a lot of unrelated, oversized letters.

WAVELY REVIEW

This nameplate, however, does a better job of symbolizing the newsletter. It reflects attention to detail. It also looks better on the page, because there's more white space at each end.

Inappropriate Typeface Choices

Each typeface speaks in its own voice. Like shouting in church or whispering "excuse me" when trying to exit a crowded New York City subway train, an inappropriate typeface can send the wrong message.

LOVELY LINGERIE

When combined with inappropriate type size and paper, the wrong typeface has an even greater negative impact. For example, small, high-stress serif typefaces are often hard to read on glossy paper because the glare creates visual confusion. Although glossy paper can enhance the sharpness of letters, it sometimes reflects so much light that it is difficult to read.

An inappropriate combination of line length, type size and line spacing is another frequent cause of difficulty.

This type
is too
large for
this nar-
row col-
umn.

Large type set in narrow columns is as difficult to read as small type set in wide columns.

Even when the proper type size/line length relationship is maintained for body copy, that relationship is often forgotten when it comes to designing captions. The result may be a caption set in small italic type, with default line spacing, placed under a photograph that extends the full width of a page.

Floating Baselines

Floating baselines occur when body copy in adjacent columns doesn't align. This is usually caused by interruptions like subheads, pull-quotes, initial caps or other internal elements.

To prevent that, the distance between baselines should be a multiple of the line spacing you've chosen for the body copy. In other words, if you're using 10-point leading, interruptions should be 20, 30, 50, 100 or 120 points deep. If you're using 11-point leading, interruptions should be 22, 33, 44, 55, or 99, 198 points deep, etc.

Too Little White Space

Type and visuals that crowd the top, bottom and side borders of a page leave little or no breathing room. As a result, pages look gray and uninviting.

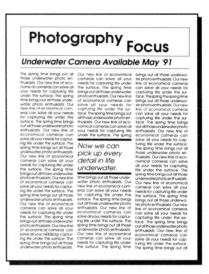

Crowded pages lack starting and stopping points; they also lack resting spots, which increases reader fatigue. In addition, readers may be frustrated when they keep bumping into page borders at the beginning or end of lines.

Too Much White Space

White space is a good thing when it frames pages and frames important words or graphics. But white space used within page elements creates unsightly "holes," often referred to as trapped white space.

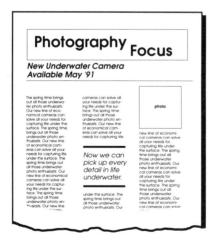

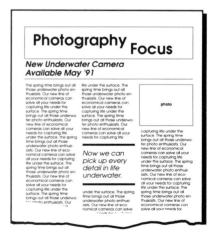

Compare the two examples above. Both contain the same amount of words and graphics. Notice the unity in the left-hand example, in which white space surrounds the text and graphics. But the right-hand version is swimming in white space, giving the impression that articles and photos were accidentally omitted from the page.

The need to use white space to frame rather than separate text and graphics is obvious in large, unkerned headlines set with default line spacing. In the above example, the headline looks like a series of letters with freeway lanes separating the lines. Here, white space destroys the vertical and horizontal unity of the headline.

Rivers of white space can appear when type is justified and word spacing becomes loose. Flush-left/ragged-right type with strong verticals along the right-hand edge of the copy can also create inappropriate holes of space (e.g., when text is wrapped around a pull-quote or squared-off photograph that extends into the column to its left).

Lack of Reader Cues

Gray pages and confusion go hand-in-hand. Without reader cues, it's difficult to draw readers into your articles. Without reader cues, readers have no relief or direction and pages lack vitality and appeal.

Consider the left-hand example. Headlines appear out of nowhere, introducing long blocks of text with no breaks. Reading this dull, uninviting page promises to be more of a chore than an adventure.

In the right-hand example, however, reader cues enliven the page. Although word density has dropped slightly, the words that remain are more accessible and inviting.

Inconsistent Reader Cues

If you don't use your desktop publishing or word processing program's style feature, you may end up with inconsistent typeface, type size or alignment for your reader cues.

Headlines reduced to fit available space instead of being shortened might be mistaken for subheads; short subheads enlarged to fill up available space can be confused with headlines. Either situation sacrifices the necessary correlation between type size and message importance.

Excessive Symmetry

Excessive symmetry is the result of too much balance among the components of your page. Culprits can be four-column grids with too much text, photographs of equal size and headlines of equal weight.

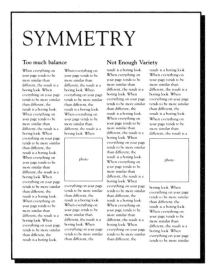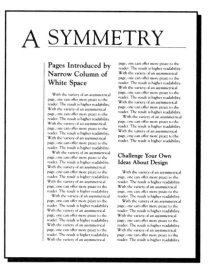

Asymmetrical column grids or column placement can cure excessive symmetry. Pages introduced by a narrow column of white space are often more inviting than ones completely filled with text, particularly if two wide text columns are being used.

Exploding Pages

Another potential pitfall is a newsletter page characterized by numerous small illustrations. It may lack the organization provided by a single dominant visual.

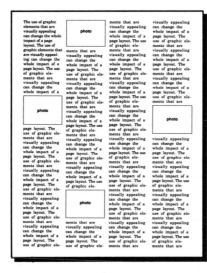
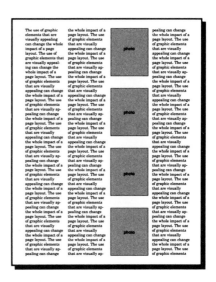

For pages that contain a lot of photographs, you're often better off grouping them in a grid at the top or along one side of the page.

Overuse of Graphic Tools

Desktop publishing and word processing programs provide us with so many graphic tools, it's easy to abuse these features.

For example, you can draw boxes around whole pages, as well as around headlines. Although boxed pages and headlines can sometimes be effective in creating a formal atmosphere, boxing an entire page can turn it into a self-contained unit. The reader must then climb over this roadblock to advance to the next page. Creating such an obstacle can discourage readership,

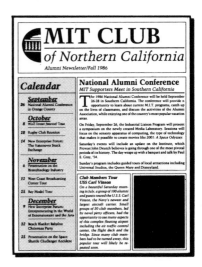

particularly when articles are continued from one page to another.

Rules also are overused; they're often added beneath headlines to emphasize them—even though rules are meant to be barriers rather than facilitators.

Exercise caution when using reversed type for department heads. Small reversed areas can attract more attention than is warranted. Also, a number of small reversed areas on a page can create a "zigzag" effect.

The rounded-corner box tool must be used with discretion. Rounded-corner boxes often create an old-fashioned or art deco atmosphere. But they also can be a dead giveaway to a newsletter's desktop-published origins! When used around features or articles, they often create visual tension. They also can be successfully used to isolate a nameplate, masthead or table of contents that appears next to the corners of a page.

Another common pitfall that even the most experienced desktop publisher occasionally can't avoid is using hard returns, tabs and indents to format copy—especially word-processed copy. Although the shortcut may appear to work and everything may line up on your computer screen, the printed results are often quite different. The problem is magnified if you reformat a page, particularly if you change column widths. It can lead to some bizarre page layouts!

Clip art is another tool that can be overused. Except in the case of maps or technical drawings, clip art shouldn't be confused with illustrations. It makes sense to use as many illustrations as necessary to communicate an idea. Clip art, however, is best used to create an atmosphere or mood. It establishes a tone, rather than communicating specific information.

As such, a single piece of enlarged clip art often does a better job of establishing a mood than numerous small illustrations, which might compete with each other.

But clip art often looks like clip art. You might want to disguise its origins by changing backgrounds and borders, or combining two pieces of clip art into one.

Always read clip-art copyright information carefully before you use it. Clip-art packages differ in their interpretation of how they can be used.

One final pitfall all newsletter editors should avoid is forgetting that not everything you see on your computer screen will necessarily be printed. It's easy, for example, to forget that on-screen page margins and borders, such as drop shadows emphasizing the page edges in view modes, won't appear on the printed page. This can lead to disappointment when newsletters with undefined borders floating on their pages emerge from your printer.

Unnecessary Folio Information

Newsletters often contain volume and issue number. This information is useful if the newsletter contains important reference material likely to be stored and referred back to in the future (e.g., *Congressional Taxation Abstracts*). But often it isn't necessary.

If your newsletter consists primarily of time-dated information that readers are unlikely to save, folio information may simply occupy space that could be put to better use.

Once again, the newsletter's purpose and content should dictate its size and whether an element is included.

Overuse of Two-Color Printing

Two-color printing can certainly add interest to a newsletter. But overuse of a second color quickly weakens an otherwise strong page design. For example, a second color that works well as a background for a nameplate and for selected page borders may become bothersome when it's also used to highlight every headline. The second-color headlines can compete with each other and even overwhelm the text.

When using a second color, remember that "less is more."

MOVING ON

All text and graphic elements in a newsletter should create an integrated whole. To evaluate the success of your design, you may want to refer to the following checklist.

✔ The front cover preserves a "family look," identifying it with previous issues, yet it's sufficiently different to distinguish it from others.

✔ Each two-page spread has repeating elements that unify it with other spreads, yet distinguish it from other pages.

✔ Each page, or two-page spread, contains one—and only one—dominant visual.

✔ The dominant visual on each page or spread reflects the most important idea being communicated.

✔ I've used the appropriate amount of copy for the space available and avoided cramming too much copy into my newsletter.

✔ The various elements of page architecture complement and don't compete with each other.

✔ Two-color printing has been used appropriately.

✔ The balance and symmetry on each page or spread create a pleasing relationship.

✔ The text and visuals properly relate to each other.

Now that you've learned about the basic design elements that must be addressed in creating a newsletter, let's translate theory into practice. In Chapter 10, you'll analyze the designs of two newsletters and delve into the reasons behind some of the design choices.

CHAPTER TEN

TRANSLATING THEORY INTO PRACTICE

By now, you're familiar with the six building blocks of newsletter design, their flexibility and the many ways they can be handled. In this chapter, we translate theory into practice by creating two sample newsletters.

Tips & Tricks, designed by
Keith Cassell, Cassell Design

Tips & Tricks is a newsletter targeted to buyers and prospective buyers of books, diskettes and reference materials for intermediate and advanced users of Autoware, a sophisticated software program. Published by a leading publisher, *Tips & Tricks* is designed to create interest in the firm's forthcoming titles and maintain enthusiasm for existing titles.

TIPS *& tricks*

Autoware Update from Outlook Press

SPRING 1990

GREETINGS

ecently, many of our readers have expressed a keen interest in knowing more about the books and software Outlook Press publishes, as well as new printings and editions. Rather than bombard you with various mailings, we thought a newsletter might prove more efficient and informative.

Outlook Press now publishes the most comprehensive library of reference materials for intermediate and advanced Autoware users. We hope you continue to benefit from our books and software, and we welcome suggestions for current and future titles.

Richard Melchus, Publisher of Outlook Press

The goal is to strike a balance between informality and seriousness. If it were too technical, it would intimidate potential buyers. On the other hand, a flippant or lighthearted approach would offend the serious user.

At the start, it was recognized that this would be a copy-oriented newsletter, with few opportunities for visuals. Thus, the decision was made to use white space as a graphic element to balance the large blocks of text that would otherwise dominate each issue.

As a standing feature, to be repeated in each issue, a book and diskette order form is prominently placed in the same layout location on page 3, to encourage reader response.

To increase its "news" value, each issue will have a theme, introduced on the cover by a short letter, signed by the publisher, that ties the contents together.

Tips & Tricks is designed to be folded and stapled as a self-mailer, so the lower half of the outside cover is the mailing label area. To entice readers inside, the table of contents is placed strategically, adjacent to the mailing label.

Since the natural reaction of most readers would be to turn the newsletter over to the back before unstapling it, the introductory "theme" letter is placed sideways on the outside back cover.

TIPS AND TRICKS

Page 1

Autoware Update from Outlook Press

TIPS & *tricks*

SPRING 1990

SECOND EDITION OF *THE AUTOWARE CUSTOMIZING BOOK* RELEASED

We're pleased to inform you that an expanded, updated version of *The Autoware Customizing Book*, by Jeffrey Gable, is now available.

Fully updated to include Autoware's recent release, the second edition features dozens of new tips and techniques for getting the most out of Autoware's exciting new version. Two new chapters expand your horizons even further:

• Chapter Two explains Autoware's new pull-down menus and how to customize them to suit your needs.

• Chapter Seven, "Customizing Tips and Tricks," offers an invaluable compilation of dozens of techniques (many of them free) that will inspire even more performance from your Autoware systems. Author Jeff Gable has headed a high-production service bureau for more than seven years, and his expertise is evident in this chapter (worth the cost of the book alone).

In addition, The Autoware Customizing Gallery has been completely updated for Re-

lease 4, and includes several important new language routines to speed your work.

Four appendices explain FIG, CREK and MGT commands to help you become more productive and give invaluable information about upgrading equipment and software to save time and money.

The Autoware Customizing Book, second edition, is 482 pages, illustrated. Suggested retail price $9.95. All Outlook Press titles are available in bookstores or through Outlook Press. See the back page of this newsletter for ordering information.

All Outlook Press books are sold with a full money-back guarantee. If within 30 days you find that a book doesn't meet your expectations, please return it to us and we will send you a full refund.

DISKETTES SAVE TIME, EFFORT, MONEY

Each Autoware book published by Outlook Press is accompanied by a diskette that contains helpful (sometimes vital!) programs that further enhance your Autoware system. If you find the book of value in your work, the accompanying diskette can save you hours of typing and debugging time, and help learn many time-saving commands you might not otherwise have tried.

Below is a description of each diskette.

The Autoware Customizing Diskette ($29.95):
Features seventy macros and

Terman routines you can use "as is," to streamline your work. These routines are completely accessible and can be modified at any time to suit your needs. Even if you use only one or two macros, you are likely to save considerable time and effort.

Mastering Autoware Diskette ($19.95):
Contains all the lesson programs in the first seven chapters, plus the twelve sample programs featured in Chapter Eight. You'll find these programs of great use as learning tools—and many are useful productivity enhancers, too.

Grid

Because of the copy-heavy nature of each issue, a three-column grid, set off by a half-column of white space, was chosen for the body copy. The three spacious columns can accommodate a lot of copy in an easy-to-read type size.

The half-column of white space on each page balances the heavy concentration of text in the adjacent columns and helps set off reader cues and the relatively small book covers that are likely to be the primary visuals in each issue. The white space also adds informality to offset the technical content of the Autoware books and diskettes.

When needed, two of the body-copy columns can be combined to accommodate screen dumps or sample pages.

Nameplate

A great deal of time was spent finalizing the nameplate design. Various typefaces were tried. Since it was likely that serif type would be used for the body copy, the natural inclination was to experiment with sans-serif faces for the nameplate.

However, sans-serif nameplates were quickly eliminated; they looked too stiff and mechanical. *Tips & Tricks* was conceived as friendly rather than a high-tech newsletter. So, it seemed clear that the friendly effect would have to be achieved with size and style contrast alone.

When all the letters of the name, including the ampersand, were set in the same size, the effect was sheer visual boredom. Instead, the size and

TIPS & TRICKS

AUTOWARE UPDATE FROM OUTLOOK PRESS   SPRING, 1990

typeface of the ampersand were changed; New Baskerville was chosen for its complexity and beauty. The ampersand creates a focal point for the nameplate.

But even with the oversized ampersand, the nameplate still lacked character. When both words were set in the same type size, *Tips* was shorter than *Tricks,* creating an imbalance.

To restore balance, *Tips'* size was increased to equal the width of *Tricks.*

Further contrast was provided by setting *Tips* in uppercase and *Tricks* in lowercase type. Although this change added more visual interest, something was still missing. The nameplate still lacked character and failed to achieve the status of a visual symbol.

It was decided to add style contrast between the left- and right-hand sides of the title. To accomplish this, *Tricks* was set in New Baskerville italics. With this refinement, the nameplate begins to look more integrated and less like unrelated words.

The last refinement was to add further left/right contrast in the nameplate by using the Palatino typeface for *Tips*. Palatino's vertical serifs in the *T* and *S* contrasted nicely with New Baskerville's diagonal serifs (such as the bottom of the *t*) and increased stress (such as the varying thickness in the *r* and *s*). Just as Palatino's formality is suitable for *Tips*, New Baskerville's playful serifs and thick-to-thin variations relate to the *Tricks* theme.

Nameplate Refinements

The next requirement was to anchor the nameplate on the page. By itself, the title would float. A heavy rule added above it divides the white space, defining the top boundary of the nameplate.

Then a subtitle was chosen. Although the normal position for subtitles is under the title, the subtitle in this nameplate competed with the title and reduced its impact. Instead, it's set flush-right in small italics above the title, tucked under the heavy rule defining the top of the nameplate.

The final nameplate item is the folio, or issue date, information—
SPRING, 1990. This was initially set in all caps, flush-right under *Tricks*.

The first refinement was to eliminate the comma between the month
and year, which allowed the neat rectangular outline formed by the
uppercase type to remain unbroken.

The finishing touch is a thin rule added above the folio to anchor it to
the title.

Another rule below the folio makes the nameplate a self-contained
element that doesn't compete with headlines and other page features.

Body Copy

Now let's examine some body-copy choices. Times Roman was an
obvious contender for body-copy typeface because of its popularity and
availability on most laser printers. However, it was precisely for these
reasons that Times Roman was rejected: Outlook Press wanted a more
distinctive typeface for this publication. Other serif typefaces considered were too wide, too open or too old-fashioned to satisfy Outlook's criteria for *Tips & Tricks*.

Finally, New Baskerville was chosen because of its moderate x-height,
readable design and ability to project authority without calling too
much attention to itself.

Eleven-point type is an ideal choice for readability and copy density.

Although the 11-point type size works well, leading had to be manually
adjusted. The software program's default line spacing was too tight.
There was a tendency to regress—to accidentally re-read the same line
of type instead of advancing to the next line. The tight line spacing
also created extremely dark pages. By opening up the leading to 13
points, both of these problems were eliminated.

> Fully updated to include Autoware's recent release, the second edition features dozens of new tips and techniques

> Fully updated to include Autoware's recent release, the second edition features dozens of new tips and techniques

Flush-left/ragged-right alignment was selected for two reasons. First, it projects a more inviting, informal appearance; it's more "conversational" and less "authoritative."

Second, when the columns are justified, the six vertically aligned parallel columns tend to lead the reader's eye up and down, instead of across each line. In addition, the lack of white space at the end of each line creates an excessively dense effect.

And the additional hyphenation required with justified type also can slow the reader's pace.

Some hyphenation was used, however, to avoid the extremely short lines that would result if flush-left/ragged-right alignment were used without hyphenation.

As a further refinement, letter spacing was reduced by 5 percent to increase word density and create a more professional appearance. This modest reduction shortens each paragraph, often eliminating one line of type. The cumulative effect is an increase in word density and in white space.

To introduce more white space within the columns of text, paragraph indents were eliminated and extra line space was added between paragraphs. This helps offset the heavy concentration of body copy.

To add visual interest and emphasis, the two columns on page 3 highlighting seminar locations are joined together.

In addition, three columns are integrated to create the large, easy-to-use mail order coupon.

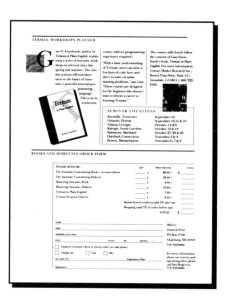

Reader Cues

The next goal was to insert reader cues to break up the copy-heavy pages. To preserve a restrained dignity, reader cues are limited to headlines and initial caps.

Headlines

One of the ways you "voice" a newsletter is by deciding how much contrast to create between headlines and body copy. Traditionally, large sans-serif headlines are contrasted with serif body copy, but this isn't always appropriate. For one thing, they can overpower the body copy and encroach on the space available for text.

Since the headlines are needed only as road signs, and Autoware users are probably already motivated to read *Tips & Tricks*, it was decided to use uppercase headlines in the body-copy typeface. Although uppercase headlines can be difficult to read, setting them in a relatively small type size and using adequate white space for separation eliminates this potential problem.

For emphasis, headlines are set flush to the left page margin, beginning in the half-column of white space.

For further contrast with body copy, unkerned letter spacing is used.

Initial Caps

Because of the restrained headline treatment and the relatively few opportunities to incorporate visuals in the design, it was decided to use large initial caps in the left half-column of white space. These graphic accents provide visual relief and add character to the publication.

 any Autoware users are beginning to work with desktop publishing technology to produce reports, forms, technical documentation, user manuals and other printed materials. Of course, those documents must be well or

 any Autoware users are beginning to work with desktop publishing technology to produce reports, forms, technical documentation, user manuals and other printed materials. Of course, those documents must be well or

When isolated in the white space adjacent to the copy, the large initial caps look incomplete and detached.

To address this problem, a small background pattern is added behind each initial cap.

But, unfortunately, the background pattern obscures the design attributes of the typeface, neutralizing the contrast between thick and thin strokes of the letters.

When the pattern is reduced in size and placed to the lower right, it tends to compete with adjacent body copy.

Moving the background box to the lower left provides definition for the left margin and integrates the initial cap by "pushing" it closer to the body copy.

Visuals

An initial inventory of available visuals indicates that most would be book covers.

Placed vertically within the column margins, the book covers tend to dominate the columns and reduce the space available for text.

Slightly reducing the size of the book covers and tilting them at a slight angle are steps in the right direction. Weight and dimension are added by using cast and dropped shadows and, in one case, a lightly screened background.

Once a strong grid has been established, slightly violating it can add variety. Placement of the book covers illustrates this: when they're confined within the column borders, they're hardly noticeable.

This simple alteration—tilting the book covers to intrude slightly into the adjoining white space—creates visual interest and an informal atmosphere to offset the highly technical nature of the contents.

The same effect is created by overlapping the photo of the seminar leader between the article describing the seminars and the box listing the locations and dates. With this treatment, the photo links the related items together and adds a three-dimensional effect to the page.

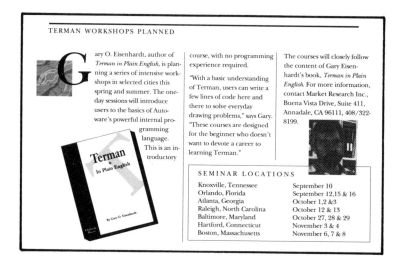

The photograph was reduced in size before being placed on the page. If the photograph hadn't been resized, it would fill the column and dominate the page.

In spite of the small book cover visuals, the inside spread didn't have enough variety. So, equal portions of the middle and right-hand columns were combined, filled in with a light background screen and used to highlight sample pages from one of the Autoware books.

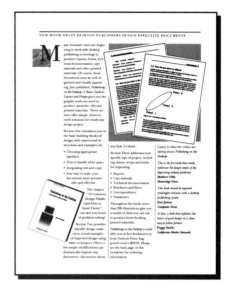

The mail order form on page 3 is generously large, occupying half the page. Its size and readable typography make it easy for readers to quickly scan Outlook Press's titles and prices. Plenty of space is provided for filling in name, address, payment method and signature.

The extra line spacing used to emphasize Outlook Press's address makes it easy for readers to find where to send their orders. And setting the billing information entries and the Outlook Press address in type of the same height provides visual linkage between the two.

Double-spacing the mailing information and single-spacing the *For more information* copy block make each block unit distinct and present a professional image.

Aligning the top of the *Mail to:* block and the bottom of the *For more information* block with the top and bottom of the billing information block unifies the two sections and creates a finished appearance.

Vertically compressing those copy blocks, leaving white space above or below, would destroy the rectangular outline of the coupon.

Like nameplates, mail order coupons benefit from the extra time and care devoted to their design, since they're repeated from issue to issue.

Graphic Accents

In spite of limiting reader cues, visuals and typeface variety, *Tips & Tricks* has evolved into a sophisticated, high-density newsletter. Therefore, graphic accents must be added with care and restraint.

Boxing the pages with top, bottom and side rules of equal weight, would change the character of *Tips & Tricks* and exaggerate page density—as the example shows. The borders compete with the heavy rule defining the nameplate and weaken the impact of the backgrounds behind the initial caps.

Also, extra white space would be needed at the bottom of each column to provide breathing room between text and page borders. This would make it necessary to sacrifice some text.

Yet, something is needed to integrate the page. The columns of type seem to float. In addition, when reading the first article, it's too easy to jump over the *Diskettes . . .* headline and continue down the left text column, into the first paragraph of the second article, instead of moving to the top of the second column.

Vertical downrules are added to give definition and direction. Equally important, a horizontal rule is used to separate the first and second articles. A small amount of white space placed above the horizontal border rule divides the downrule between the first two columns and reinforces the two articles' separate identities. Joining the lower half of the downrule between columns 2 and 3 with the horizontal rule, to form a corner, provides further separation.

Refinements

To succeed as a whole, the six building blocks that make up a newsletter must be integrated. Otherwise, the newsletter looks haphazard and thrown together.

Something is still missing in the newsletter—it lacks "wholeness." The nameplate doesn't seem to be organically related to the remainder of the publication. It almost looks like one person designed the nameplate, and another designed the remainder of the newsletter.

Once the problem is identified, the cure is simple. Design integrity is dramatically improved by simply duplicating in the first letter of the nameplate the background treatment used with the initial caps.

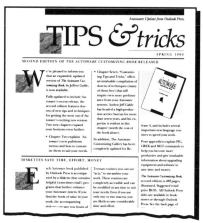

This simple refinement ties the nameplate to the rest the newsletter, creating a visually integrated whole.

Conclusion

As you can see from these examples, although newsletters are designed on a piece-by-piece basis, they don't take on a life of their own until their various parts are considered in relationship to each other. The refinements show that success is directly related to the time invested in the finishing touches that tie the various parts of a newsletter together.

Tips & Tricks Type Specifications

Masthead:	84-point and 76-point Palatino, 96-point New Baskerville Italic
Headlines:	10-point New Baskerville
Body Copy:	10/14 New Baskerville
Column Width:	10 picas, 10 points

kidscope, designed by Keith Cassell, Cassell Design

**Front
Page**

OCTOBER 1989

A NEWSLETTER FOR PARENTS & KIDS

kidscope

Child Care Zoning Change Requested

On November 28, the Blair County Planning Board and the Blair County Commissioners will hear public testimony on a proposed zoning change affecting child care. Zoning now requires anyone operating any kind of child care program in a residentially zoned area covered by Blair County Planning to have a special use permit. This requirement is generally unknown and many family day care homes and play-groups have operated for years without awareness of this regulation.

The Planning Board will consider staff recommendations and public testimony in its December 19 meeting and make a recommendation to the Commissioners. The Commissioners should act on the recommendation at its January 3 meeting.

The zoning change will require only those who wish to operate a program that requires state licensing in a residential zone to obtain a special use permit. It would not cover those who are required to register as family day care homes (3-5 children) or who are operating a half-day program.

ChildCare Resource requested this final change to prevent half-day programs that put no limits on the numbers of children in care. If a program operates fewer than four hours per day, there are no state regulations about adult/child ratios.

Big Bulb Sale

Those interested in selling bulbs to raise funds for the KidsCare Center must pick up their order forms by October 2 at the Center. Completed forms must be returned by the 30th. All proceeds go toward playground equipment.

Speech Therapy Now in Hillendale

Speech Therapy is now available in Hillendale at the Penn Rehabilitation Services. Pamela Henderson, Speech-Language Pathologist, has recently joined the Speech and Hearing Clinic.

Children and adults can receive both Physical and Speech Therapy at 118 Church Street. Contact the Speech and Hearing Clinic at 966-1006 or Penn's secretary, Debbie Cook, at 732-6600. Look for them at the December 11 Hillendale Christmas parade.

The primary purpose of *kidscope*, circulated to parents of preschool children by a nonprofit group, is to foster a feeling of community among parents. In today's fast-paced world—where single-parent and two-income households are becoming the norm, this type of publication provides valuable information and support.

A second *kidscope* goal is to help parents locate resources available locally—ranging from private and state-funded agencies to informal child care support groups and children's play groups.

A third goal is to provide a low-cost way for parents to sell children's outgrown clothing or furniture, announce yard sales or even give away kittens and puppies.

Although its intent is serious, *kidscope* is deliberately designed to communicate in a friendly unintimidating way. A more formal design would be inappropriate.

Nameplate

In order to attract young parents and project a playful, informal approach, a hand-drawn nameplate is chosen. The title is crafted with a "felt-tip marker on cardboard" technique.

It took several tries to achieve an image that looked informal yet legible—scribbled but not sloppy. (Some attempts looked messy, while others were so letter-perfect they looked like press-on type.)

Using all lowercase type, including the initial letter, *k*, gives the nameplate a childlike spontaneity that clearly identifies the newsletter's orientation to parents of young children.

The finalized design was then converted into a computer graphics file using an image scanner. The file was slightly enlarged to create the desired "coloring book" effect.

Placed on the page by itself, the title lacks definition. A heavy rule added under the name helps separate the nameplate from the headlines and body copy and at the same time provides visual interest.

To add to the playful, informal effect, the word *kidscope* is enlarged slightly so that it extends beyond the horizontal rule on the left and on the right.

Notice how the descender of the p in *kidscope* drops deep into the page, almost touching the first headline. This deep descender helps unify the nameplate with the rest of the page.

Subtitle and Date

A lighter rule above the name frames it at the top. The top rule also makes a horizon for the date and subtitle, *A newsletter for parents & kids.*

The date and subtitle are set flush-right, to balance the width and height of the k in *kidscope.* And, to create contrast with the handwritten *kidscope* title, the date and subtitle are set uppercase in a relatively small point size of a sans-serif typeface, Futura. An extra space is inserted between letters, with three extra spaces between words. Additional letter spacing is gained by using the software program's tracking feature. Stretching the words to the left helps integrate the date and subtitle with the primary title.

A comparison of an early version of the nameplate with the final version shows the major improvement achieved by moving the date and subtitle from the left to the right and replacing the boldface type (which competed with the title) with a smaller, lighter typeface and exaggerated letter spacing.

Department Heads

In order to strengthen visual identity and maintain page-to-page continuity throughout the newsletter, internal department heads are created in the same style as the newsletter title: *more news, calendar* and *classifieds* were created with crayons and then scanned.

It takes constant vigilance and a conscious effort to maintain consistency. At one point in the design process, everyone looking over the editor/designer's shoulder agreed that "something was not quite right";

it was quite a while before the culprit was identified as an inconsistent uppercase initial letter.

Department heads are given the same border treatment used with the nameplate—on the bottom a thick horizontal rule and on the top a thinner horizontal rule—to define the white space at the top of the page and add visual interest.

The same scanned marker-on-cardboard technique is used to announce the theme of each issue in the mailing label area. Since this is what the reader sees first when the newsletter arrives in the mail, it's important to use this area to begin selling the issue's contents.

Grid

A four-column grid is chosen to accommodate *kidscope*'s layout since each issue will likely include both long and short articles, plus numerous short calendar listings and classifieds. The four-column grid allows maximum flexibility for article placement and makes it easy to join two columns together—as illustrated by the table of contents and upcoming-issue teaser information on the front page.

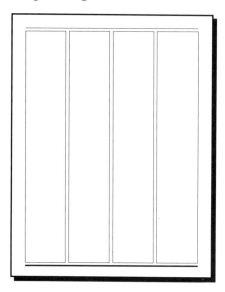
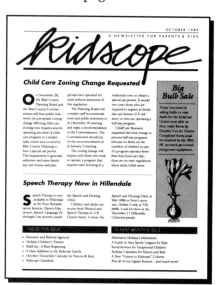

Reader Cues

Futura bold italic is used for headlines. The bold adds impact and legibility to the small type size; the italics suggest an informal, conversational tone, in keeping with the character of the nameplate.

For consistency, all headlines are set in the same point size, flush-left, spanning one, two or three columns, depending on the length of the article that follows. Flush-left placement creates a pool of white space to the right of the headline, which adds to its impact.

A placeholder created with the software program's drawing tool ensures consistent spacing above and below each headline.

The importance of consistency is again illustrated by an earlier version of the newsletter in which a different headline treatment is used for each article. The effect is an awkward, disjointed, unorganized effect. A great deal of impact was added simply by using one typeface, type size and type style for all headlines.

There are two exceptions to consistent headline treatment. The lead article on page 2 is introduced by a one-word headline. Since a one-word headline is limited in communicating power, it's supported by a two-line, boldface explanatory subhead, *A Busy Beginning for New Program.*

The other instance is on page 3, where *Hey! Look!* is used to introduce a calendar item of parks and recreation department class offerings. This strong italicized headline on a page without other headlines has the same effect as a bull in a china shop—it gets attention!

Table of Contents

One of the most important reader cues, the table of contents, appears on the front page. Bullets are used instead of page numbers to lure readers into opening the newsletter. With only four pages, it's unlikely readers will need page numbers to find the articles they're looking for. Furthermore, four of the six entries in the table of contents would be introduced by the same number, 2.

In fact, page numbers are omitted throughout the newsletter, since it's only four pages long.

The table of contents box on the lower left of the front page is balanced by a teaser announcing the contents of *kidscope*'s next issue. This technique helps arouse reader interest and maintain enthusiasm for future issues.

Initial Caps

Each article is introduced by an oversized Futura bold initial cap. These large initial caps reinforce the smaller type size of the headlines. Once again, the importance of consistency was demonstrated during the process of design, redesign and revision. Originally, only a few articles had initial caps. This seemed to imply that articles beginning with an initial cap were more important than the others. Confusion and ambiguity were eliminated by beginning *all* articles with initial caps.

Identical initial caps are used on the calendar page to relieve the monotony of the visually similar short items.

To signal their separate-but-equal status, sidebars are introduced by headlines set in a serif typeface, Galliard italic. This distinctive headline treatment helps the sidebars emerge almost as "advertisements" against the text that surrounds them.

Subheads

The front cover and pages 3 and 4 are further organized by subheads reversed out of boxes that span two columns. Uppercase Futura bold type provides maximum legibility. For consistency, box size and type size are the same in each case. (Serif type would not work as well because the detail of the thin serifs would probably be lost against the black background.)

Body Copy

Ten-point Galliard type on 13-point leading is used for the body copy of all articles. A slightly smaller type size is used in the classifieds to increase word density and make them look more like newspaper classifieds. Leading in calendar listings is slightly reduced to permit more white space above and below each entry.

Introductory words in each calendar listing are set in boldface type as lead-ins. This technique saves space and avoids the clutter that individual headlines would add. Since boldface type is used so sparingly in the newsletter, the lead-ins capture the reader's attention and provide a natural transition into each item.

Flush-left/ragged-right alignment is used throughout to reflect the desired informality. Justified copy would create a style at odds with *kidscope*'s purpose.

The uneven line endings also add variety and white space to the page. If justified text were used, white space would be dissipated *within* each line instead of providing visual contrast *at the end of* each line.

Graphic Accents

To avoid the visual grayness resulting from four parallel columns of text, sidebars are set against a screened background. Thin hairlines around the screens help define them and make them look deliberate.

Thin horizontal rules separate articles as well as calendar and classified entries.

Heavy horizontal rules—one at the bottom and one at the top of each page—balance each other, define the body copy area of the newsletter and create page borders.

The horizontal rules and Futura bold italic headlines are similar in weight, adding further unity and consistency to each page.

A vertical rule is used on page 3 to divide the calendar listings into parents' events and children's events. This is an excellent example of restrained use of a software program's line-drawing tool to create graphic accents only where they're appropriate or necessary.

Visuals

Visuals are used with great restraint. Clip art used in the back-page mailing label area provides a seasonal theme. The clip-art visuals of young girls are an effective accent for the *Mothers of Twins Group* calendar listing.

Note how a software program's COPY and PASTE or DUPLICATE tools can transform a basic clip-art illustration into a unique image.

kidscope

Calendar Page

calendar

PARENTS

Infant/Child Nutrition and Healthy Support Group offers free classes on first and third Wednesdays, 9:30 - 10 a.m., Blair County Health Department, Hillendale. Call Mary Malloy, 486-4343 ext. 32.

A pre- & post-natal exercise class offered Thursday evenings, January 19 to February 9, 7-8:30 p.m. at the Hickory Hill/Portage YMCA. Individualized program designed to strengthen and stretch the major muscles involved in pregnancy, childbirth and after; develop balance, coordination and good posture. $15 for all Y members, $30 for nonmember. Financial assistance is available.

Young Mothers' Group/ Children's Play Group seeking new members with children aged 0-3 years. Group meets 10 a.m.- noon Monday–Thursday at Blair Co. Rec. and Parks Dept., 110 Elm, Hillendale. Contact Tim McGee at 439-8181.

Tri-Adopt parent support group for adoptive parents meets bimonthly. Call Judy Hammond, 483-9808 or 488-9726.

Free parent call-in service sponsored by the Center for the Study of Development and Learning. Parents can call with questions about children's growth and development, behavior, developmental disabilities, and parenting. Provides referrals, classes, group sessions, and library of child development reference tools. Mons. and Weds. 8 - 9 a.m. 1-800-391-KIDS.

Support groups for parents of children with emotional and behavioral problems meet Mondays from 7:30 to 9 p.m. at the Mental Health Association, 119 Blair St. in Hillton. Call 434-1111.

Parent's Day Off! Every third Saturday of each month. Call Child Care Support Group for info. 486-4589.

Mothers of Twins group meets 2nd Tuesdays, 7:30 p.m. at Blair Baptist Church. Call Kate Klapp at 842-8383.

KIDS

Laird Planetarium... Saturday classes for Young Astronomers (grades 1-6). Call for information.
• *Planet Search* M-F at 8 p.m., S/S at 1 & 3 p.m., Dec. 19 thru Jan. 27.
• *Winnie the Pooh* Sat. only at 11 a.m.
• *Cosmic Cat* M-F at 11 a.m., S/S at 4 p.m.

The Play House Theatre Company presents "A Holiday Gift," a puppet show for children of all ages. November 12–Dec. 31. For groups on Wed./Thurs., 10 a.m. General public on Sats., 2 p.m. 302 Pettigrew St., Hazelton 689-5523.

Hey! Look!

Parks & Recreation Department of Hazelton is offering classes for school kids in piano, drawing, tennis, tumbling, jazz dancing, baton, ballet, & Tae kwon do; for preschoolers in music and tumbling. Dates, times, fees vary. Most classes begin mid-September. Registration is open. Watch for news of First Friday Family Nights and contests for you and your parents! Call Sharon Glass at 483-7897 for all the info!

Museum of Life and Science in Hazelton is open Mon.-Sat. 10 a.m.-5 p.m. and Sun. 1-5 p.m. Children 4 & under free. Computer Creations art display, Oct. 11–Nov. 18. Dinosaur Art, Oct. 6–Dec. 5. Santa Train, coming Nov. 26–Dec. 29. The Discovery Room is always open... where you can handle fascinating objects and learn by touching, smelling, listening and seeing.

Swimming Lessons for all ages. Held during open swim hours at Community Center Swimming Pool. One or two students per lesson. Call 968-2790 for more information. The Department offers the following swim classes: Parent Tot Swimming, Preschool Swimming, Red Cross Cert. Swim Classes, Advanced Beginners Swim.

In the *Swimming Lessons* entry, notice how the clip-art fish has been rotated vertically and is cut off by the horizontal rule at the bottom of page 3. This is an excellent example of how you can not only disguise commercially available clip art but make it appear to be an organic part of the newsletter.

Notice how the clip art accompanying the PlayHouse Theater entry interrupts the vertical rule dividing parents' and kids' items. This helps unify and integrate the page.

In the sidebar on the front cover, notice how the roots of the flowering bulb extend below the screened background into the white space. If the roots were contained within the screened area, the page would be far less interesting.

The small cluster of leaves used in the mailing-label area is an effective accent to reinforce the autumn theme of the October issue. Similar clip art can be used for other months of the year.

In an earlier version of the newsletter, the leaves were significantly larger and placed lower on the page, creating a "hole" of white space between the leaves and the newsletter's return address. By making the leaves smaller and moving them up, they become an integral part of the newsletter's title and return address. The increased white space below now does a better job of setting off the leaves, the return address and the line introducing the newsletter's monthly theme.

Layout

Front page and page 2 articles are laid out in a combination of horizontal and vertical modules resembling a newspaper format. The long article on the front cover appears shorter by being placed in three shorter columns. The "newspaper resemblance" of the front page is reinforced by headlines that extend across all three columns.

Both vertical and horizontal article modules are used on page 2. Articles are placed within one-, two- or three-column rectangles.

The effectiveness of this modular approach can be observed by comparing page 2 with an earlier alternative approach. Here, the page is divided into four smaller modules, which seem static and fail to communicate a "news" feeling. The wider columns with shorter headlines make for slower reading and compromise page unity.

Conclusion

kidscope illustrates the important role design elements play in attracting targeted readers, as well as the importance of consistency and attention to detail in producing a newsletter.

Although *kidscope* will be read primarily by parents, it's orientation toward children's issues and activities is strongly communicated in the nameplate and department heads that resemble a child's efforts with a crayon. In spite of the simplicity of these elements, the newsletter projects a professional image because it is consistently organized and disciplined. The fact that the editor and staff take their job seriously is reflected in the consistent use of the four-column grid throughout the newsletter and consistent treatment of headlines and body copy.

The results of consistency can be appreciated by comparing earlier trial-run versions of *kidscope* with the final newsletter. Redesign—with more attention to grids and consistent treatment of headlines and body copy—contributed to a stronger, more readable newsletter.

Other improvements contributing to the success of the final version of *kidscope* involved reducing the size of some visuals, making them more proportionate to other page elements while at the same time creating more white space; and the addition of rules to separate the nameplate from the body copy and define page borders.

Once again, we see that success in newsletter design is directly related to the amount of attention paid to consistency and details.

---

kidscope Type Specifications

Masthead:	Hand-lettered
Headlines:	18-point Futura Bold Italic
Body Copy:	10/14 Galliard
Subheads:	12-point Futura Bold
Column Width:	10 picas

CHAPTER ELEVEN

THE NEWSLETTER GALLERY

One of the best ways to learn how to design effectively is to study the attractive newsletters that come across your desk.

By analyzing newsletters in terms of the six building blocks (grids, nameplate, body copy, reader cues, visuals, graphic accents), you'll see how designers work with each of these elements to create balanced, interesting pages.

The ten favorites I have included in this gallery illustrate how strength and communicating power can be achieved by using specific techniques described in earlier chapters. As you analyze these diverse examples, notice that each is unique. Yet, with the exception of one tabloid, all are produced in the same standard 8 1/2- by 11-inch page format.

The purpose of these examples isn't merely to judge or praise, but to help you sharpen your skills and improve your ability to relate the information in the preceding chapters to an ongoing analysis of newsletters all around you.

SMALL BUSINESS SOURCE

Front Page

S M A L L   B U S I N E S S
SOURCE

A CLOSER LOOK AT SMALL BUSINESS DEVELOPMENT CENTERS

Small Business Development Centers are one of the most important resources available to small business owners and entrepreneurs. The centers are designed to help those interested in starting a business and to provide management assistance for those already in business. SBDCs accomplish this with one-on-one counseling, training sessions, publications, and educational programs designed and managed by academic and professional consultants.

Upstart Publishing recently completed a survey of Small Business Development Centers throughout the United States. The survey results help shed some light on the role of SBDCs in small business education, the nature of the services provided by the centers, and the types of resources they offer their clients. We spoke to more than 35 directors or assistant directors in locations throughout the country. Here are some of the facts we uncovered.

* *How many people are counseled each year through the SBDC system?*

Estimates given in response to this question indicate that over 500,000 people take advantage of the services of SBDCs each year. Given the total

SBDC FUNDING

- SBA Funds — 44.0%
- School Funds — 32.6%
- State Funds — 18.0%
- Other Funds — 5.4%

number of start-ups in the U.S. each year, this indicates that SBDCs are reaching and helping a significant percentage of new businesses.

According to estimates, over 500,000 people take advantage of SBDCs each year.

* *How are SBDCs funded?*

While funding for each Center varies, the overall survey results indicate that, on average, 44% of SBDC funds come from the Small Business Administration, 32.6% from the college and/or university system affiliated with a particular center, 18.0% from state moneys, and

5.4% from other sources, which include donations from individuals, private corporations, and local municipalities.

Total budgets vary widely, ranging from an annual budget of $250,000 to $7,700,000, depending on location, activites, and clientele served. The average budget fell near the $2,000,000 mark.

What sort of materials do SBDCs provide for their clients and where do these materials come from?

Just about every SBDC provides some sort of printed reference material for their clients, with 51% indicating that they provide handouts or reproduced material for their clients. Some 19% use video tapes as part of the education process, 16% use books (the majority of these focus on business planning) and 12% use software in working with clients. Another 2% report

continued on back page

NOTEWORTHY

David H. Bangs, Jr., author of Upstart's bestselling Business Planning Guide, will present "A Marketing Primer" at Inc. magazine's First Annual Conference on Growing the Company. The keynote speech will be presented by Tom Peters, author of In Search of Excellence. The conference will be held on November 9–10th in Boston. For information, contact Sue Knapp at Inc., 44 Commercial Wharf, Boston, MA 02110 or call 1-800-255-1080.

British Commonwealth rights to Upstart's Cash Flow Control Guide have recently been sold to London-based Kogan-Page Ltd., which also specializes in small business titles. The agreement licenses the British publisher to sell the Guide in a number of foreign countries, including Great Britain, Hong Kong, Singapore, New Zealand, and Australia.

UPSTART

Volume 1, Number 4
Source is published quarterly by Upstart Publishing Company, Inc. © UPCO 1988.

Upstart Publishing's *Small Business Source* illustrates how a lot of information and a professional image can be communicated cost-effectively with a two-color newsletter printed on both sides of an 8 1/2- by 11-inch sheet of paper.

Nameplate

If the words *Small Business Source* were all set the same size, the nameplate would be dull and wouldn't really identify it as *the* source of small business information. Therefore, the title is broken into two components, with *Source* set in a significantly larger, bolder typeface and emphasized by white space and a heavy rule.

Body Copy

Because *Small Business Source* is output on a high-resolution phototypesetter and printed on coated paper stock, a relatively small type size can be used successfully. A four-column grid offers plenty of vertical white space and wide gutters.

Despite its small type size, body copy is extremely readable because line spacing (leading) and letter spacing (tracking) have been decreased and word spacing increased. The resulting increase in word count creates an authoritative tone that attracts readers.

Although the newsletter is based on a single long article, notice how that feature uses only three of the four columns on the front page and continues on the back. The remaining column, devoted to two additional features, is set in italics with extra leading, which adds visual interest to the page.

Because the feature article continues on the back page, readers have a reason to turn the newsletter over. Notice how three of the four columns are grouped together to form a box that becomes the dominant visual on the page. Two columns of text fit within the three-column box, adding further interest.

Publication Information

Notice how the folio—volume and issue numbers—and the publisher's name have been moved from their usual location in or near the nameplate to a less prominent place at the lower right corner. Thus, the information repeated in each issue doesn't conflict with either the nameplate or the feature article headline.

Details

When used with restraint, initial caps set in screened boxes add color to a page and provide contrast with the straightforward headline treatment. Because the initial cap is dropped into the paragraph, it gives breathing room to the content.

The combination of vertical downrules and dot-leader patterns to separate adjacent columns creates a contemporary sophistication.

Notice how the top border on the back cover is formed by repeating the symbol from the Upstart logo, and the way the logo itself anchors the lower right corner of the page.

Small Business Source Type Specifications

Nameplate:	Albertus
Headlines:	14-point Palatino Bold
Body Copy:	9/11 Palatino
Pull-Quotes:	14/15 Palatino Italic
Column Width:	9 picas

inFidelity

**Front
Page**

*in***Fidelity**™

The Newsletter of Keith Yates Audio / Summer 1989

Absolutely, Resolutely First-Class

Our new store opens this Fall

**Great sound in small
spaces! Page 5.**

KEITH YATES
AUDIO

A purpose-built, state-of-the-art facility at 2440 Fulton Avenue will be our new home beginning this Fall. Now under construction, the new store will offer:

- Four well-isolated audio-only soundrooms, two of which are larger than our current main soundroom
- Two ambitious Home Theater rooms with high resolution video and Surround Sound
- A custom installation display room for in-wall speakers, multiroom A/V systems and furniture
- An easily accessible service department
- A software area for top-rated CDs and DATs
- A concert-hall type floor plan that will accommodate

MOVING SALE

Keith Yates Audio's first—and we hope last—Moving Sale will be held Tuesday, October 3 through Saturday, October 7 at our existing (D Street) location.

This rather peculiar sale will include opened and sealed inventory, as well as odds and ends accumulated over eight years—including the new and improved, the old and obsolete, the scratched and dented, and a few items that were, to put it plainly, mistakes.

The sale will begin at 11 a.m. All sales will be considered final.

a live chamber ensemble and seat an audience of up to 100.

To promote home-like acoustics, all walls are being constructed entirely of wood 2-by-4s set sixteen inches on-center, and half-inch sheetrock—the same as most residential projects.

Located in Fulton Point just south of El Camino in Sacramento, the store was found after a seven-month search throughout the Sacramento area. At 7,600 square feet, we believe it to be the most comprehensive specialty audio/video facility on the West Coast. Our present location at 3019 D Street will be retained for custom installation crews and inventory.

Projected move-in date is mid-October! Watch for us!

An audio/video retailer publishes this newsletter to keep customers up-to-date on the latest advances in audio/video home entertainment and custom home installation services.

The newsletter's design is entirely in keeping with reader expectations, since the market for expensive audio/video components includes many design-conscious individuals. This design is as exciting as the high-technology components it describes.

Image-building and a density of information come together successfully in *inFidelity*.

Nameplate

inFidelity's nameplate demonstrates the effects that can be achieved by using different screen values for letters and their backgrounds.

The first two letters, *i* and *n*, are emphasized with a light (approximately 40 percent) tint screen, enhanced by being placed against a darker (approximately 80 percent) background screen.

Notice how the lightly screened *in* forms a striking contrast to the darker *Fidelity* and how the screened background behind the nameplate bleeds to the top and sides of the page. If this screen didn't bleed and instead were framed in white space, the impact of the nameplate would be diminished.

Notice how the lowercase *in* and uppercase *F* in *Fidelity* also create a play on words, making it clear that the title refers to audio systems, not extramarital activity. (Consider how the meaning of the title would change if the letters were reversed, with the *i* uppercased and *F* lowercased.)

Title and subtitle are separated from the body copy by a generous amount of white space.

The three thin rules separating the title from the subtitle and folio span three of the four columns, creating a balance within the nameplate and reinforcing the newsletter's underlying grid. Because the rules bleed off the right-hand side of the page, readers are subtly encouraged to open the newsletter and continue reading inside.

Production Quality

High-resolution phototypesetting and printing on quality paper enhance *inFidelity*'s look. Bleeds at the top of each page also reflect high production standards. The screens are even in value, devoid of the mottled look that can result when artwork is printed on a laser printer.

Body Copy

Repeating the *inFidelity* nameplate at the top left and the firm's name in the lower corners of each page of the spread provides unity, as well as an attractive frame for the pages.

Page-to-page unity is also enhanced by the consistent use of typeface, type size and type style for body copy and prices throughout the newsletter design.

Although the four-column grid is used in different ways, it mostly provides the structure for four single text columns.

In other locations, it's used as a container for two columns of text that surround a photo or graphic, plus other combinations of text and illustrations.

Notice how the introductory information on pages that describe music systems is grouped in the third column from the left. Placement and typography are consistent for the *System* heading, number and component listing (e.g., *speakers, receiver,* etc.).

Further unifying the newsletter is the consistent amount of white space at the top of each column.

Back Page

inFidelity's back page illustrates how a mailing panel can be an integral part of a newsletter. This is done by using text and graphics that fit under the return address, postmark and address label area.

Front Page

By using a screen and a bleed, the *Moving Sale* column adds immediacy to the page. The bleed also helps separate this article from adjacent body copy.

The screened box and the reversed, tilted *Moving Sale* headline create a lot of contrast, as does the article's bold type next to the medium-weight body copy used in the regular text columns.

Restraint is a wonderful thing. Consider how this page might look if the screened article were boxed. The effect of the vertical lines of the box next to the column downrules would create unnecessary clutter.

Handling Photographs

Contrast is provided by the placement of photographs. For example, on the two-page spreads showing new systems, a rectangular photo for *System 1* extends across all four columns. The relatively square photo accompanying *System 2* spans three columns.

Further contrast is provided by the photo used with *System 4*, silhouetted so that vertical speakers break into the body copy.

This newsletter design gives flexibility so that photographs can be as large as necessary to effectively communicate. Photographs can bleed off a page or into adjacent columns. If the photographs on page 3 were formatted horizontally to fit the width of the column grid, they would shrink to a size that would make them ineffective. If they were reproduced to be two columns wide, they would dominate the page.

When the photos bleed to the left and right, however, they remain anchored to the appropriate columns and are large enough to create visual impact.

Notice how the featured inventor's photo spans two columns, breaking up excessive page symmetry and balancing the two other photos on the page—almost forming a visual triangle.

---

inFidelity Type Specifications

Nameplate:	Approximately 128-point Bodoni Italic, Condensed and letter-spaced
Headlines:	26-point Bodoni Regular
Subtitles:	16-point Bodoni Italic
Body Copy:	10/12 Helvetica Condensed Light
Pull-Quotes:	9/10 Helvetica Black
Column Width:	10 picas

THE CHANNELMARKER LETTER

**Front
Page**

THE
Channelmarker™
L E T T E R

Volume 1, Number 2   *A Publication of Merrin Information Services, Inc.*   April 1989

IN THIS ISSUE

Published by **Merrin
Information Services, Inc.**
Suite 800
2479 East Bayshore Road,
Palo Alto, CA 94303

(415) 493-5050

A Little Light to Brighten Stygian Dealer Profits

These are the best and worst of times for relations between vendors and resellers of personal computers and related products.

Heated customer demand for these products in the late 1980's has been unflagging. Volume should therefore drive revenues...and profits. At the same time competition between suppliers for space on dealers' shelves has been positively incendiary. Thus the battle for market share intensifies daily, while dealer margins continue their decade-long slide.

All participants loudly tout their desire to get margins and/or profits up...while they continue all the practices that drag them down. We believe one of the major weapons in the vendors' struggle to improve dealer profitability—on which this issue focuses—is the clumsily wielded, so-called 'dealer agreement,' which, we assume, is intended to increase sales of the vendor's products while it fattens dealers' profits.

Can a dealer agreement actually be designed to boost a manufacturer's sales? If so, how? Observation and research reveal abysmal ignorance among vendors on both questions. After reviewing a host of such agreements, we find that most are legalistic nightmares. Only one major computer-maker demonstrates

any true savvy: Apple Computer with its Earned Investment Program (EIP). We think the EIP reflects an intelligent analysis of the situation and a commendable attempt to refine and hone the dealer agreement as a sales tool and a mechanism to help increase dealer profits. The agreement is far from perfect and still has much room for improvement. But we see it as a small, brave candle in Carlsbad Caverns, a tiny light in that massive labyrinth of Stygian darkness—but at least a light. As for the others, all we can do is curse the darkness....

The standard dealer agreement offered by vendors is a monster of bureaucracy and legalese, stuffed with clauses in which vendors and dealers spell out certain promises to each other concerning discounts, terms for delivery and order cancellation, among other matters. To an outside observer of the personal computer dealer channel, they might just as well be totems or fetishes or mantras. Unlike those devotional objects and incantations, however, our analysis shows that there is evidence the typical dealer agreement really harms both dealers and vendors. This is because, in essence, the only carrot specified gives larger discounts for shipping more of a

(continued on Page 3)

T*he Channelmarker Letter* illustrates the importance of using white space with long articles that don't include photos or illustrations. It also shows how careful design and typography can add value to expensive newsletters, helping to make subscription costs more acceptable to readers.

Color

The Channelmarker Letter is printed in two colors on a heavy, textured white stock. Page borders, rules and the illustrations in the nameplate are printed in a PMS green. Type is a complementary dark gray.

Graphic Accents

Consistent typography and abundant white space are the distinguishing features of this newsletter. White space is built into the body copy by using paragraph indents, extra space between paragraphs and flush-left/ragged-right alignment that adds a varying amount of space to the end of each line.

More breathing room is also provided by *scholar's margins*—white space that frames each two-page spread. On page 2, the scholar's margin is used for masthead and subscription information.

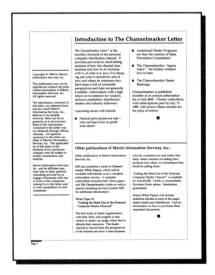

On other pages, they're used to balance two text-filled columns and for pull-quotes. (Notice how the italic type's conversational tone encourages you to read the pull-quotes.)

White space on the left-hand side of the front page, used for the table of contents and publication source information, balances the two text columns beside it.

Although pages are boxed, notice how the horizontal and vertical rules between and within the columns approach but don't touch the boxed borders. This prevents the newsletter from looking like a maze of lines and adds breathing room to the layout.

On the inside pages, page numbers, located in the lower outside corners of the spread, are emphasized by short horizontal rules directly above them. This subtle touch adds character and distinctiveness to an otherwise ordinary boxed page.

On page 2, deep indents and solid boxes used as bullets and end signs emphasize the listings.

For consistency and to further reinforce *The Channelmarker Letter*'s professional image, the column endings are aligned at the bottom of each page. Articles are placed so that text fills the first column, then stops in the second column at the point where the article ends. This often creates a block of white space that acts as an exclamation point, further emphasizing the article and preparing the reader for the start of a new article.

Channelmarker Type Specifications

Nameplate:	18- and 40-point Palatino Bold
Headlines:	16-point Palatino Bold
Body Copy:	10/12 Palatino Regular
Pull-Quotes:	14/15 Palatino Italic
Column Width:	14 picas

PROFILES

**Front
Page**

PROFILES

GOVERNMENT CONTRACTING
NOVEMBER - DECEMBER 1988

Tysons Office Sparks Government Contractors' Interest

In one year, the new Don Richard Associates office in Tysons Corner has been overwhelmingly received. Employers seeking qualified accounting and financial help in all fields have sought out DRA. And while we are well-represented by applicants in other areas, we are particularly excited by the strong demand for top financial talent from the government contracting industry.

Our DRA Government Contracting Specialist, **Bill Shontell**, is committed to answering that demand by offering the best recruiting service available anywhere for government contractors. Bill has designed the program to highlight the talents and strengths of candidates with varying degrees of experience. This first issue of Profiles, devoted entirely to financial candidates with the background you need, does just that.

Remember, if you don't see the employee that matches your job requirements profiled, **call Bill at (703) 827-5990.** This is just a small sample of the applicants we represent. Chances are, the candidate you seek is available and ready to go to work.

You can depend on Bill to understand the needs of government contracting because he's been there. With 6 1/2 years in financial management with two major government contractors and several years in public accounting with Price Waterhouse, Bill knows the importance of putting the right person in the right position.

Call on the professionals at Don Richard Associates to make the right calls for government contracting.

Special Report:
Greater Washington's Labor Shortage
By George Grier, condensed from Board of Trade report

The Problem

On Saturday, June 4, the top story in the Washington Post carried an alarming headline. It read: "AREA HIT BY LABOR SHORTAGE. JOBS GO UNFILLED AS UNEMPLOYMENT DROPS TO 2.7 PERCENT."

A booming economy, the Post reported, has reduced the local unemployment level to less than half the rate for the nation. A level as low as 2.7 percent is generally considered "frictional." This means that virtually all unemployed workers are in the process of switching jobs — not looking for them. And this condition has sent many area employers on a desperate search for workers who are not already committed. A labor market as tight as this has not existed in the Washington area for many years.

Evolution of a Labor Shortage

How did the Washington area get into its difficult situation?

1. Strong job growth. Throughout most of the 80s, and especially since 1983, job growth has been strong in this area. Even in the recessionary year of 1982, there was a net loss of fewer than 10,000 jobs out of a total of about 1.6 million, or a bit over one-half of one percent.

Fortunately, the recession's impact on the Washington area was only tempo-

rary. An astonishing one out of every five jobs that now exist in this area has been created since 1983.

2. Private sector growth predominates. While the trend in government employment has been slightly downward, the trend line for private jobs has resembled the trajectory of a jet plane take-off. In percentage terms it amounts to a 34% in six years.

3. Federal Contracting fuels private business expectations. But statistics like these should not be permitted to obscure the role of the federal government. It is true that the federal government declined in importance as an employer in the D.C. area. By 1986, fewer than one area job in five was in the federal government, compared to one in three in 1960.

Yet at the same time as federal government has not been growing, the national government has played an increasing role as a purchaser of goods and services. Since 1983 the growth in federal purchases in this area has been substantially greater than the increase in federal payroll. Thus, more and more, the employment growth of this area has been in the private sector; fueled largely by federal procurement.

Will Federal Belt-tightening Hurt?

This relationship with the federal government of course, makes the area vulnerable to future changes in federal

(Continued Page 3)

A newsletter for government contractors should be a no-frills communications vehicle, free from frivolous or unnecessary elements. Practicality and accessibility are paramount. Busy readers should be able to assimilate information quickly. *Profiles* fulfills these goals.

Nameplate

Profiles' nameplate contains all the necessary information. The title clearly emerges from a reversed box. The supporting subtitle and dateline are set in smaller black type inside a small white box. Because of the date's importance, the months are set in uppercase type only slightly smaller than the subtitle type.

The box containing the subtitle and dateline slightly overlaps the title area of the nameplate and the text area, tying the nameplate together with the content. A heavy rule at the bottom of the subtitle box adds a slight three-dimensional effect and unifies it with the rest of the nameplate.

Further integrating the title and subtitle are the oversized first and last letters, which add visual interest to the nameplate.

Profiles' title is set in a serif typeface that contains enough stress to add interest to the page without being so ornate or stylized that it attracts too much attention. Goudy might look too academic here; Palatino might look too expensive. A simple, sans-serif typeface would look dull.

Logo Box

Centered at the bottom of the front page, the publisher's logo provides a third focal point to complete an invisible triangle formed with the oversized first and last letters of the title. The screened box emphasizes the logo. (Note how the oversized *A* in *Don Richard Associates* unifies the three lines of the logo.)

The logo box slightly overlaps the boxed border that defines the text area, creating an interesting three-dimensional effect.

Body Copy

Based on a very flexible three-column grid, *Profiles'* copy area is boxed for formality. Downrules define the columns and allow closer column placement, reinforcing *Profiles'* no-frills image. Justified alignment permits maximum word density per line and per page.

Reader Cues

Profiles uses a lot of reader cues, so that each issue can be quickly scanned. Headlines are set flush-left, keeping them separate from headlines in adjoining columns and making it easy for the reader's eyes to move straight down and find the first line of an article.

Numerous subheads let the reader scan the major points of an article and decide whether to read it. Extra white space above the subtitles helps separate them from the preceding paragraphs.

Flush-left eyebrows, such as *Special Report*, categorize headlines. Bylines list the author and the source of the information (e.g., *by George Grier, condensed from Board of Trade report*).

Reader cues and body copy are set in several different sizes of the same typeface used for the *Profiles* title, subtitle and dateline.

Careful attention has been paid to small details. For instance, ample space is provided between the jumpline and the end of the article. Notice that the jumpline and the other column endings are aligned on the same baseline. Too often, jumplines extend below the baseline of text columns—intruding into the white space that should separate the last line of text from the bottom page border.

Back Page

Because *Profiles'* back page is the first part of the newsletter readers see, a lot of thought has gone into designing it. Although typographic restraint was used throughout the newsletter, one departure from that is a teaser, simulating a quickly written note, added in a script typeface below the mailing label. It offers an immediate reason to begin reading the newsletter: *Inside—31 Specific Talents for Government Contractors!* How many prudent and responsible government contractors could resist reading that?

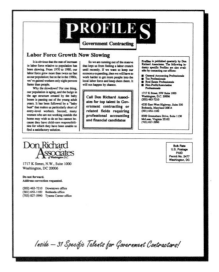

A miniature version of the name-plate and subtitle placed on the top half of the back page reinforces *Profiles'* identity. Because it contains an article, the page takes on an editorial look, yet it gracefully segues into an advertisement for the publisher's products. Centered in the middle of the page, a box describes the firm's recruiting services.

Another box contains the *Profiles* masthead, which lists not only the names and addresses of Don Richard Associates offices, but the firm's other publications as well.

Profiles Type Specifications

Nameplate:	Times Extra Bold
Headlines:	18/22 Times Bold
Body Copy:	10/12 Times
Subheads:	12-point Times Bold
Column Width:	14 picas

SECOND WIND

Front Page

SECOND WIND

REFRESHING INSIGHTS ON THE ADVERTISING BUSINESS

April 1988

Give your Copywriter a Macintosh...

If you do, it will save you lots of money in the long run.

Before we explain our copywriter's strategy, let's talk about the Macintosh computer in general as it relates to advertising agencies. In our opinion, the Macintosh is the best computer for a smaller agency to have. There are several reasons: First, because of its design, the Mac is very easy for a novice to understand and operate. We are novices! Most advertising people don't know a ram from a byte, and shouldn't! Our job is to create advertising, not become computer nerds.

Next, the Mac has a graphics potential that is beginning to be fully appreciated. This graphics capability is beneficial to us in both desk-top publishing and graphics. The desk-top publishing aspect of the Macintosh will allow us to make new business presentations that are far superior to our competition's. Second, the Macintosh is starting to creep into creative departments. Some venturesome art directors are using the Mac equipped with a scanner and laser printer to input the various layout elements of an ad or brochure, etc.: type, logos, illustration, photography. After input, the art director has the ability to reposition, resize, change typestyle...all at the push

of a button. Saves much time!

Of course, there is a whole other business, financial, accounting aspect of the Macintosh that makes it perfect for a smaller advertising or graphics firm. Several companies are now publishing business/financial advertising agency software that runs on the Macintosh.

I will speak in detail about fully computerizing a small advertising agency in an Advanced Seminar. Look for details and attend! Your whole future in this business may depend on computerizing your agency.

Now, back to the copywriter. Think about how most agencies create their copy. A copywriter writes it by hand or types it on a typewriter. If the agency has word processing, (which, by the way, is a good idea because of its ability to store documents in a logical way

continued on page 6

The Billings Hocus Pocus...What you say is what you're not

When asked how large your agency is, what do you say? Do you give the billings number, the capitalized billings number or the gross income number? Or, are you confused as to what is what. I think it's time we spoke about the different numbers, because if you don't fully understand them, they can get you into trouble.

continued on page 2

Often, one of the best ways to attract attention is to do the opposite of what everyone else is doing. *Second Wind: Refreshing Insights on the Advertising Business* does just that.

Characterized by exaggeration and flamboyance, the advertising business often succeeds by making products seem larger than life. In such an environment, *Second Wind* is a quiet but effective change of pace.

Nameplate

Second Wind's unique approach is evident in its unpretentious nameplate. Its modest size is accentuated by the generous pool of white space surrounding it.

The title and subtitle are set in relatively small type sizes. The title typeface is interesting enough to avoid a "plain vanilla" feeling, but simple enough to allow the message to emerge.

Second Wind's soft tone is reinforced by the strength and visibility of the boldfaced dateline. The thin horizontal rule separating title and subtitle is centered and set off by white space.

Crowning the title, subtitle and dateline is a stylized *S* that looks like a Chinese brush stroke, subtle but strong. Together, these elements can project an image of serenity—a welcome relief from the typical chaos of a busy advertising executive's desk.

Visuals

The stylized visuals reinforce the newsletter's direct personalized approach. In many ways, these visuals reflect the adage that "opposites attract." One look at the cartoon-like illustrations and you know the content *has* to be meaningful—otherwise the newsletter couldn't possibly succeed!

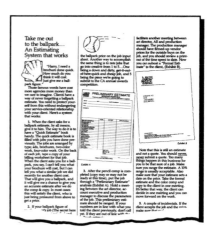

On the front page, the informality of the visuals is reinforced by the hand-drawn boxes around the illustrations and table of contents.

On the inside pages, the levity of the illustrations contrasts with the seriousness of the estimate form and cover sheet. These contrasting styles work together to provide emphasis and visual interest.

Note how extending the preliminary estimate form across the downrule and into the margin of the next column provides visual relief from the monotony of the dense body copy. A similar effect is created by having elements of the illustrations extend into the outside margin (e.g., the thumb of the baseball glove). Interest is also provided by tilting the estimate and cover sheets.

Reader Cues

In keeping with the newsletter's informal tone, the headline treatment is relatively restrained. Instead of introducing another typeface, headlines are set in a large size of the body-copy typeface. The flush-left/ragged-right alignment creates a conversational feeling and adds breathing room between columns.

On page 4, white space is used both horizontally and vertically to emphasize listed items. Extra space is added between numbered items, and the numbers themselves are indented. Extra space also emphasizes the articles listed in the table of contents box on page 1.

Second Wind's primary selling message—a paragraph promoting a seminar on computerizing a small advertising agency—is set in boldface italics. Placing it in the center attracts the reader's attention.

All in all, *Second Wind* shows how a whisper can attract more attention than a shout.

Second Wind Type Specifications

Headlines:	18/18 Palatino Bold
Body Copy:	11/11.5 Palatino
Pull-Quotes:	11/11.5 Palatino Bold Italic
Column Width:	14 picas

THE AutoCAD PRODUCTIVITY NEWSLETTER

Front Page

Winter Spring 1989

The AutoCAD
Productivity Newsletter

News and notes from
Ventana Press

Publisher of the
AutoCAD Reference Library

New Book Focuses on 3D

We're pleased to announce the February publication of *The AutoCAD 3D Book*, by George O. Head, Charles A. Pietra and Kenneth J. Segal. The book was written to help you quickly learn the many new 3D features found in AutoCAD's powerful, yet complex Release 10.

Written for those new to 3D, the book covers all commands, including a complete overview of AutoCAD's sometimes confusing User Coordinate System (UCS). You're led step by step into dynamic viewing, perspective, multiple viewports, surfaces and meshes. A special chapter, "New Twists to Old Commands," alerts you to many traditional AutoCAD commands that behave differently in 3D (ouch!). And "3D Tips and Tricks" provides dozens of time-saving techniques that can make your transition to 3D most rewarding (see excerpts on page 2).

In addition, three chapters cover AutoSHADE™, AutoSOLID™, and the more popular, established third-party 3D applications.

Finally, "The AutoCAD 3D Library" features 25 AutoLISP programs that you can enter directly into your computer to speed your 3D work, including automatic perspective, snap and zoom; automatic 2D/3D symbol replacement; rotation on any axis, 3D parametric programming and more.

"Most new Release 10 features deal with 3D," says coauthor George Head. "We wrote *The AutoCAD 3D Book* so that users wouldn't have to go out and buy the umpteenth version of their introductory book just to find out what's new with AutoCAD."

The AutoCAD 3D Book is the fourth title of The AutoCAD Reference Library (see related article on page 3), designed to help beginning and intermediate users get the most from AutoCAD's considerable new capabilities. "AutoCAD users can become two or three times as productive by learning a few tricks and techniques," says coauthor Charles Pietra. "This is one area where a little extra training goes a long way."

The AutoCAD 3D Book is 7-3/8" by 9-1/4", with more than 200 figures and illustrations. Suggested retail price is $29.95 for book only; $79.90 with optional diskette. The book is available from your authorized AutoCAD dealer, bookstores or Ventana Press.

3D Workshops Planned

Many professionals who learned traditional drafting methods need to rethink their skills in 3D, which opens new levels of performance for them.

George Head and Charles Pietra, two of the authors of *The AutoCAD 3D Book*, will conduct workshops on AutoCAD's Release 10 this winter and spring.

George Head will offer **AutoCAD 3D Workshops with Release 10**. These one-day seminars will focus on 3D and all commands and functions now offered with Release 10. "Early students have found that my workshop will save a good 30 to 40 hours of digging and frustration," says George.

The workshops will be held in six cities this year at a cost of $295 per person per seminar.

Associated Market Research
Suite 380
Capital of Texas Highway South
Austin, TX 78704
(512/445-6482).

Chuck Pietra, president of MicroCAD Managers of Syracuse, NY, offers a two-day hands-on workshop, **3D with Release 10**, now being held every three weeks.

Pietra's workshops help users "think in 3D" and make the difficult transition from traditional drafting techniques to the third dimension. "The class is for current AutoCAD users who want to quickly get up to speed on Release 10." Cost for the two-day seminar is $395.

MicroCAD Managers
The Pickard Building, Suite 121
5858 E. Molloy Road
Syracuse, NY 13211
(315/454-9360).

T *he AutoCAD Productivity Newsletter* illustrates how white space can be used to balance a text-heavy publication and how an effective nameplate can be created by greatly increasing the shortest word in a title.

The overall look of the newsletter, with its combination of bold letters, white space and gray areas of text, is appropriate for its design-conscious audience—engineers and architects. Anything less would repel them from wanting to read what's inside.

Nameplate

A newsletter's nameplate becomes even more important when content offers limited or no visual opportunities. *The AutoCAD Productivity Newsletter* features a strong, attention-getting nameplate that creates a good balance with the articles and program listings, which for the most part lack visual interest.

The nameplate illustrates the benefits of augmenting a page layout program with a powerful drawing program. The drawing program makes it possible to overlap and layer the letters that form the word *AutoCAD*. Notice how the large outline letters are layered on top of each other: the *t* (of *Auto*) is on top of the *o*, which is on top of the *C*, which overlaps the *A*, which is on top of the *D*. This treatment saves space and creates a three-dimensional effect.

The title is set in a screened box spanning slightly more than two of the newsletter's three columns, and the box is placed flush-right on the page.

Contrast within the nameplate is created by using different typeface families, sizes, styles and spacing. *AutoCAD*, set large enough to attract the attention of anyone interested in computer-aided design, provides the visual magnet. The large, condensed, sans-serif type forms a striking foil for *the* and *Productivity* set in italics in a smaller serif typeface. The tight letter spacing of *the* and *Productivity* also contrasts with the overlapping type in *AutoCAD* and the spacious lettering in *Newsletter*.

The third element in the nameplate, *Newsletter* is set in narrow, sans-serif type with exaggerated letter spacing. Tying the nameplate together is a narrow horizontal rule above the title that equals *Newsletter* in length.

Dateline and publisher's information, clustered to the left of the nameplate, are set flush-left. Dateline information is aligned with the top of the nameplate, and *AutoCAD Reference Library* with the bottom.

Content

A generous amount of white space separates the body copy from the nameplate. Set in a large, condensed, sans-serif typeface, headlines echo the typography of the primary visual on the page—the word *AutoCAD* in the nameplate. Set flush-left, headlines are characterized by extremely tight letter and line spacing, made possible by the relatively low descenders of the condensed typeface.

Because of the amount of white space on the page, a relatively small type size was chosen for the body copy, set flush-left/ragged-right in a serif typeface. Like the headlines, letter spacing within the body copy was tightened slightly to increase word density and white space at the end of each line.

Graphic Accents

A horizontal layout is used for pages containing more than one article. Articles are stacked, separated by white space and horizontal rules.

Extra breathing room is provided by the white space between the thin downrules and the thick horizontal rules dividing the pages.

Visuals

The visual used on the front page is rotated left on a screened background similar to the one used behind the nameplate. This treatment provides emphasis and unity, reinforcing the nameplate and the newsletter's visual identity. The background also softens the strong and sometimes jarring contrast that occurs when a very dark image (in this case, a book cover) appears against a white background.

Inside Pages

The highly technical, copy-intensive inside pages are made more readable by generous amounts of white space that frame the pages, and low-key but interesting reader cues. Flush-left/ragged-right alignment opens the pages, as does the extra space added between numbered topics within articles.

Articles are introduced and organized with several reader cues. A review of an updated book is introduced with the kicker, *An excerpt from.* Generous leading in the byline allows each name to be easily read.

A long, italicized summary between the byline and the article helps the reader identify salient points.

Within the article, uppercase boldface type is used to separate program commands and subcommands from the narrative text. The boldface type not only lets readers quickly locate commands they're interested in, but also helps visually separate the commands from the narrative.

Continuity between the front and inside pages is provided by the consistent white space framing each page and the use of horizontal rules of similar weight.

The AutoCAD Productivity Newsletter Type Specifications

Nameplate:	Garamond Bold Italic, Megaron Condensed and Megaron Condensed Extra Bold, reversed, letters overlapped by hand
Headlines:	24-point Helvetica Black Condensed
Body Copy:	10/11.5 Modified Times Roman, 80 percent Condensed
Subheads:	12-point Times Roman, 80 percent Condensed
Column Width:	14 picas

THE NETWORK NEWS

Front Page

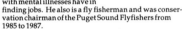

THENETWORKNEWS

Washington State Community Support Network
Mental Health Division, Jack Bartleson, Director

SUMMER 1988

Mental Health Consumer
Gets Law Changed

House Bill 1952, which will create work opportunities with the Washington Conservation Corps for individuals who have experienced mental illness, was signed into law March 16 by Governor Booth Gardner.

"I was very pleased that the bill passed the Legislature and that I had the opportunity to see it signed into law," says Vernon Young of Gig Harbor.

The idea for the bill came from Young, a mental health consumer who is aware from personal experience of the difficulties individuals with mental illnesses have in finding jobs. He also is a fly fisherman and was conservation chairman of the Puget Sound Flyfishers from 1985 to 1987.

Vernon Young of Gig Harbor

"I knew there was plenty of work that could be done on streams in the state, so I met with Conservation Corps officials two years ago to see if mentally ill persons could do some of this work through the Corps," he explains. "I found that the program was only open to people aged 18 to 25."

Knowing that mental illness often strikes young people who are just recovering when they reach their mid-20s, Young asked about the possibility of waiving the age limit. He was told that the law would have to be changed. "That seemed like an impossible task," he recalls. "I didn't know anything about how to get a law changed."

Shortly after this, the Alliance for the Mentally Ill of Washington State (AMI/WS) held a workshop on the legislative process, and Young, a member of AMI/WS, attended. Once armed with this knowledge, he approached his local legislator, Representative Wes Pruitt. Pruitt was enthusiastic about the idea and sponsored the measure in the Legislature this year.

Though the bill met with little opposition in the Legislature, Young did spend one day in Olympia lobbying for it, and Jean Lough of Clark County AMI/WS, lobbied extensively for it. The final result is a law that waives the upper age limit for Conservation Corps workers with sensory and mental disabilities.

Even though the law now has been changed, Young is not giving up his efforts to see that it is implemented and to continue to look for ways to fund employment for the mentally disabled in conservation efforts.

He recently submitted a proposal to the Puget Sound Water Quality Authority with Dr. Murry Hart of the Greater Lakes Mental Health Center, who worked closely with Young on the concept for HB1952.

Though the proposal has a similar goal as the legislation Young has been involved in, it is not related to the new law or prohibited by any law.

The aim of the proposal is to establish and maintain an organization made up of clients of the Greater Lakes Mental Health Center to identify, contract for, and work on conservation projects, such as stream clean up, rehabilitation, and flood mitigation in Pierce and other counties.

"I guess I'm like a little bulldozer," Young states. "I go around shoving and pushing to find ways to employ persons with mental illnesses in conservation projects that will benefit both the individuals who do the work and the quality of the environment in the state." ■

INSIDE

T*he Network News* illustrates the importance of choosing a nameplate visual that symbolizes the editorial focus of the newsletter. The newsletter is designed to share information and create a sense of community among social workers scattered throughout the state of Washington.

The Nameplate

The newsletter's design illustrates the critical role a strong nameplate plays in establishing a graphic identity for a newsletter. It also demonstrates the importance of selecting an appropriate visual and sizing it to be effective but not competitive with the title.

The hand-holding figures in the nameplate visual are large enough to make the network theme obvious. Because the figures are silhouetted, your attention is drawn to the joined hands, rather than the individuals. The shapes of the figures suggest that young and old, male and female are included, broadening the newsletter's scope and appeal.

Cropping the figures at the right- and left-hand margins suggests that the illustration could go on forever, further reinforcing its theme. The sharp vertical cropping of the figures at both ends indicates that there's more to come, but space didn't permit including it.

The actual title is set on a single line, which extends the width of the illustration. Because it's significantly smaller than the illustration, it lets the visual dominate the nameplate. Otherwise, the two would compete with rather than complement each other. Since recognition more than legibility is the desired effect, the title is set in uppercase type. After the first issue, the nameplate is seen by readers as an icon, or visual symbol, rather than words to be read.

Dateline and Publication Information

Because *The Network News* contains timely information, the dateline is emphasized in large uppercase type. Set flush-right, the design is simplified by eliminating the comma between *Summer* and *1988*.

Balancing the large dateline are two flush-left lines of information, placed below the nameplate, acknowledging the state agency that publishes the newsletter. A heavy horizontal rule separates the dateline and publication information from the title above, emphasizing the title and setting it off from the headline and body copy that follow.

Reader Cues

The Network News was designed for quick scanning. A large, centered headline and prominent table of contents quickly inform readers about the issue's content.

The headline is reinforced by the large, bold initial cap that serves as a magnet to draw readers into the first line of the article. The article's end sign is a solid box.

A short, concise title, *Inside*, introduces the table of contents. Because it's shorter than *Table of Contents*, it can be set in larger, more noticeable type. Consistent with the dateline, *Inside* is set in uppercase type. The article titles and page numbers are set in slightly larger type than the body copy, to attract more attention and distinguish them from the body copy.

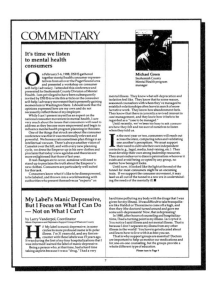

Inside Pages

The inside pages of *The Network News* reflect the visual identity and consistency established on the front page. Pages are boxed; thin downrules separate the two columns. Heavy horizontal rules emphasize the top border of each page and serve to separate articles. Solid boxes are used as end signs. As on the front page, text is aligned flush-left/ragged-right.

Article categories are introduced with large, uppercase eyebrows set above the top page border. Initial caps are used to begin each article and, when appropriate, within articles to introduce new topics.

Long headlines establish a conversational tone for the newsletter.

Visuals

Articles are personalized by setting a small photo of the author into one of its text columns. Using mug shots is an excellent way to add graphics to newsletters that don't offer other photo or illustration opportunities. Head shots with captions also eliminate the need for bylines, which can sometimes interfere with the transition from headline to body copy.

The personal nature of the articles is reinforced by the way the subjects in the photos are looking directly into the camera. This gives readers the feeling that the authors are talking directly to them.

Note that authors' photos on inside pages are slightly larger than the front-page photo and that they extend into the top page border, providing visual interest. The slightly larger photo requires more white space at the top of the second column, which in turn can be used to align the last lines of the left- and right-hand text columns, establishing a formal, serious page layout. A slightly larger type size for the author's name and title also helps to use up the extra white space.

All too often, two-column newsletters suffer from static, overly balanced pages. *The Network News* shows how to avoid excessive page balance by using relatively heavy headlines in the left-hand columns and by carefully sizing and placing photographs in the right-hand columns.

The Network News also reflects the importance of using great care in choosing typographic elements. By using uppercase type with restraint and carefully orchestrating type size and style, you can build a lot of typographic color into a one-typeface newsletter.

The Network News Type Specifications

Nameplate:	56-point Palatino
Headlines Page 1:	36/36 Palatino
All Other Heads:	18/19 Palatino Bold
Body Copy:	10/11 Palatino
Initial Caps:	56-point Palatino Bold
Column Width:	21 picas

LABLINES

Front Page

June 1989

LABLINES

Product News from IBM's Cary, NC Software Development Laboratory

■ *For CSP/AD/AE, DB2, and SQL/DS Installs*

Application Enabling: Triple Option Savings Available

Triple Option is a term most often associated with the offensive scheme employed by high-powered collegiate football teams. IBM has given additional meaning to this term, however, with the availability of a unique plan for customers to take advantage of IBM education and services and save money if they install in test CSP/AD/AE Version 3, DB2 Version 2 or SQL/DS Version 2 prior to July 31, 1989.

Here's how our Triple Option plan works: customers who install one or more of these products prior to the expiration of this promotion can receive (1) a three-month waiver of the Monthly License Charge (MLC), (2) a three-month deferral of billing for One-Time Charge (OTC) customers, or (3) a credit for IBM education classes taken.

To become eligible, customers must agree to one of the following options for each product installed:

◆ Sign an agreement with an IBM Authorized Industry Application Specialist (AIAS) or an Authorized Application Specialist (AAS) — known as "IBM Business Partners" — for applications and/or services specific to the installed product. This agreement must be for an amount equal to or greater than three months MLC.

◆ Sign a contract with IBM Systems Integration Division-Professional Services (SID-PS) for services specific to the installed product. This contract must be for an amount equal to or greater than three months MLC.

◆ Complete and be invoiced for product specific IBM education classes. The customer pays the invoices and sends copies of all invoices to the IBM branch office. IBM then issues a credit for the amount of the invoices, up to a maximum of three months MLC. Education classes must be completed by December 31, 1989.

Certain restrictions, of course, apply to this Triple Option plan. First, a customer can receive only one three-month waiver, deferral or credit for each of the eligible

products installed.

Second, the Triple Option plan is limited to those customers who have not licensed the current or preceding versions of the products that comprise this offering at the same location.

Third, waiver of payment, deferral, or credit of OTC billing may not be added to any other promotional discount or allowance. Further, none of these options may be used in conjunction with any special bids or other special offerings.

Lastly, the Triple Option plan is effective only during the specified time period and may be withdrawn at any time upon written notice.

Football season isn't here yet, but now is a great time to make IBM's Triple Option part of your application enabling plan of attack. You can save money, get leading-edge software products that can make your organization more productive, and you can sign up for services and education that will get your programmers off to a fast start.

Contact your local IBM marketing representative for more detailed information. Tell him or her you want to know all the details about IBM's Application Enabling software promotion, announced March 28, 1989, in Announcement Letter 389-046.

CUSTOMER INSTALLS PRODUCT

CHOOSES 1

BUSINESS PARTNER	SID–PS	EDUCATION
3 MONTH **MLC WAIVER**	3 MONTH **MLC WAIVER**	UP TO 3 MONTHS **MLC CREDIT**

IBM

T abloid newsletters like *LabLines* offer their own special excitement. Their large size gives a billboard effect that can dramatically showcase large nameplates and visuals. In addition, you can use large type in comfortably wide columns, which makes them more readable, especially for older or visually impaired readers.

Nameplate

The framing effect provided by the horizontal rules visually reinforces *LabLines'* title, and the thick ascending and horizontal strokes of the *L*'s enhance the effect.

The bold italic, sans-serif type used in the *LabLines* nameplate adds motion to the title, suggesting action and a fast read. The subtitle, also set in a slanted, sans-serif typeface, echoes this effect.

Reader Cues

The design of the reader cues in *LabLines* pulls you into the first article on the front page. For example, notice the invisible diagonal line created by the subtitle and the horizontal rules above and below the *A* in *Lab*. This diagonal continues down to the horizontal bar that introduces the eyebrow over the featured article and eventually to the initial cap, *T*, on the first line of the article. Anyone interested in *CSP/AD/AE, DB@, and SQL/DS Installs* will want to read the article.

Graphic Accents

The dateline is reversed out of a diamond-shaped box tilted across a heavy horizontal rule. The diagonal shape is echoed in the bullets within articles and in the diagonal boxes used for the headers on the inside pages.

The horizontal rules—in the dateline box, at the top of each page, and above and below the masthead—reinforce the "lines" theme of *LabLines*. On the front page, the white space in the left column is defined and emphasized with a horizontal rule of the same thickness as the rules framing the nameplate.

Note that the ends of these rules are cut at an angle, giving the sense of motion, also conveyed in the slanted type and angled rules in the nameplate typography.

The IBM logo appears in the lower left corner of the front page, where it balances the dateline information in the upper left corner. These elements help define the white space in this column. Overall, the left column provides an open feeling that balances text-dense columns to the right.

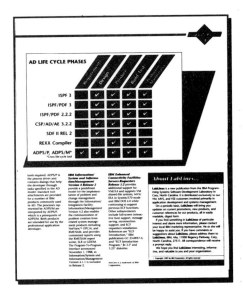

Typography

Sans-serif type is used for headlines and masthead information. Reversed sans-serif type, which contrasts with the serif type used for the body copy, is used for the large organization chart on the front page and the applications table on page 3. However, eyebrows and headlines for boxed stories on inside pages are set in the italic version of the serif type used for the body copy. These soften the harder lines of the sans-serif type and heavy rules.

On the inside pages, boldface introductory sentences are used as reader cues within articles to mark new topics and help readers quickly scan a story.

Scalloped column endings provide white space within articles. Whenever possible, new paragraphs begin at the top of a column, creating a significant pool of white space at the bottom of a short column that can provide a welcome foil for the extremely technical information in the articles.

Visuals

LabLines' tabloid format lends itself to the use of large visuals integrated into articles with wraparounds. On page 1, notice how the text columns have been shortened to accommodate the organization flow chart, and how the bottom row of the chart defines the bottom of the page.

In the table on page 3, softer, less angular checkmarks give an informal feeling, contrasting with the formality of the sans-serif type used for the row and column identifiers.

Screens and shadow boxes create a three-dimensional effect. Notice how the angle of the shadow box reinforces the diagonal of the horizontal rules and the box used for the header.

LabLines illustrates the importance of details like this. It shows that the difference between good and excellent is often defined by the tender loving care used in maintaining consistency between the various page elements. The page would lose some of its integrity if the diagonal behind the table's shadow box appeared at a different angle.

Inside Pages

Concentrating white space along the left-hand border provides continuity between the front and inside pages. The space is used to highlight calendar listings and emphasize screen shots—electronically created snapshots of a computer screen.

The headline introducing the article on page 2 is surrounded by white space. Flush-left headline alignment makes it easy to read down to the initial cap at the beginning of the article.

A serif, italic headline, sans-serif body copy and extra leading visually separate the boxed seminar announcement from adjacent text. The box emerges as an interesting sidelight, both visually and content-wise.

LabLines Type Specifications	
Nameplate:	Hand-drawn and Franklin Gothic Black
Headlines:	28/32 Stone Sans Bold
Subtitles:	18-point Stone Serif SemiBold Italic
Body Copy:	12/15 Stone Serif
Column Width:	17.5 picas

PROVIDENCE TODAY

Front Page

P R O V I D E N C E

TODAY

Downtown Edition

A NEWS AND HEALTH LETTER FROM PROVIDENCE MEDICAL CENTER

SPRING 1989

❑ Comprehensive multispecialty services in the heart of downtown Seattle:
  Internal medicine
  Family medicine
  Women's health
  Ophthalmology
  Dental care
  Sports medicine
  Physical therapy
  Allergy
  Orthopedics
  Plastic surgery

❑ Parking in the Fourth Avenue Plaza garage ($1 per visit).

❑ Extended hours. We're open 7 am to 7 pm, Monday through Friday.

❑ A preferred provider for King County Preferred, Blue Cross Prudent Buyer, Sound Health, CIGNA; Health Plus, Good HealthPlan, HMO Washington, Pacific Health and other major insurance plans.

Special clinic section.
Pages 5-8

Dental implants—an alternative to dentures.
Page 7

Providence Downtown
1001 4th Ave. Plaza
Suite 420
Seattle, WA 98154
326-5577

Lowering your cholesterol

Deaths from heart disease in the United States are declining rapidly...and the reason has a lot to do with lifestyle and diet changes.

According to a recent Centers for Disease Control (CDC) study, the death rate from heart disease since 1960 has been reduced by one-third. This has been accompanied by a three to four percent drop in blood cholesterol levels. The CDC attributes about half the decline in the death rate to changes in lifestyle, about a quarter to a third to changes in diet and the rest to improved control of blood pressure.

However good this news is, the fact remains that heart attack is still the most common cause of death in the United States. A high cholesterol level, which is associated with coronary heart disease, can double a person's risk of having a heart attack. Yet a 1987 nationwide survey by CDC indicated

LISTEN TO YOUR HEART

that fewer than one in 10 persons knew what their cholesterol level was. You can find out your cholesterol level through a simple blood test. Providence Medical Center offers a cholesterol test for $5, as well as a complete cardiac risk assessment for $12. Call Providence Health Resources at 340-2669 for an appointment.

Once I know my cholesterol level, what does it mean?
The level of cholesterol in the blood is measured as milligrams (mg) of cholesterol per 100 milliliters (ml) of blood. According to Heart, Lung and Blood Institute recommendations, a blood cholesterol level below 200 (each 100 ml of blood contains 200

mg of cholesterol) is considered desirable. Levels over 240 are considered high.

How do I control my cholesterol level?
There are nine basic steps:
1. Lose weight.
2. Reduce the amount of total fat from all sources in your diet.
3. Especially reduce the amount of animal and saturated fat.
4. Eat low-cholesterol foods (check the labeling on prepared foods).
5. Eat high fiber foods every day, especially those with the soluble fiber pectin, such as oatmeal, oatbran and apples.
6. Exercise aerobically on a regular basis.
7. Limit alcohol to none or no more than one drink per day.
8. Stop smoking.
9. Practice stress management techniques.

For more information on maintaining a low-cholesterol diet, call Providence Health Resources at 340-2669 for a free copy of the 1989 edition of the Providence Diet.

PROVIDENCE
D O W N T O W N

Providence Today reflects the sensitive application of reader cues to communicate a lot of information in a small amount of space.

Nameplate

The nameplate reflects restrained use of three forms of contrast: size, spacing and background. Providence is set in uppercase sans-serif type with exaggerated letter spacing reversed out of a colored background.

Today, however, is set in a significantly larger, tightly kerned, serif typeface. Note the way O fits underneath T, and A is tucked between D and Y. The letters reproduced at large size become significant design elements. For example, your eye picks up details like the stress (contrasting stroke thickness) in the O and D. The details of the serifs, especially the left-hand tail of the Y, are important design elements. Also notice that the top of the D is slightly curved.

Consider how much less interesting the nameplate would be if Providence and Today were set in the same typeface or size.

The title is clarified by the subtitle, A News and Health Letter from Providence Medical Center. It's set in tightly spaced, uppercase type, below the nameplate and to the left of the dateline. Note the clarity achieved by omitting the folio, which isn't important in this kind of seasonal publication.

Each issue of Providence Today is regionalized by the triangular flap in the upper right-hand corner. Setting Downtown Edition at an angle prevents it from competing with the nameplate. A drop shadow adds a three-dimensional effect to the page. Note the similar type treatment in Downtown Edition and Providence Today. The longer word is set in uppercase, sans-serif type with exaggerated letter spacing, the shorter word in serif type.

The nameplate and regional identification span three of the newsletter's four columns, separated from the editorial material below by a heavy horizontal rule. Bleeding the rule off the page provides motion and continuity with the rest of the newsletter.

The Providence Today title is centered over the two inside columns of the grid. The centered Providence Downtown logo at the bottom of the page helps unify the top and bottom of the page.

Graphic Accents

The *Providence Downtown* logo, placed discretely at the bottom of the page, is small enough so that it doesn't compete with the nameplate, but large enough to define the white space. Without the logo, the bottom of the page would look empty.

Editorial material on the front page is concentrated in the three right-hand columns. The left-hand column highlights services and information with ballot boxes and contents page numbers. Providence's services in downtown Seattle are marked by a thick vertical rule that bleeds to the edge of the page. The medical center's address and phone number are set at the bottom of this column. All copy in the column is set in bold, sans-serif type, differentiating it from adjacent body copy.

Inside Pages

The four-column grid on the inside pages has a lot of white space built in. A deep sink at the top of the page is defined by the heavy horizontal rule, oversized page number and banner, reinforcing the corner banner on the front cover. Notice that the weight of the page number is appropriate in relation to the horizontal rule below it.

Within the text columns, extra space between paragraphs is used rather than paragraph indents. Flush-left/ragged-right alignment provides visual variety by creating white space at the line endings.

A significant amount of white space at the bottom of the page also gives valuable breathing room, as does the absence of downrules between columns.

The inside pages are bordered by a distinctive box with internally curved corners. The space between the border and the outside edge of the page is defined on the right by a heavy vertical rule that repeats the rule on the front cover, again providing integration and publication identity.

Typography

Providence Today reflects a lot of restraint. One typeface is used for headlines, subheads and body copy. The style and size of headlines, subheads and body copy are consistent throughout the newsletter. Boldface type emphasizes headlines and subheads.

Extra leading enhances the readability of both reader cues and body copy on the inside pages.

Visuals

Several techniques enhance the effectiveness of the clip art used in *Providence Today*.

The racing bike visual is made more effective by its large size and by the horizon/vanishing perspective created with the page layout program's line-drawing tool. Placing the lines closer together at the top of the drawing than at the bottom creates an illusion of distance. Another technique used successfully with the racing bike image is extending the bicycler's head above the top horizon line—creating the clip-art equivalent of a silhouetted photograph!

The running-shoe illustration becomes stronger by surrounding it with plenty of white space, created in part by reducing the depth of the two center columns.

Together, the sophisticated use of reader cues and restrained use of clip art not only communicate a lot of information but also build confidence in the institution publishing the newsletter by projecting an image of good health.

Providence Today Type Specifications

Nameplate:	Palatino and Helvetica Condensed
Headlines:	16/18 Palatino Bold
Body Copy:	11/13 Palatino Bold
Subheads:	11/13 Palatino Bold
Column Width:	11 picas

THE STRING INSTRUMENT CRAFTSMAN

**Front
Page**

THE STRING INSTRUMENT
CRAFTSMAN

VOLUME 1
MAR/APR 1988

IN THIS ISSUE

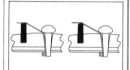

THIS FRET
TO BE
REMOVED

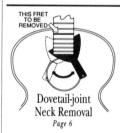

The Toxics In Your Workshop

By Ervin Somogyi

Solvents, finishes, and thinners are the most poisonous and immediately toxic substances with which luthiers work. The harmful agents here are fumes, with particles (or droplets) on the order of 1 micron or less in size. (Smoke particles measure 1/2-micron and below in diameter.) The smaller the particle, the easier time it has being inhaled straight into the lungs.

Of course, many chemicals are absorbed directly through the body's skin and tissues. *Chemical toxicity* is formally defined as "irritation to mucous membranes and respiratory tract and more or less ready absorption through the skin, which causes general poisoning of the organism" [according to *Dangerous Properties of Industrial Materials*, by Irving Sax (Reinhold Book Corp., 1968)]. The "organism," needless to say, is you.

Let's take a look at the chemicals most commonly used by instrument makers and repair specialists. Most of them are solvents, and *all have a high rating for chemical toxicity*. In chemical and industrial handbooks, this is expressed in terms of a ***Threshold Limit Value***, or **TLV**. This is the lowest exposure known to have no permanent adverse effect on the organism. The

higher the TLV rating, the *less toxic* the substance is to users.

RATING THE SOLVENTS

Most solvents used in string instrument work fall into two main chemical categories: ***aliphatics*** and ***aromatics***.

The *aliphatics* are saturated hydrocarbons, such as methanol, gasoline, kerosene, painters' naphtha, alcohols in general, and mineral spirits. Compared with aromatics, these substances have higher TLVs for measurable irritation and harm done to the organism upon repeated contact. That is, they don't make you as sick as fast.

The *aromatics*, on the other hand, have low TLVs. They are more toxic (strongly suspected to contribute to cardiac arrhythmia, depression, and increased intra-cranial pressure), and generally are proven carcinogens. Also, since the body doesn't eliminate these as rapidly, there are *cumulative* dangers of contact. Aromatics include benzene, toluene, xylene, tylene, and naphthalene. Old paint-strippers, old-style rubber cement, and other long-popular solvents have been made with aromatics, formulations that common sense — and law — are now changing. However, they are the best solvents, and are readily

Continued on page 9

Troubleshooting Electric Guitars

By Mike Metz

When an instrument with "sick" electronics comes into a shop for repairs, the first thing to do is find the problem, and then make a diagnosis. Symptoms may come from sources other than the guitar itself, like the amplifier, the cable — even the instrument's owner. If you will be the person doing the repairs always play the instrument yourself to verify the complaint. Even if no problem is evident at first, take the time to check

the controls, flip the switches, and wiggle the jack, and make sure you understand how the instrument's builder intended it to function.

After verifying that there is something wrong, it's time for a diagnosis. Sometimes, by tinkering with all the controls, you can get some sound to come out. An intermittently balky pot, switch, or jack often can be smoked out this way, and you can then start the repair. Here are some general points to

Continued on page 11

T*he String Instrument Craftsman* is an excellent example of a newsletter design that matches tone to content. People interested in hand-built instruments wouldn't relate to a newsletter that's trendy, modern or loud. *The String Instrument Craftsman* readers expect a newsletter that reflects careful attention to detail—in a word, craftsmanship.

Nameplate

The nameplate communicates an appropriate feeling by using a clean, classic typeface with carefully detailed serifs and contrasting thick and thin strokes.

The key word, *Craftsman*, is emphasized by being set significantly larger than the rest of the title, in uppercase letters that extend all the way across the top of the nameplate.

The title is reversed out of a double box frame that separates it from the rest of a rather dense page. The reversed type highlights the details of the typeface design; this treatment also makes it reminiscent of an architectural blueprint.

Dateline

Because the content of *The String Instrument Craftsman* is timeless, full folio information is provided so back issues can be archived. Three-hole punching the newsletter makes it easy for readers to organize them in notebooks.

Located below the nameplate and above the table of contents, the folio is reversed out of a lightly screened box.

Nameplate and dateline information are repeated at reduced size on each inside page. This helps readers identify issues and the title itself, in case an enthusiastic subscriber photocopies an article for a friend.

Graphic Accents

To enhance the newsletter's classic image, each article and feature is bordered. This technique helps distinguish each article. The double borders used between adjacent boxes create a formal effect.

No downrules are used between columns in multicolumn articles, to emphasize the relationship of the columns to each other.

Visuals are boxed to anchor the irregularly shaped illustrations, which might otherwise float on the page. On the inside page, portions of illustrations extend outside the border and adjacent white space, adding visual interest and avoiding a confined effect.

A light screen highlights the sidebar, to keep it from being dominated by the larger article above it.

Typography

Excessive typographic contrast would be inappropriate for *The String Instrument Craftsman*'s readership. Sans-serif reader cues contrasted with serif body copy would be out of place. Instead, headlines and body copy are set in different sizes of the same typeface. Author bylines are set in boldface type. Jumplines and captions are set in italics for differentiation. Illustration credits are positioned vertically.

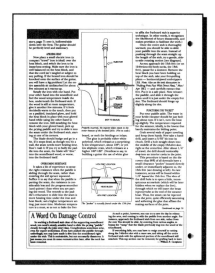

Headlines and body copy are aligned flush-left/ragged-right to contrast with the centered type in the table of contents box that occupies the entire left column of the front page. The illustrations within the contents box further enhance the newsletter's attractiveness.

Table of contents categories, headlines and page references are centered, giving them further distinction from the flush-left body copy.

Subheads within articles are set in uppercase type and centered. They create barriers that force the reader to stop and note a new topic being introduced. They also make it easier to skim an article for specific items of information.

Uppercase, sans-serif type used within the illustrations is easy to read, even at small sizes. Using contrasting type in the illustrations also separates it from adjacent body copy.

The String Instrument Craftsman Type Specifications	
Nameplate:	32- and 64-point Garamond Regular and Expanded
Headlines:	32-point Garamond Condensed
Body Copy:	9/10 Garamond
Column Width:	13.5 picas

CHOOSING THE RIGHT HARDWARE

Because of the bewildering range of computer hardware available, choosing the right hardware for your desktop publishing activities can be a lonely journey.

Most computer store salespeople are spread thin, knowing a little about a lot of different products and not developing in-depth knowledge in one area. Consider the plight of the typical salesperson: one minute they're discussing a $49.95 game, the next they're describing accounting packages for CPAs. Somewhere in the middle they're talking to you, a newsletter publisher.

Finally, most computer stores have a high staff turnover—more than 40 percent a year! This means that the person you're talking to today about a computer system for your newsletter might have been selling office copiers or home stereo components a few months ago.

The exception is the computer store with a sales staff that specializes in different areas such as desktop publishing. Desktop publishing specialists are rare but are worth searching for.

DO IT YOURSELF

Even if you're lucky enough to find a local computer retailer who understands desktop publishing, you should make it your business to stay abreast of the latest hardware technology and learn how it can be applied to your needs. Subscribe to the major desktop publishing magazines, such as *Publish!*, *Personal Publishing* and *PC Publishing*, and free publications, like *TypeWorld* and *MacWeek*. (See the bibliography for a complete list of publications focusing on newsletters and desktop publishing design.)

Being informed will also help you avoid one of the most frequent problems encountered when choosing hardware: underbuying. Many people new to desktop publishing don't buy—and many vendors don't sell them—the equipment needed to do the job right.

By staying up-to-date on hardware and software developments and working with a vendor who specializes in desktop publishing, you can bypass these problems and get up and running the day your hardware is delivered.

APPLE VERSUS IBM

If you're buying your first desktop publishing system, you'll probably find yourself comparing the Apple Macintosh to an IBM-type computer. "IBM" doesn't refer to just computers manufactured by International Business Machines Corporation. Rather, it generally includes any computer that uses the MS-DOS operating system, a standard established by IBM. The IBM world includes computers made by Compaq, AST, Leading Edge, Tandy and so-called "generic" computers, which local retailers often assemble themselves.

The division of the desktop publishing world into Apple or IBM-type computers shouldn't be considered absolute, however. Files can be exchanged between Apple Macintosh and IBM computers in many ways. So, it might make sense for you to choose a "Mac" for desktop publishing even if your office already has MS-DOS computers. Every year, IBM- and Mac-based computers get friendlier with each other.

THE MACINTOSH

If you're starting from scratch—if you're buying your first computer and/or are self-employed—you'll probably appreciate the straightforward simplicity and ease of use offered by the Macintosh. If you're planning to have your files produced with high-resolution typesetting, you might also find that local service bureaus have more experience working with Macintosh files than with MS-DOS files.

Apple Macintosh computers offer straightforward elegance and simplicity which, once experienced, make for dedicated converts. At first glance, you might feel there's something childish about deleting a file by dragging its name across the screen to a trash can. But this straightforward visual orientation saves time and is easy to remember.

It's also easier to name files in an Apple Macintosh environment than in MS-DOS. Instead of being limited to eight-letter file names, you can use up to 30 characters. You can also add spaces between words; "June 1988 Newsletter" is a lot friendlier than "Jun88nws."

A final benefit of the Apple Macintosh is the interface (the way you communicate with a program), which is similar for all programs. For example, different programs often accept the same commands for opening and saving files, a great time-saver and one that has yet to find widespread acceptance in the MS-DOS world. "Command S" usually saves files, "Command Z" undoes your last instruction, etc.

It's important to note that Macintosh computers were originally designed for graphics applications. Desktop publishing, and Aldus PageMaker in particular, is credited with a lot of the Mac's success.

The Macintosh is basically a plug-in-and-go computer, which means that it's easy to load new software programs and downloadable typefaces. Adding a new software program to a Mac is easy. Once loaded, it automatically recognizes the type of monitor, mouse and printer being used. However, each time you add a new software program to an MS-DOS computer, you have to go through a complicated set-up routine.

The same is true of adding downloadable fonts. Installation in a Macintosh is fast and easy, and the fonts become instantly usable in all programs. In the MS-DOS environment, you have to go through a relatively complicated installation process so that your software will recognize the font.

The Macintosh SE

The design of the original Apple Macintosh, continued today in the Apple SE/30 series, is so compact that the monitor (screen) and CPU (central processing unit), combined within a single small unit, take up less than a square foot of desk space.

This design offers both advantages and disadvantages. The advantage is that the SE takes up very little desk space and is relatively easy to move from desk to desk, office to home, etc.

The disadvantage is that the SE has a relatively small, nine-inch diagonal screen. Although numerous books and newsletters have been written and designed on the Macintosh's small screen, most desktop publishers agree that working on the SE's small screen isn't easy.

Because you can see only part of a page at once, you're forced to switch back and forth between full-page and partial-page views. This can slow you down and makes it hard to see what spreads will look like when they're printed.

The Mac SE family also provides space for only one plug-in accessory card and expansion card. This keeps you from customizing your SE by adding both a big-screen monitor and internal modem, for example.

The Macintosh II Family

The Macintosh II family costs more than the SE but offers better performance and more flexibility. The original Macintosh II and IIX contain space for five plug-in circuit boards. The more recent IICX and IICXI offer a slightly smaller footprint with the space to add three plug-in expansion cards. The Macintosh II series was also designed for use with color monitors and software.

Unlike the SE computers, the Mac II lets you choose from a variety of monitors. The black-and-white monitors show either a single page or two-page spread. You can also choose from different color monitors in various sizes. If you're going to be working with electronic airbrushing, you can also choose a grayscale monitor that will make it easy to perform darkroom magic on your computer screen and see the results as you work.

Advances in the Macintosh world involve Apple's new system software and the Adobe Type Manager. These give a much more accurate on-screen representation of how typefaces will appear when printed.

MS-DOS COMPUTERS

Although desktop publishing first became popular on the Macintosh, desktop publishing in the MS-DOS world is larger in terms of the number of users.

Because of the numerous third-party accessories and hardware options available, a bewildering array of choices are available.

When choosing an MS-DOS computer for desktop publishing, it's important to buy the fastest model you can afford, but at least an AT model that uses the Intel 80286 chip. Better yet, Intel's 80386 chip offers even more speed. If you're working with scanned images or complex page layouts, you'll particularly appreciate the added speed of the 80386 chip.

One reason speed is so important in the MS-DOS world is because of the extra memory required by the Microsoft Windows operating environment. The Windows environment lets you have more than one software program available at one time. Using the clipboard (temporary memory-based file storage) you can exchange information between one program and another.

A graphics monitor is required for desktop publishing with MS-DOS computers. Three quality levels of graphic monitors are available: CGA, EGA and VGA. The latter two offer the best performance. Color versions of all three types of video monitors are available. Color monitors help separate the text and graphics of the page layouts you're working on from the screen background and the tools provided by your desktop publishing program. Color monitors also let you adjust background and text colors to your personal preference. Used with the appropriate software, color monitors also let you preview background, text and graphic-accent colors.

The minimum amount of memory you'll need in the MS-DOS world using today's sophisticated software programs is 640K, although performance improves as you add *extended memory*, which exists as a separate memory bank addressed differently than the computer's normal memory.

By placing your program and the document you're working on in appropriately configured extended memory, you can work much faster. However, you must remember to save your work to the hard disk more often. (Otherwise, a momentary popular interruption could cost you hours of work.)

OS/2 and Presentation Manager

Microsoft's new operating system, called OS/2, is the latest advancement in PC-compatible computers. OS/2 was designed to overcome the limitations of MS-DOS, which cannot directly access more than 640K of memory. OS/2 can directly access virtually unlimited amounts of memory, speeding up program execution and allowing multi-tasking, which lets your computer perform one function—like printing—while simultaneously being used for another function such as page layout or word processing. OS/2's primary disadvantage is that it requires considerably more computer memory to operate.

Just as Microsoft Windows is the operating environment—or interface—that allows immediate access to more than one program in the MS-DOS world, Microsoft Presentation Manager is the operating environment in the OS/2 world. With OS/2 and Presentation Manager, computers in the IBM world more closely resemble Macintosh computers in the way they can exchange information between programs.

The large number of established and emerging operating systems, including OS/2, Unix, Xenix and others, can be confusing when you're trying to choose among them. Your best bet is to stay informed and not buy technology for technology's sake.

MULTI-COMPUTER OFFICES

Even if your office is entrenched in the MS-DOS world, you shouldn't automatically choose an IBM-compatible computer for desktop publishing. Files can be shared between Apple Macintosh and MS-DOS computers in a number of ways.

Computers can be hooked together to create networks, which can save time and money—particularly if more than one person works on your newsletter. Instead of copying files onto diskettes, which must be physically transmitted from the writer to the editor to the layout person, the computer simply accesses the file stored on the writer's or editor's computer.

Networking systems let you share files between Macintosh and MS-DOS computers. The TOPS system, developed by Sun Microsystems, operates through the AppleTalk network, which lets more than one Macintosh share a single Apple LaserWriter printer. If you add an AppleTalk card to your MS-DOS computer, the TOPS software will let you share files between a Macintosh and an MS-DOS computer.

MacLink Plus, another option, consists of software plus a special cable. The software translates most word processing formats to and from the Macintosh and MS-DOS environments.

Another option is the Dayna File, a floppy drive that attaches to your Macintosh and lets it read and write 3 1/2- and/or 5 1/4-inch MS-DOS diskettes.

Finally, Macintosh (beginning with the IIX) and SE/30 computers include a special high-density drive and software that let you read and write 3 1/2-inch high-density diskettes, which can be shared with MS-DOS computers.

UPGRADING OLDER COMPUTERS

If you have a computer with the older 8088 chip and monochrome text, you may wonder if it's worth trading it in on a new AT model or upgrading it by adding a graphics monitor and an accelerator board.

Unfortunately, trade-in values on older computers are ridiculously low. You'll probably be offered just a few hundred dollars for a computer that cost you thousands several years ago. There's usually very little relationship between the trade-in value of a computer and its original price—or its ability to smoothly perform routine word processing or mailing-list management functions. Computer prices haven't increased as fast as performance has, so older equipment is less desirable to many buyers.

Upgrading your computer is another option. However, the cost of upgrading an older computer can often approach the discount price of a brand-new one. And there are no guarantees that an upgraded computer, based around a mixture of circuit boards, will perform as well as a new one. Plus, new computers come with warranties.

So, buying a new computer and using your older one at home or as a backup workstation may be your best solution.

COMPUTER ENHANCEMENTS

Few computers come complete, out of the box. Several categories of enhancements can improve the performance of both Macintosh and MS-DOS computers:

Computer Memory

One of the most effective ways to produce your newsletter more efficiently is to add more memory to your computer. Extra memory speeds up all types of programs and is a virtual necessity with today's most sophisticated software programs, which have grown larger and more powerful. For example, if you load your word processing or desktop publishing program into extra memory, it operates faster because it doesn't have to access the hard disk every time you execute a command.

Additional memory also lets you have more than one program loaded and ready for use, so you can quickly move between programs. You can write an article with a word processing program and immediately switch to a page layout program to see how the article fits into the design. Or, you can switch between your drawing and page layout program, or between image-enhancement and page layout programs, to see how a revised nameplate or an enhanced photograph will appear.

In general, extra memory speeds up working on large files or large graphic images. You can move more quickly from page to page, or from one portion of a graphic to another, if the entire document is stored in computer memory. Otherwise, you have to load portions of it piecemeal from your hard disk.

Both Macintosh and MS-DOS computers have the space necessary for adding memory. (Adding memory to the Macintosh II series is easier than it is for the SE.)

Things are more complicated in the MS-DOS world, because you're typically limited to 640K of directly accessible memory. To get around this limitation, Intel, among others, offers extended memory boards that can be configured with up to 8 megabytes of additional memory. When installing this memory, you have to inform your software that this space is available.

OS/2 offers the promise of faster operation by allowing direct access to additional memory without the 640K limit.

Hard Drives

Most computers used for desktop publishing have a built-in hard drive, which operates faster than a floppy disk drive. You don't have to remove and insert disks when going from program to program. Indeed, many of today's programs are too large to fit on a single disk. Both internal and external hard drives are available.

Internal models save desk space and eliminate the noise of a second fan. Some external hard drives, like the Iomega Bernoulli Box, feature removable storage media, which means you can enjoy virtually un-limited storage.

You'll find that the more you use your computer, the faster hard-disk capacity disappears. Unless you're strict about deleting files you no longer need, you're likely to find that hard-disk space is rapidly used up—especially when you add downloadable fonts or begin working with scanned images.

Not long ago, 10-megabyte hard disks were considered a luxury. Now, as application files have grown larger and hard-drive prices have dropped, the standard in both the Apple Macintosh and MS-DOS worlds appears to be 40-megabyte hard disks.

Hard-disk access time often improves as disk space increases. The performance curve accelerates faster than the cost curve, especially in the MS-DOS world. So, if you're buying your first system, it might pay to buy at least double the hard-disk capacity you anticipate using.

For a frame of reference, the storage capacity necessary for a typical text-oriented, eight-page newsletter ranges from 250K to over 600K, depending on the software program used. If the newsletter contains several scanned graphic images, this could dramatically increase.

Extra hard-drive capacity also allows for printer spooling, which permits background printing. When printing a program, complex newsletter pages can be saved on the hard disk, then downloaded to the printer while you continue working on different pages.

Backups

Regardless of whether you're using a built-in or external hard disk, it's important that you regularly back up your files. Hard disks occasionally crash—and it's always at the most inopportune moments, such as deadline time. So consider these backup options.

You can back up your hard disk every week on floppy diskettes. This method may require numerous floppy diskettes, however, and can easily take an hour or longer.

Tape backups are another alternative. Available in both the Macintosh and MS-DOS environment, they copy the entire contents of your hard disk in just seconds.

However, tape backups can't be used by themselves. They create archive copies that must be copied onto another hard drive before the information stored on them can be used. For this reason, you might consider purchasing an external hard drive the same size as your built-in hard drive. This means you can simply copy to the second drive everything on the original drive, and it will be instantly usable.

Big-Screen Monitors

One of the most important ways to improve your newsletter's quality and produce it more efficiently is to add a big-screen monitor. It lets you see an entire page or two-page spread at a glance. You can see how headlines relate to each other and to adjacent body copy, and whether photographs are proportionately sized to the page. It lets you look at your layout from a reader's perspective, seeing how the whole relates to its individual parts.

The two types of big-screen monitors available are portrait monitors and landscape monitors. Portrait monitors are vertical, generally showing a single 8 1/2- by 11-inch page at or near actual size. Landscape monitors are horizontal and let you see two facing pages at once. This helps you avoid page designs that look good individually but fight each other when viewed side by side.

Input Devices

The keyboard is your primary interface with the computer. Keyboards differ in "feel"—some have stiff keys that must be firmly pressed; others have soft keys that respond to a gentle touch. Some click as they're pressed; others are silent. Keyboards also differ in the placement of function keys, which can be arranged in a row across the top of the keyboard, or grouped in two vertical rows to the left of the keys.

Some keyboards are lightweight and easy to move around. Others are heavier and won't slide around on your desk.

The location of the cursor controls also varies. Some keyboards offer separate cursor control and numeric keypad controls, while others combine them, which requires toggling back and forth, using the NUM LOCK key. Keyboards also differ in the placement of the CONTROL, COMMAND (or Apple symbol) and ALT (or OPTION) keys, which are often used in conjunction with other keys. Some offer only one set of these alternate keys; other keyboards repeat them on both the left- and right-hand sides of the space bar.

Two keyboards are available with the Macintosh. The Apple extended keyboard is preferable, with more comfortable key spacing, a separate numeric keypad, and a row of function keys along the top of the keyboard to use for frequently repeated keystroke sequences.

Future software programs will undoubtedly use these keys for direct access to frequently used commands (such as CUT, PASTE and NEXT PAGE). Or, using a macro program, you can assign your own specific commands to them.

Most keyboards are interchangeable. If you don't like the one that comes with your computer, shop around for one that feels better.

Next to the keyboard, the most popular input device is a mouse. A variety of mice are available for Macintosh and MS-DOS computers. Some people instead prefer to use a trackball, which can be considered an upside-down mouse. Whereas a mouse is physically moved around the top of a desk, a trackball remains in one place, with cursor movement manipulated in the palm of your hand.

Scanners

Scanners are used to make electronic files out of both text and graphics, including your firm's or association's logo. Once scanned, enhanced with a drawing or paint program and saved, your logo can be increased or decreased in size without loss of quality.

You can also use a scanner to create a distinctive nameplate by combining downloadable typefaces with hand-drawn letters. Or, you might want to scan the signature of your president or director to personalize his or her monthly column. Scanners are especially useful for copying public-domain clip art, available from several sources.

Types of Scanners

Three types of scanners are available: hand-held, sheet-fed and flat-bed. Hand-held scanners must be used carefully, since the quality of their output will be affected by any movement.

Sheet-fed scanners have rollers that pass the photograph over a stationary imaging drum. One drawback of this type of scanner—in addition to the possibility of wrinkling your artwork—is the amount of care that must be taken in inserting the artwork into the scanner. If inserted at a slight angle, the image will be scanned at an angle. Another difficulty is the size limitation—large artwork, or artwork mounted on boards, can't be scanned.

For these reasons, flat-bed scanners are preferable. They're easier to use, more accurate and can accommodate a wider range of artwork. Flat-bed scanners also let you preview the entire image before it's scanned, so you can decide which portion of the image you want to scan. This saves time and preserves hard-disk storage space.

As with other types of hardware, the price of scanners has remained relatively constant, although performance has increased dramatically. Hewlett-Packard's ScanJet Plus, for example, can be used with either Macintosh or MS-DOS computers. Because it's an 8-bit scanner, it captures and stores more information than 4-bit scanners. It can capture 256 levels of gray, which means it can preserve the original contrast range of high-contrast photographs and reproduce subtle transitions between black and white.

Scanner Software

The software that comes with most scanners saves images as a single graphics file. Thus, if you scan a book page, it's saved as a file in which individual words can't be removed or replaced.

Most scanners, however, can be used with OCR (Optical Character Recognition) software, which creates text. Instead of storing a page as a single piece of art, a scanner equipped with OCR software recognizes individual words and saves them in a word-processed file, letting you edit or rewrite the original article. This can be a good solution for archiving back issues of your newsletter or avoiding having to retype a typewritten speech.

Frame-Grabbers

This category of input device includes video boards that can capture images stored on videocassette recorders or photographed by a video camera attached to your computer.

Frame-grabbers allow you to replace traditional silver-emulsion, film-based photography with totally electronic photography. Frame-grabbers can also be used in conjunction with electronic cameras (e.g., the Sony Mavica), which record images on a floppy diskette or captured with portable video cameras or camcorders—combination VCR's and video cameras.

Electronic photography eliminates the delays involved in developing film, choosing and enlarging the best negatives, and then airbrushing or otherwise manipulating photographs. A frame-grabber can perform all these functions on the screen of your computer, expediting production and reducing costs.

PRINTERS

Although acceptable newsletter quality can be achieved with 24-pin dot-matrix printers, most desktop-published newsletters are produced using laser or inkjet printers.

Silent and fast, laser printers, like office copiers, use heat to bond precisely placed toner (particles of carbon) to paper. Most laser printers create text and graphic images out of a grid of 90,000 dots per square inch, arranged 300 dots vertically by 300 dots horizontally.

Available for both black-and-white and color applications, inkjet printers operate slower than laser printers, but offer considerable cost-savings. Like laser printers, inkjet printers create text and graphics out of a grid consisting of 90,000 dots per square inch. Inkjet printers usually use heat to bond the ink to the paper.

Laser Printers

The three categories of laser printers are determined by the particular way the printer exchanges information with a computer. These include laser printers that use the Hewlett-Packard Printer Command Language, laser printers that use the PostScript Page Description Language and laser printers that use Apple's QuickDraw technology.

Hewlett-Packard Printer Command Language printers are the most popular. The main advantages of these printers are their relatively low initial cost, their high-quality output and their quiet operation. Although primarily designed for use with MS-DOS computers, interface software is now available that lets these printers communicate with Macintosh computers.

The primary disadvantage of laser printers based on the Hewlett-Packard Printer Command Language is that they're not easy to use for proofreading newsletters that will be produced with a high-resolution phototypesetter. At present, they aren't compatible with the systems used to transmit information to high-resolution phototypesetters. They're also somewhat limited in their typeface options.

Printers that use the PostScript Page Description Language create letters and numbers using typeface outlines, which increase or decrease in size and can be filled with various shades of gray at the time of printing.

The PostScript Page Description Language also drives high-resolution phototypesetters such as the Linotronic, which means you can proof your newsletter on an Apple LaserWriter or its equivalent and take the files to a service bureau for high-resolution output.

A third way computers can communicate with printers is with the Apple QuickDraw method. QuickDraw laser printers offer the same 300-dot-per-inch resolution as PostScript-based printers, but fewer typeface options are available; and fonts—specific typeface, type size and type style—must be created in advance and stored on your hard disk before printing.

Inkjet Printers

Emerging as inexpensive alternates to laser printers, inkjet printers offer the same 300-dot-per-inch resolution that laser printers do. However, inkjet printers operate more slowly and aren't designed for the continuous operation most laser printers can handle. But they still can produce excellent results. Type can be set in a variety of sizes.

They're a good choice if you want the quality, flexibility and quiet operation of laser printers but want to spend a lot less. Ideally, you should compare inkjet with laser-printer quality by printing a sample newsletter page on both printers. After producing the pages, copy them on an office photocopier to check the quality of the second-generation copies.

Printer Enhancements

Like computers, laser and inkjet printers are designed to be improved upon on a modular basis. Most include expansion slots that let you customize them. As your needs change, you can step up to better performance.

You can improve your printer's performance in four basic ways.

Additional Printer Memory

Additional memory can significantly improve the performance of your laser printer. It lets you download more typefaces to the printer. (Do this at the beginning of the day, so they'll be available for immediate printing and you won't have to wait for the computer to transmit the typefaces to the printer.)

Additional memory also lets you print larger graphic images. If you regularly print large scanned photographs or large charts and graphs without the additional memory, you may find they come out printed on two sheets of paper!

And additional memory lets you print larger type sizes on Hewlett-Packard LaserJet printers.

With PostScript printers, if your pages contain several downloaded fonts, you may get a warning that the page cannot be printed because there isn't enough room in the printer memory for all the typefaces to be downloaded. Additional memory solves that problem by letting you store downloadable fonts.

Font Cartridges

Inkjet and laser printers typically come with only a few resident, or built-in, typefaces. Resident fonts are typically limited in typeface variety as well as size and style options, and are rarely sufficient for desktop publishing needs.

To overcome this limitation, Hewlett-Packard and others now supply a variety of font cartridges for both laser and inkjet printers. Font cartridges—plug-in cards containing sets of carefully matched fonts—typically include a selection of typefaces, type sizes and styles that work well together as headlines, subheads and body copy. Often, both serif and sans-serif typefaces are included.

The advantage of font cartridges is that the typefaces are immediately available. You don't have to wait for type to be downloaded from your hard disk to the printer. Installation is also easier. You simply plug the font cartridge into the printer and perform an installation routine, which informs the software that the type specifications are available for use. Font cartridges are also economical.

They're great to use with nameplates previously created with a drawing or paint program, or even with nameplates prepared as camera-ready art using traditional typesetting and pasteup techniques.

The disadvantage of font cartridges is that you're limited to the typefaces, sizes and styles already on the cartridge. If it contains a 12-point typeface, for example, you can't choose 11- or 13-point type. Maximum type size is also limited, in many cases to 14 or 24 points— less than a quarter inch high. This limits your ability to create headlines that dramatically contrast with body copy.

Font cartridges offer you less flexibility in letter spacing. They typically limit you to portrait orientation or fewer landscape options. Thus, all typeface, type-size and style options cannot be rotated. Font cartridges won't let you set type at random angles between 90 and 180 degrees.

Before you purchase a font cartridge, however, be sure that it's fully compatible with your page layout program.

Plug-in Circuit Boards

The performance of Hewlett-Packard laser printers can be further enhanced by two categories of plug-in circuit boards, which add flexibility and improve performance.

One category includes various boards that can add PostScript compatibility to your Hewlett-Packard LaserJet printer. These let you proof newsletters at 300 dots per inch in your office and then transmit the files to a service bureau for high-resolution phototypesetting. In addition to providing access to the wide variety of PostScript typefaces, these boards typically increase printing speed as well.

Another category of enhancement includes performance boards that speed up printer operation by adding on-the-fly font scaling and increased resolution. Instead of being forced to create and store each typeface, size and style in a separate file on your hard disk, you can create the particular type specifications you need while your pages are being printed.

In some cases, these boards also increase the resolution of a Hewlett-Packard LaserJet printer. Instead of working with 300 dots per inch, they can offer 600- by 400-dot, or even 1,000- by 1,000-dot resolution, which creates distinctly sharper characters and smoother backgrounds.

Plug-in circuit boards (e.g., the Intel Visual Edge) are also available that improve the quality of scanned photographs. They let you increase the grayscale of reproduced photographs as well as their detail or resolution. They also dramatically increase speed, reducing the time it takes to reproduce a photo from minutes to seconds.

Printer Hard Disks

A final printer enhancement is adding a hard disk to PostScript printers. A hard disk lets you store typefaces where they're needed. This frees up valuable disk space and eliminates the need to download fonts at printing time.

A hard disk attached to your printer also allows printer spooling, which frees your computer while complex files are being printed so you can continue working. You can even download several files for printing at one time. This feature is especially useful if a single laser printer is shared by several computers.

As a final refinement to the printer hard disk, Adobe provides its entire typeface library on an Apple hard disk, ready to be attached to an Apple LaserWriter IINTX. If you're in an environment where several newsletters are being prepared simultaneously, this can save you installation and printing time and money, since fonts on the hard disk cost significantly less than those bought individually.

CONCLUSION

This appendix barely scratches the surface of hardware and software options available for producing desktop published newsletters; it's simply a starting point for your exploration. Find out as much as you can through magazines and your business associates. It's extremely important to be aware of all alternatives—even if you never move beyond the most basic system.

It's also important to view your computer and printer as tools, or working partners. Just as you wouldn't expect a carpenter to make a beautiful wooden cabinet with a dull saw and a toy hammer, you shouldn't expect to prepare attractive, effective newsletters without the necessary tools.

As a writer who's been involved with computers for a long time, I can attest to the importance of investing in the proper hardware. Indeed, I've found that with computer hardware, *purchase price always increases arithmetically, but productivity increases geometrically*. Thus, for every $10 you spend improving your computer or printer performance, you receive $100 worth of added productivity.

There's nothing more frustrating than watching a page being slowly redrawn on a computer screen, or watching your laser printer blink at you. Conversely, there's nothing more satisfying than a computer that responds quickly to a moving mouse or a printer that begins printing immediately after you tell it to.

Computer and printer enhancements quickly reward you with improved productivity and better-looking newsletters. Once you experience the joy of working with a big-screen monitor, a fast computer, or a laser printer that can store downloadable fonts or scale them on the fly, you'll wonder how you ever got along without them!

CHOOSING THE RIGHT SOFTWARE

One of the first decisions you'll make about your desktop publishing system is which type of software you'll use—word processing or dedicated page layout. Although differences between them are gradually disappearing, each still offers distinct advantages and disadvantages. You'll need to become familiar with the features and functions of both systems so you can decide which will work best for you. Often, it depends on the complexity of your newsletter design.

After you've chosen the type of software, you'll need to select a specific program. Microsoft Word, Word for Windows and WordPerfect are examples of word processing programs that offer desktop publishing capabilities; Aldus PageMaker and Xerox's Ventura Publisher are among the choices of dedicated page layout programs.

WORD PROCESSING

Most word processing programs today can perform functions once available only in dedicated desktop publishing programs. For instance, they can create multicolumn documents and offer a variety of typefaces, sizes and styles appropriate for headings and body copy. Most advanced programs also let you enhance your publication with rules, boxes and imported graphics.

Advantages

One practical advantage of choosing a word processing program is that you probably have experience using it. Instead of going through a long learning curve, you may have to master only those commands specifically related to desktop publishing, such as setting up multicolumn formats, importing graphics, and drawing rules and boxes.

Word processing programs make it easy to go directly from writing and editing to placing the article into the finished page. These programs also include helpful utilities. A spell-checker can prevent embarrassing errors; the thesaurus feature helps you find precisely the right word.

In general, word processing programs are ideal for simple-format newsletters prepared under last-minute deadline conditions. A two- or three-column newsletter with only a few typefaces would be a typical candidate. Word processing is also an excellent choice when you plan to mark photo placement and have your commercial printer strip your glossy photos into place.

Disadvantages

Word processing programs lack some of the advanced capabilities, output alternatives and ease of use that dedicated page layout programs offer. For instance, you can't see exactly how your finished page will look until you switch from the editing screen to a preview or page view. As a result, you can spend a lot of time switching back and forth between views.

Some programs do let you edit in preview mode, but it's usually much slower than editing in text mode.

Although you can see parallel columns of type in a text-editing view, you don't see graphic accents—page borders, rules, bars—or imported graphics. Unless you've added a Hercules graphics card, another limitation is that differences in type size aren't shown on your computer screen. Headlines, subheads and pull-quotes are the same size, making it hard to visualize your finished pages.

Page-preview image fidelity also varies from program to program. In most cases, a generic representation only distinguishes serif from sans-serif type, rather than giving you accurate font characteristics. Type size and letter spacing are often approximations, which means you may need to review numerous printouts to assure effective letter spacing in headlines and precise copyfitting throughout your pages.

With word processing programs, it's harder to set up formats that automatically repeat from page to page.

Summary

In general, word processing programs are adequate for creating good-looking vertically oriented, two- or three-column newsletters, even under a tight deadline. They're ideal for text-oriented, simply formatted, 8 1/2- by 11-inch newsletters that contain a limited number of imported graphics.

PAGE LAYOUT PROGRAMS

Desktop publishing programs offer more convenience and precision than do word processing programs. They do a quick and effective job of integrating previously prepared text and graphics. Instead of constantly switching between edit and preview modes, you're always operating in a WYSIWYG (what-you-see-is-what-you-get) environment. As a result, you see pages take shape as you work.

Advantages

Page layout programs offer a variety of layout aids, such as movable on-screen rulers for accurate placement of text and graphics, and sophisticated background grids with automatic "snap to" features that help you line up adjacent items.

You get far more graphics capability with a page layout program. Aldus PageMaker, Quark XPress, Letraset ReadySetGo! and Ventura Publisher let you adjust the contrast range of imported graphics and add a variety of halftone and screen effects. Most can produce creative negative or high-contrast posterization effects.

Page layout programs let you prepare color separations for spot-color emphasis or four-color images.

Used with PostScript typesetters, most programs can prepare film negatives, which can cut costs as well as production time.

Reduction and Enlargement

In conjunction with PostScript printers, you can prepare thumbnail sketches, then print out a reduced version of your newsletter on a single 8 1/2- by 11-inch sheet of paper. This helps you preview your publication and see how individual pages interact with each other.

Most word processing programs work best with standard page sizes, but desktop publishing programs let you create oversized or undersized pages. If you have access to a phototypesetter or a laser printer that can print 11- by 17-inch pages, you can have the "billboard" effect of large tabloid pages.

If you do have access to such a printer, you can create tabloid-sized publications by tiling—printing portions of an 11- by 17-inch page on several 8 1/2- by 11-inch pages, which are then pasted together.

Reduction capabilities let you print pages with bleeds at slightly reduced size, which your commercial printer can compensate for by slightly enlarging them.

Other Features

You can add registration marks that indicate the exact dimensions of your printed page to help your commercial printer align the various layers of color-separated pages.

Page layout programs make it easier to set up left- and right-hand master pages that contain repeating elements; to copy or move text and graphics from one page to another; and to create pages with flexible, multicolumn layouts.

Finally, these programs usually contain import filters that let you connect with and integrate files from a wide variety of sources. If your writers are using more than one word processing program, you'll be better off using a page layout program.

Layout Tools

Page layout programs offer many tools that make it easy to place text and graphics on a page. Most offer a variety of on-screen rulers and layout guides that can be moved to allow you to accurately measure the distance between page elements. In many programs when text and graphics approach the ruler or guide, they're "pulled" into perfect alignment. This magnetic attraction can usually be turned off if you want to place an element near, but not precisely aligned with, a ruler or guide.

Most page layout programs also include a "Send" command that lets you place a text or graphic element behind another one—or move an element from the front to the back. This is used when elements are layered or must overlap each other in a particular way.

Another command typically found in page layout programs, but often missing from word processing programs, is the "Group" command that lets you create a single graphic out of several individual parts, or move or resize several individual pieces of text and graphics as a single unit.

Another advantage offered by many page layout programs is their capability of saving files either as publications or templates. Template files are locked, which means they can be later opened and used as the basis for other files, but can't be modified themselves.

Disadvantages

A primary disadvantage of a dedicated page layout program is its cost, which can easily equal—or even surpass—the cost of a word processing program, which also must be purchased. Although some page layout programs boast word-processing features, such as spell-checkers and search-and-replace capability, you still need a word processing program to prepare your initial text.

Whereas a word processing program can be used for many functions (routine office correspondence, proposals, etc.) a page layout program's utility is primarily limited to preparing camera-ready artwork for desktop publishing projects.

Another issue involves training. Because they offer so many options, the most powerful programs are often the most difficult to master.

Although page layout programs have built-in HELP programs that let you access topics by the name of command or desired effect, the plethora of available features can be intimidating to new users.

A variety of books and video training materials are available for most page layout programs, but it can take weeks for a new user to become proficient if he or she is already familiar with basic computing and word processing skills.

Before committing to such an investment, be sure the program's capabilities will, indeed, result in time-savings and more effective, better-looking newsletters.

Summary

Dedicated page layout programs offer a richer portfolio of features than even the best word processing programs. If you have the time and resources to indulge your creative abilities to the fullest, you'll surely benefit from these features. Even if you don't need the features now, you may find they'll save you a lot of time and money in the future.

WHICH PROGRAM?

Having chosen the type of software you need, your next concern is which program to choose.

If possible, try out the programs friends and co-workers are currently using. Whatever program you choose, you're bound to encounter some stumbling blocks along the way. Or, test it out at a computer store and attend retailers' workshops. You may want to contact a local computer users' group for "get acquainted" hands-on opportunities.

It's an advantage to be able to ask advice from someone familiar with the program, rather than searching through a cumbersome reference manual or trying to get through to the software manufacturer's customer support phone line.

As you evaluate various page layout programs, keep your future needs in mind. Don't buy capabilities you don't really need. If short documents such as newsletters are likely to be your primary format in the years to come, it makes little sense to buy a program designed for producing books and other long documents.

Also consider the program's relative popularity. Market leaders want to maintain their position, so they offer periodic updates to accommodate new releases and enhancements.

A program's popularity is important in other ways. If you need to hire a freelance or graphic artist part-time to help produce your newsletter, you'll be able to choose from a larger pool of candidates if you're using popular software.

AUXILIARY PROGRAMS

Even if you're totally satisfied with the performance of your word processing or desktop publishing program, it's unlikely that the program by itself will be enough. You may want additional programs to augment and enhance your capabilities.

For example, although word processing and desktop publishing programs give you a lot of typographic control, you can get even more from an auxiliary drawing program, which offers more refinement. You can set type at larger sizes and adjust letter spacing more precisely. (Many desktop publishing programs are limited in the maximum type size they can create.)

In addition, you can set type at an angle (e.g., a special "Inside This Issue!" announcement run diagonally across the upper right-hand corner of the front cover).

Or you can compress or stretch the type of your nameplate to extend it all the way across the top of page 1.

Drawing Programs

Drawing programs can be categorized by the types of files they create.

Paint-type programs create images out of a series of dots and offer a variety of background screens and textures. Although paint programs have always been popular, they're limited in that the images they create must be used at the original size. They let you modify letters by working on them at enlarged views. However, they're more useful as artistic tools than as typographic tools.

Draw-type programs create images out of lines and shapes, but are relatively limited in their typographic flexibility.

The most useful programs are illustration-type programs (e.g., Aldus Freehand, Adobe's Illustrator 88, Corel Draw and WordPerfect's Draw-Perfect), which create encapsulated PostScript (EPS) programs that can be increased or decreased in size without loss of quality. EPS illustration software programs often contain autotrace features, which can be used to enhance scanned images or graphics created with other files.

EPS illustration-type programs offer the most typographic flexibility possible. You can set type in larger sizes, fill the letters with graduated fountain effects, stretch or compress type, and adjust letter spacing with more flexibility than conventional draw-type or paint-type programs.

Another popular use of drawing programs is infographics—pictures that combine illustrations with charts or graphs. Often, the starting point for a strong visual is a chart or diagram that's later manipulated by a drawing program. Popularized by newspapers like *USA Today*, these charts and diagrams translate numbers into attention-getting visuals.

Type Enhancement Programs

Type enhancement programs (e.g., LaserMaster's Special Effects Program and SoftCraft's Font Solution Pack in the PC world, or Altsys' Fontographer in the Mac world) help create distinctive typography for nameplates, banners, logos and association seals. By manipulating typefaces, you can join or overlap letters, add or eliminate serifs, and enhance a letter character with artwork.

Image Enhancement Programs

Image enhancement programs (e.g., LetraSet's Image Studio in the Mac world and Astral Publishing's Picture Publisher in the PC world) can increase or reduce the contrast range of part or all of imported photographs; combine two or more images into a collage; airbrush out distracting elements; or add missing elements.

Charting and Graphing Programs

It's easy to translate numbers into visuals that can be understood at a glance using a charting and graphing program. You simply type in the relevant numbers and the type of chart or graph you want, and the program does the rest.

UTILITY PROGRAMS

A variety of software utilities, many published by small, specialized firms, are available to meet your specific needs. One utility helps users of Ventura Publisher keep track of stored style sheets. Another helps WordPerfect users easily share styles from one document to another.

Two utility programs, Suitcase II and Font Juggler, let Macintosh users group families of typefaces together and prevent typeface identification conflict problems (see Appendix C). They can load more typefaces than Macintosh system software is designed to accommodate. These programs also let you preview typefaces loaded on your hard disk.

Timeslips, available for both the Macintosh and MS-DOS environments, helps you keep accurate time and cost records for newsletter design and production. It can also document increased production efficiency when you enhance or add hardware and software.

Another category of utility software includes programs that let you predefine kerning requirements for sizes and combinations of letters. By defining kerning pairs in advance, you don't have to manually reduce letter spacing every time the letter pairs are used in headlines.

The best way to stay abreast of these utilities is to read the small ads in the back sections of desktop publishing magazines, or read publications like *Aldus Magazine* or *Ventura Professional*, prepared specifically for users of these popular software programs.

DOWNLOADABLE FONTS

We saved a very important software category for last: soft—or downloadable—fonts, which you access as files on floppy disks.

Literally thousands of typefaces, sizes and styles are available for both the Macintosh and MS-DOS environments. In contrast to the relatively limited options available as resident fonts built into laser printers or as font cartridges, there's virtually no limit to the selection of downloadable fonts—and the number is growing.

In addition to more typeface, size and style alternatives, downloadable fonts offer more weights. Many faces are available in light and heavy weights and condensed or expanded versions, giving you more tools for adding "color" and variety to your newsletter.

The two main types of downloadable fonts are outline fonts, such as the Adobe PostScript fonts for Macintosh and MS-DOS computers (and others); and scalable bit-mapped fonts, available from Bitstream and Hewlett-Packard.

Outline Fonts

PostScript fonts are mathematically generated from lines and arcs. Because one mathematical set can define a typeface in all sizes, ranging from very small to very large, PostScript outline fonts are easier to install and occupy less space than bit-mapped fonts on your hard disk.

Outline fonts offer the most flexibility because they can be quickly generated and printed at any size and in varying shades of gray. Outline fonts can also be rotated (or set at an angle) at a moment's notice.

One big advantage of outline fonts is that as they're being scaled to small sizes, the fonts are automatically hinted, or adjusted to preserve correct proportions between thick and thin strokes. This avoids problems like small enclosed areas (e.g., the inside of a lowercase e) filling in when reproduced on 300-dot-per-inch laser printers.

Bit-Mapped Fonts

Bit-mapped fonts, particularly at large sizes of 60 points or more, occupy significant amounts of hard-disk space because they must be generated, or scaled, and stored as files before you use them. Bit-mapped fonts thus force you to plan ahead. If you need 12-, 24- and 48-point type, you have to generate these font files and save them on your hard disk before you begin working on your newsletter.

Offsetting the negative aspect of having to plan ahead, Bitstream fonts offer redeeming advantages. These fonts are automatically refined as they're generated, which improves their sharpness when printed on laser printers.

You can buy software programs (e.g., Hewlett-Packard's Type Director font management program) that conserve hard-disk space by letting you generate fonts selectively. If you're going to use only a few letters in a large headline size, you don't have to generate the entire alphabet.

It's hard not to get excited about the design potential of downloadable fonts. The cost of purchasing additional typefaces is usually a small fraction of your original hardware and software investment, but they give you dramatic design ability.

Compatibility Issues

When choosing from the numerous typeface alternatives available, it's important to anticipate possible quality improvements down the road.

For example, typefaces from larger firms, such as Adobe and Bitstream, are more likely to be available at local service bureaus than products from lesser-known firms. If your newsletter will always be printed on your own laser printer, typeface availability won't be a problem; but it might become an issue if you decide to send your files to a service bureau for high-resolution typesetting.

TECHNICAL SUPPORT

No matter which software programs you choose, it's important to register them with the software publishers and keep your address current in their files so you can be notified of current developments and other information of interest.

Software programs are in a continual state of improvement. No program can ever be considered "complete." Interim releases are one form of improvement. These are often indicated by version numbers following a decimal point (e.g., 3.0 becomes 3.01 or 3.1, etc.). Also, although software programs undergo thousands of hours of pre-release testing, occasional problems crop up after shipping has started. Sometimes problems occur only when certain keyboard command sequences are executed; other glitches emerge when importing files prepared with other word processing or graphics programs. In such cases, new disks are often shipped at little or no charge to registered users.

More important are the major version upgrades, usually indicated by new series numbers (e.g., 3.0 becomes 4.0). If you're a registered user, you can usually upgrade to the latest version for a small portion of the fee—often 10 percent or less.

Telephone-support access is often limited to registered software customers. Often this support is offered for a limited amount of time. After that, you can continue to call the software company with problems if you subscribe to its extended technical support program. These programs often include an informative newsletter, as well as free upgrades when new versions of the software are introduced.

HIGH-RESOLUTION OUTPUT

Why do some newsletters look better than others? Chances are, they were sent to a service bureau for high-resolution phototypesetting.

Most newsletters are produced on laser printers with ouput resolutions of 300 or 400 dots per inch. But there's an alternative that reaches beyond desktop publishing capabilities: high-resolution typesetters, using a grid of 1,270 to 2,450 dots per inch, can give your publication sharper, more clearly defined letters, smooth gray backgrounds and highly detailed photos.

Whether high-resolution phototypesetting is appropriate for you depends on the expectations of your readers, the paper your newsletter is printed on, the way you're handling photographs and—most important—your budget.

WHEN TO USE IT

Upgrading the quality of your publication by using high-resolution output makes good sense when the image is as important as the content. For example, you'd need to project a very polished image if you were producing a newsletter that cost subscribers more than $100 a year. And it's worthwhile if your newsletter is designed primarily to enhance your organization's image.

Paper is an important factor as well. The advantages of high-resolution output are lost when newsletters are printed on porous paper. For example, type edges can spread and bleed when printed on newsprint.

So, if you're going to invest in typesetting, you should also invest in coated paper.

Phototypesetting is also a good choice when you're providing your commercial printer with scanned photographs, which lack impact when reproduced at 300 dots per inch. (An exception might be Hewlett-Packard printers equipped with Intel's Visual Edge.) Output from a 2,540-dot-per-inch Linotronic typesetter reflects the quality capabilities of today's finest scanners and image-editing software.

High-resolution typesetting also lets you use bleeds (text or graphic elements that extend to the very edges of a page). Most laser printers can't print a full 8 1/2- by 11-inch page, which precludes using bleeds. Phototypesetters, however, can cover an image area up to 20 inches wide, which means they can not only print bleeds on 8 1/2- by 11-inch pages, but can also typeset tabloid-size newsletter pages.

COST CONSIDERATIONS

The cost of high-resolution phototypesetting equipment puts it beyond the reach of most newsletter publishers. Although an increase in competition will undoubtedly bring down the cost and make equipment easier to buy or lease in the future, most phototypesetters will probably continue to cost more than $25,000.

Rather than making an investment like that, it makes good sense to hire a phototypesetting service on a per-job or per-hour basis.

USING SERVICE BUREAUS

Most service bureaus offer 24- or 48-hour turnaround. While-you-wait service is sometimes available for last-minute corrections, if you're willing to pay the price.

Service bureaus usually have a standard charge per page, typically based on text-only pages. Plan to pay more if your job contains complex graphics or scanned photographs, since these pages take longer to print. (Some pages can literally take hours to prepare!) Most service bureaus begin charging more after a certain number of minutes per page—ask what that charge is before the job begins.

OUTPUT OPTIONS

Most service bureaus offer a choice of either 1,270- or 2,540-dot-per-inch resolution. The lower resolution works well if your newsletter is text-oriented and photographs will be added later by the commercial printer. Higher resolution is best for newsletters containing complex graphics and scanned photographs.

In either case, you'll get back camera-ready galleys (typeset pages that can go directly to a commercial printer).

If your newsletter contains spot color, the service bureau can provide color separations; each page will emerge in two or more layers. One layer will contain all the text and graphics to be printed in black; additional layers will have accent colors used for headlines or graphic emphasis.

If your newsletter calls for four-color artwork, the service bureau can prepare four-color separations, with separate layers for each of the primary colors that together create a four-color image.

Finally, service bureaus can prepare film negatives for newsletter pages. This saves time with your commercial printer, since the negatives can be placed directly on the printing press.

SUBMITTING WORK TO A SERVICE BUREAU

There are two ways to handle transactions with a service bureau. One way is to physically hand over the floppy disks containing your files to the service bureau. (You'll probably need to use high-density floppy diskettes, since page layout files can quickly grow large, especially if they contain scanned graphics.)

If your project contains complex illustrations or scanned images, you may have to divide your project files among several floppy disks.

A removable storage medium, such as the Iomega Bernoulli Box, can make it easier to transmit files to a service bureau. Because it can contain up to 40 megabytes of information, this device is large enough for even the most complex, graphics-filled newsletter.

Another way to send files to a service bureau is with a modem connecting your computer to your telephone. You can send files directly from your computer's hard disk to the service bureau computer's hard disk via modem. Modem transmission eliminates delivery charges and allows files too large for one floppy disk to be sent without being divided into smaller files.

It's always a good idea to also provide the service bureau with laser proofs of your project. These can help the service bureau maintain quality control and solve unanticipated problems by seeing a representation of the finished page.

Since many offices and service bureaus now have facsimile machines, you can send copies of your finished pages to the service bureau by fax.

AVOIDING THE PITFALLS

In spite of all its benefits, high-resolution phototypesetting is not without problems. For this reason, it's important to establish a working arrangement with your service bureau well in advance of your first deadline, and to be aware that you may run into some unexpected difficulties that will have to be ironed out.

First, be sure your laser printer files are compatible with your service bureau's phototypesetter. This can present a problem if, for example, you're using a Hewlett-Packard LaserJet Series II printer and you want to step up to high-resolution phototypesetting. Most service bureaus use PostScript phototypesetting machines, which require different files than those prepared for output on LaserJet printers.

Although it's sometimes possible to use a LaserJet-type printer to proof line endings and approximate headline placement, the copy won't be set in the typeface your newsletter will eventually appear in. So, if you plan to step up to high-resolution output, consider upgrading your LaserJet with a PostScript board (available from several suppliers), which lets you prepare high-fidelity page proofs in your office.

Font Compatibility

Your next concern is to make sure your service bureau has the same typefaces you use for your newsletter. This is one good reason to choose typefaces produced by the major typeface publishers. Most service bureaus already have a large investment in Adobe typefaces, for example, since they're long-time leaders in the field. If you know you're going to work with a particular service bureau, you might want to choose the typeface brand it recommends.

Another major problem concerns font ID conflicts, especially in the Macintosh environment. When the original Macintosh was designed, each typeface and style was assigned a unique number. Because no one anticipated the explosive growth of desktop publishing and the development of thousands of typeface designs, not enough numbers were made available.

Soon, the same numbers were assigned to more than one typeface. In addition, the way fonts were loaded into your computer's hard disk related to the way they were numbered. As a result, problems soon began to surface at service bureaus. Newsletter pages that were supposed to be printed in Adobe's Helvetica Black were coming out in a totally different typeface or, even worse, appearing in typewriter-like Courier (the typical system default).

Several utility software programs, like Suitcase II and Font Juggler, can get around the problem of font ID conflicts, and Apple's NFNT font renumbering scheme sidesteps the issue. But, it's still important to be aware of the problem and work with your service bureau to make your files compatible with their systems.

Test Files

Phototypeset output may look more or less different from laser-printed proofs. For example, phototypeset letters and numbers may appear thinner than the originals. The differences may weaken the impact of your text. Another problem occurs when hairline and vertical rules come out much thinner than you intended.

One of the best ways to test your computer's compatibility with a service bureau's phototypesetter is to prepare a test file containing a few sample newsletter pages.

When preparing it, include large and small samples of all the typefaces you're using in your newsletter. Include both roman (upright), regular-weight type and boldface and italic type.

By including all these samples, you'll find out if there are any unexplained font conflicts. It's also a good opportunity to ensure that the service bureau has all the typefaces you need.

Your test file should also include both justified and flush-left/ragged-right paragraphs to make sure that line endings remain the same when output on a phototypesetter.

Test rules of different thicknesses and boxes containing a variety of screen tints. Be sure to identify the shades, or percentages of black, used in these boxes. (Indicate the percentages of gray of each box screen next to the box.)

Print out a sample page on your laser printer before you take the test file to the phototypesetter.

You can compare the rules produced by your laser printer with the rules produced by the phototypesetter. Likewise, you'll be able to see whether the phototypesetter produces lighter or darker screened boxes than your laser printer.

If your newsletter includes clip art or scanned photographs, you might also include typical samples in your test files to see how phototypeset output compares with laser proofs.

You'll get the best results if you establish a working partnership with your service bureau and commercial printer before your first deadline. By working with them and giving yourself plenty of time to correct problems, you'll get the quality you're expecting from high-resolution phototypesetting.

A

Airbrushing — A process that allows distracting details to be eliminated or de-emphasized. Can be performed on a Macintosh or PC computer with special software.

Alignment — The placement of type on a page or in a column. Includes flush-left, flush-right, justified and centered.

Anchoring — Linking an imported graphic to a specific location on a specific page; or linking it to adjacent text, in which case a graphic moves with the text if preceding text is added or removed.

Ascender — Vertical stroke of lowercase letters that extends above the x-height of a typeface. Examples include b, d and t. Ascenders are usually shorter than the height of uppercase letters.

ASCII — Unformatted computer files, sometimes used to exchange information between different types of computers (e.g., Macintosh and MS-DOS computers). ASCII files lack typeface, type size and style information.

Autotrace — A feature of many drawing and scanning programs that can smooth out the borders of scanned images or translate graphic images from one file format to another. Autotrace can also translate characters into graphic images, letting you manipulate them to create distinctive initial caps, logos or nameplates.

B

Ballot box — An open box, available as a character with some typefaces, which can be used as a response device or indicate the end of articles.

Banner — A newsletter's title set in a distinctive way on the front page, often using a special typeface, type size and style. The banner is consistent in design and placement from issue to issue. (See *Nameplate.*)

Bars — Thick rules—or lines—often used horizontally to separate articles within columns, or the banner from front-page headlines, or to emphasize pull-quotes or visuals.

Baseline — The invisible line upon which a line of type rests.

Bit-mapped font — Specific typeface alphabet, created in user-defined size and style, stored on your computer's hard disk. Bit-mapped fonts offer great accuracy, but they occupy a lot of hard-disk space and must be downloaded to your printer before they can be used. (See *Downloadable fonts*.)

Bleed — A photograph, rule or other graphic element that extends to the edge of a page.

Blurb — A sentence or two above or below the headline that summarizes a feature article. Blurbs are typically set in a type size between that used for headlines and for body copy. (See *Subtitle*.)

Bowl — White space enclosed within the circular parts of letters such as b, d and o. Bowls may fill in when heavy typefaces are reproduced at small sizes on 300-dot-per-inch laser printers. (See *Counter*.)

Byline — Author credit line placed at the beginning or end of an article. Bylines sometimes include the author's title, professional affiliation or location.

C

Caption — A phrase or sentence that identifies the content of graphics like charts, graphs and photographs.

CGA — (Color Graphics Adaptor) An inexpensive type of color computer monitor capable of previewing newsletter pages as they will appear when printed. (See *EGA* and *VGA*.)

Clip art — Previously created illustrations, available as either line art or on disk. Line art can be scanned in or reduced to size by photographic techniques.

Clipboard — A temporary file, used to copy or move text or graphics from one part of your publication to another. The clipboard also lets you share text and graphics between different programs (e.g., word processing and page layout) without storing the file.

Clustering — A technique used to improve a newsletter's design by organizing small, scattered visuals on a page together into a single, large visual. Clustering is often used to create a grid out of a series of individual photographs. (See *Mug shot*.)

Color separation — An overlay, or separate layer, of a primary color of an image. Together, separate overlays create four-color printed images. Many desktop publishing programs let you create separations.

Composite newsletter — Newsletter created using both traditional and desktop publishing techniques (for example, the nameplate might consist of camera-ready phototypeset artwork, while article headlines and body copy are prepared using a word processing program and a laser printer).

Condensed type — Typeface style that retains the design integrity and legibility of the original face, but characters are narrower, permitting a higher word count. Many sans-serif typefaces have condensed versions that are especially useful for headlines, subheads and pull-quotes.

Constraining — Maintaining the original proportions of an image when reducing or enlarging it, by pressing the SHIFT key. Many desktop publishing and drawing programs have this feature.

Continuous-tone photograph — An original photograph that contains an infinite number of shades of gray, ranging from black to white. These photographs must be screened either at the scanning or commercial printing stage before they can be printed. (See *Halftone*.)

Contrast — The range of black to white tones in a scanned photo. A low-contrast photo has relatively light blacks and relatively gray whites. A high-contrast photo ranges from full black to full white.

Copy — Type or textual matter.

Copyfitting — Writing to fit available space. Copyfitting is made easier by "nonsense" files, which can be used to determine article length before the story is written. (See *Nonsense file*.)

Counter — Space inside letters, such as c and s, that opens onto the white space between letters. Care must be taken not to fill in counters when reproducing heavy typefaces at small sizes on laser printers. (See *Bowl*.)

Crop marks — Printer marks that bracket the part of a page, photograph or illustration to be printed. Crop marks are often placed on tissue-paper overlays covering a photograph or illustration. (See *Registration mark*.)

Cropping — Cutting or manipulating photographs and drawings to eliminate distracting detail along the top, bottom or sides. Cropped visuals remain square or rectangular. (See *Silhouetting*.)

Curly quote — Quotation mark that curves toward the quoted material. Opening quotes curve to the right, toward the quotation; closing quotes curve to the left, enclosing the quotation. Often called smart quotes. (See *Smart quote.*)

Cursor — A blinking rectangle or underscore mark on the computer screen, indicating the position where text or graphics may be entered or edited.

Cursor advance — A command in many word processing programs that lets you use keyboard commands instead of a mouse to position text and graphics. You can move the cursor up, down, left and right by specifying the distance to be moved in inches or points and picas. (See *Mouse.*)

D

Default — Automatic format setting used by a word processing or desktop publishing program, unless the user changes it. For example, most word processing and desktop publishing programs automatically set line spacing for 12-point type at approximately 14 points. Most programs also let you set up your own custom default files.

Descender — Portion of lowercase letters, such as g, p and y, that drops below the baseline. (See *Baseline.*)

Desk accessory — A type of software program that can be accessed from within another software program, such as appointment calendars and calculators. Desk accessories useful to newsletter editors include scanning software, spell-checkers and drawing programs.

Dingbat — A symbol such as a bullet, small box, pointing hand, map symbol or copyright notice. It can be used to emphasize lists, ballot boxes (for forms and surveys) or to indicate the end of an article, among other things.

Discretionary hyphen — Used in words such as proper nouns that must be divided in a specific way if they break at the end of a line. Discretionary hyphens let you override your software program's built-in hyphenation feature.

Dot leader — Row of periods often used as a replacement for vertical downrules. (See *Downrule.*)

Downloadable fonts — Bit-mapped and outline fonts—loaded from floppy disks—that can be loaded into your printer to provide a variety of typefaces, weights, sizes and styles, in addition to your printer's resident fonts and stored on your hard disk. (See *Resident font*; See also *Font cartridge*.)

Downrule — Vertical line used to separate adjacent columns of type. Downrules often are most effective with justified columns in which word spacing is adjusted to achieve lines of equal length.

Drop — White space added to the top of a page, above the columns of type. A drop can add consistency to a newsletter's design and emphasize headlines or visuals.

Drop cap — Oversized initial capital letter, used to highlight the beginning of a paragraph. The top of a drop cap is usually aligned with the tops of ascenders and uppercase letters in the first line of type. (See *Initial cap*.)

Drop shadow(or shadow box) — A graphics technique that creates a three-dimensional effect on a page. It involves copying a nameplate or masthead box, shading it black, and placing it behind the original image, offset slightly below and to one side.

E

EGA — (Enhanced Graphics Adapter) A type of color monitor that provides midlevel quality graphics for previewing colors and finished page design.

Ellipsis — A three- or four-dot punctuation mark that represents omitted text.

Em dash — A dash used in typeset text to introduce a subordinate phrase. Often expressed as two hyphens in word-processed manuscript copy, an em dash equals the width of a square of the type size, usually an uppercase M.

Em space — A horizontal measure equal in size to a square of the type size, usually an uppercase M. The first line of a new paragraph is often indented one or two em spaces.

En dash — A dash used in typeset text, usually to indicate continuing or inclusive numbers, or in place of a hyphen in a compound adjective that has one element hyphenated. An en dash is equal in width to an uppercase N.

En space — Half an em space.

Expansion card — An electronic circuit board that plugs into most computers, allowing them to work with customized peripherals such as image scanners, big-screen monitors or modems. Many laser printers can use expansion cards that provide extra memory for printing larger, more complex graphics.

Exporting — Sending files from one program back to another; e.g., while working in a page layout program, sending a block of text back to a word processing program for spell-checking.

Extended character set — An expanded version of the standard 256-character typeface, which contains additional characters, such as European accent marks, ligatures and other symbols usually accessed through special keyboard combinations. (See *Ligature*.)

Eyebrow — Word or short phrase used as a department head. Eyebrows are typically centered over the headline they introduce.

F

Feathering — Tiny changes in line spacing made to line up the bottoms of adjacent columns. Although some feel it creates more professional-looking pages, others object to the way it throws off baseline alignment in adjacent columns.

Folio — Information that identifies an issue, usually by date, volume and issue number. The folio is generally placed next to the nameplate.

Font — The full alphabet, number and symbol set for a particular version of a typeface. Separate fonts produce bold, italic and bold-italic versions, as well as weight variations of a typeface. *Font* can also refer to a single type size.

Font cartridge — A plug-in circuit board containing one or more fonts that can be added to your printer to supplement its resident fonts. Font cartridges are cheaper, easier to install and quicker to access than downloadable fonts, but offer limited typeface and type size options. (See *Downloadable font*.)

Font editor — A type of software program that lets you alter letters, adding or removing serifs, tilting, changing stroke widths or adding background fill effects. Useful for creating type for distinctive nameplates and logos.

Fontware — Bitstream's font installation program, which creates and stores bit-mapped fonts at specific sizes on the hard disk, ready to be downloaded or sent to the printer as needed.

Formatting — Choosing consistent typeface, type size, style, margins, line spacing, alignment and indents for each category of type (e.g., headlines, subheads, body copy) in a word-processed file.

Fountain effect — A smooth background transition from light to dark. Radial fountain effects have the light area in the center getting darker near the edges. Linear fountain effects go from light to dark, moving from top to bottom, left to right or diagonally (from upper left to lower right, etc.).

Frame — A fundamental building block used in Xerox Ventura Publisher. Frames can contain either text or graphics and can extend over more than one column of the underlying grid.

Frame-grabber — Hardware and software that create electronic photo files from a previously recorded videocassette or a video camera hooked up to a computer. Frame-grabbers let you capture and edit images on your computer, bypassing traditional photographic methods.

G

GEM — Digital Research's operating environment and graphics file structure, used by Ventura Publisher.

Graphics monitor — A device that shows text and graphics as they'll appear when a page is printed. (See also *Text monitor.*)

Grayscale — The levels of gray in photos or artwork captured by an image scanner or reproduced by a laser printer or phototypesetter. Grayscale relates to the smoothness of the transition from black to white. A grayscale range of 256 levels approaches the quality of an original photo.

Grayscale monitor — A monitor that can reproduce up to 256 levels of gray, making it useful for airbrushing or manipulating the grayscale range of scanned photographs. Most computer screens are limited to either 4 or 16 levels of gray when reproducing scanned images.

Greeking — Creating files of randomly chosen words forming sentences and paragraphs of varying size, for use in preliminary page design. *Greeking* also refers to the way that many software programs convert small-size type on a computer screen to rows of symbols, which speeds up screen redraws.

Grid — A matrix of nonprinting vertical and horizontal lines that guides the placement of text and graphics on the page.

Grouping — Locking together adjacent text and visuals so that they can be moved, saved or resized as a single element.

Gutter — The vertical space between columns of type. Gutter width should be proportional to typeface, type size and alignment. In two-page spreads, *gutter* also refers to the space between the right column of the left-hand page and the left column of the right-hand page.

H

Halftone — A photo that's screened—broken into a series of dots or lines—to make it suitable for printing. (See *Continuous-tone photograph*.)

Hanging indent — Indent in which the first line of a paragraph extends to the left of the body copy that follows. Hanging indents can emphasize short calendar items, association news or personnel milestones (e.g., Fifty Year Club members). (See *Indent*.)

Hard hyphen — A special command that prevents awkward hyphenation at line endings. (See also *Discretionary hyphen*.)

High-resolution output — Newsletter artwork prepared by image-setters, usually phototypesetters, operating at more than 1,200-dot-per-inch resolution.

Hints — Small changes in letter-stroke thickness and character proportions found in Adobe typefaces, designed to improve reproduction at small sizes on 300-dot-per-inch PostScript laser printers.

Hotlinks — An emerging technology that immediately exchanges information between programs. For example, changes in a chart created with a spreadsheet program can be made automatically as a copy of the chart is placed in a newsletter page produced with a compatible word processing or page layout program.

Hyphenation — Breaking a word or compound after a syllable and placing the remainder on the next line.

I

Image scanner — A hardware accessory that converts a glossy photo into an electronic file, which can be manipulated and placed in a newsletter created with a word processing or page layout program.

Import filter — Allows desktop publishing programs to accommodate various word processing programs. An import filter automatically eliminates unnecessary information, but retains text and formatting information.

Indent — Moving a line of type to the right to indicate the start of a new paragraph or list. Both right- and left-hand indents can be used to adjust the margins of text placed in a box, such as a sidebar or masthead. (See *Hanging indent*.)

Infographics — Stylized visuals that combine elements of both drawings and charts or graphs, adding interest to otherwise dull numbers and statistics.

Initial cap — An oversized first letter of the first word in an article. Initial caps can be dropped into the copy (see *Drop cap*) or extend into the white space above the first paragraph (see *Raised cap*).

Inkjet printers — Printers such as the Hewlett-Packard DeskJet and DeskWriter, which offer much of the quality and flexibility of laser printers at far less cost.

J

Jumpline — A phrase used when an article continues on a following page (e.g., "Continued on page 5," "Continued from page 1," etc.).

Justified text — Copy set flush-left/flush-right in lines of equal length. Copy is justified by increasing or decreasing word spacing of each line.

K

Kerning — Increasing or decreasing letter spacing to improve appearance and readability. (See also *Kerning pairs* and *Tracking*.)

Kerning pairs — Predefined pairs of letters in a particular typeface and size, for which custom letter spacing is specified in advance. Several page layout programs automatically substitute desired letter spacing when these letter pairs are encountered.

Keyboard shortcut — A way to highlight text or quickly access frequently used commands without using a mouse. Often combines COMMAND, CONTROL, SHIFT, ALT or OPTION keys with selected function keys or any other keys. (See *Mouse*.)

Knockout — Text or graphic accent that appears in outline against a photograph or a reversed, screened or colored background.

L

Landscape orientation — Type is printed across the 11-inch direction of an 8 1/2- by 11-inch sheet of paper turned sideways to give it a horizontal orientation. Landscape monitors are wider than they are tall and typically display two 8 1/2- by 11-inch pages side by side.

Laser printer — A printer that creates text and graphic images from a grid of 300 dots or more per inch. Similar in operation to photocopiers, laser printers use high heat to bond toner to sheets of paper. High-resolution laser printers operate at 400 to 600 dots per inch.

Leading — Vertical spacing between lines of type. Leading is typically measured from the baseline of one line to the baseline of the next line.

Ligature — Special combination of letters often spaced so closely together they're available as single characters accessed through special keyboard commands. Examples include "ff" and "fl."

Linking — Continuing articles or text between frames or text boxes, even if they aren't located on the same page. This speeds up laying out articles that jump from the front page to inside pages.

Linotronic — Popular high-resolution desktop publishing equipment manufactured by the Linotronic Corporation. Linotronic image-setters produce camera-ready pages at 1,270 or 2,540 dots per inch.

Live area — The portion of a page that's printed. The live area is typically smaller than the paper size, to leave room for a gripper area (a blank part of the page, by which it's pulled through a printing press). (See *Bleed* and *Trim size*.)

Local Area Network (LAN) — A network confined to a specific or limited area (a room, department or building) that links computers together to facilitate file exchange or allow several computers to share a single printer. A LAN can let one person write an article on one computer; someone else scan a photo on a second computer; and a third person assemble the article and photo into a finished page without having to copy the files onto floppy diskettes and physically transfer them.

Logo — Your firm or association's name, set in a distinctive typeface, size and style. A logo is often set against a distinct background and accented by horizontal rules and/or other graphic devices.

Low-resolution output — Usually refers to camera-ready artwork prepared with a 300-dot-per-inch laser printer. (See *Resolution*; *High-resolution output*.)

M

Macro — Short computer program of previously stored command sequences. Macros can provide word processing programs with much of the power found in page layout programs. (See *Master pages*; *Style*.)

Master pages — Left- and right-hand page layouts automatically repeated throughout your newsletter. Featured on most desktop publishing programs, master pages save you the time of adding borders, adjusting column placement and setting margins for each page. (See *Macro* and *Style*.)

Masthead — The block of information printed in a newsletter that lists staff, publisher's address and subscription information.

Mezzotint — A photograph or illustration to which a distinctive dot pattern has been added. This is done by scanning the image at small size and greatly enlarging a portion of it, or by using software programs that let you manipulate previously scanned images.

Modem — A hardware accessory that connects a computer to phone lines. Modems are often used to send camera-ready files to a service bureau or transmit files too large to be stored on a single floppy diskette.

Moiré pattern — The result of scanning and screening a previously screened halftone photograph. The pattern is confusing and destroys detail, creating uneven tonal values.

Mouse — A hand-held device that lets the computer user quickly locate and execute commands and move the cursor to any point on the computer screen. (See *Keyboard shortcut*.)

MS-DOS — The Microsoft Disk Operating System—a protocol that governs how PC-compatible computers process and store information.

Mug shot — Head-shot photograph of a person often accompanying a short article recognizing achievements or promotions.

N

Nameplate — The title of a newsletter that appears in the same distinctive typeface, size and style in every issue. (See *Banner*.)

Networking — A way of linking two or more computers to let them quickly and easily share information. It lets you transmit files between computers using word processing, drawing and page layout programs.

Newspaper columns — Text continues from the bottom of one column to the top of the next. Often referred to as "snaking" columns.

Nonbreaking hyphen — See *Hard hyphen*.

Nonbreaking space — A way to lock characters or words together in word processing or page layout programs so they won't be separated by line breaks. Nonbreaking spaces can be used with proper nouns to eliminate middle initials isolated at the end of a line, for example.

Nonsense file — A word-processed file of random letters and syllables that contains the same number of words, sentences and paragraphs found in a typical newsletter article. Nonsense files can be used to try various layouts without using actual text. (See also *Copyfitting*.)

O

OCR — Optical Character Reading software designed for use with image scanners to store a page as individual words rather than as a graphics image, letting you edit the original page.

On-the-fly scaling — Accessories that let you create and manipulate typefaces and sizes for immediate output on laser printers. This conserves valuable hard-disk space and eliminates the delays involved in transferring bit-mapped typefaces from your computer to your printer.

Orphan — Less than one-third of a line carried over from the end of one column or page and left isolated at the top of the next. (See *Widow.*)

Outline font — Typeface alphabet stored on hard disk as a series of lines and arcs scaled to the desired size during printing. Outline fonts occupy less hard-disk space than bit-mapped fonts, and can be infinitely scaled or rotated.

P

Paint program — A software program that stores files as collections of dots. Paint-type files can contain numerous levels of gray, but should be produced and reproduced at approximately the same size. (See *EPS.*)

PCL — (Printer Command Language) A Hewlett-Packard software protocol that defines how computers exchange information with Laser-Jet printers.

Phototypesetter — A high-quality output device that creates text and graphics by exposing light-sensitive film at either 1,270 or 2,540 dots per inch. (See *Linotronic.*)

Pica — A unit of measurement used by graphic artists and printers. There are about six picas to an inch, 12 points to a pica. (See *Point.*)

PICT files — Object-oriented files, stored as definitions of lines. PICT files don't contain the many levels of gray stored in TIFF files. (See *TIFF.*)

PICT2 — Object-oriented files that can include colors. (See *PICT files.*)

Placeholder — A square, rectangle or one-sided ladder created with drawing programs and used with page layout programs to ensure consistent spacing between text elements such as headlines, subheads, pull-quotes and body copy, or between photos and their captions.

PMS color — Stands for the Pantone Matching System, universally agreed-upon specifications for colors created by precise mixtures of the red, blue and green primary colors.

Point — A subdivision of a pica. A pica has 12 points: an inch 72 points.

Portrait orientation — Type set on the 8 1/2-inch dimension of an 8 1/2- by 11-inch page. Also refers to vertical monitors that typically display a single page at or near actual size.

Posterization — Effect created by eliminating the gray tones in a scanned black-and-white image, leaving a high-contrast image. Posterization can transform an ordinary photograph into a piece of art.

PostScript — Adobe's PostScript Page Description Language, which stores text and graphics as lines and arcs that can be filled with a variety of different backgrounds. PostScript files can be previewed on laser printers, then typeset without change on high-resolution typesetters.

PPM — (Pages per minute) An often misleading measure of an inkjet or laser printer speed, often based on the time it takes to apply an image to a page and mechanically move it through the printer. This doesn't take into account the time it takes to process the page before printing.

Pre-printing — Printing logos, nameplates, nameplate backgrounds, blank spots or second-color accents prior to printing the actual newsletter. When the second color has been printed, only a single pass through the printing press is needed, resulting in cost savings.

Printer-spooler — A device that lets you save a printed file to a hard disk, where it will be downloaded to the printer in increments, allowing you to continue working on your computer.

Process color — Premixed "out-of-the-can" colors that don't offer the range of tints and hues that are available in custom-mixed colors. (See *PMS color.*)

Proof — A preliminary printout of your newsletter. Proofs let you make last-minute refinements and check for typographical errors.

Proportional scale — A handy, traditional layout tool that's basically a plastic wheel used for resizing photographs. Helps you determine new width and length dimensions when only one new dimension is known, so that you can provide your printer with the exact percentage of increase or reduction needed.

Proportional type — Typefaces characterized by varying letter spacing, in contrast to typewriter letters that occupy the same amount of horizontal space. For example, w and m are wider than i. Proportional typefaces improve a page's appearance and increase the number of letters that fit on a line.

Pull-quote — A short phrase or sentence extracted from an adjacent article. A pull-quote can make page design more interesting and spark reader interest in an article.

R

Raised cap — An initial capital letter that extends into the white space above a paragraph. Raised caps add visual interest by adding extra white space to a page. (See also *Drop cap* and *Initial cap*.)

Registration mark — Printers' symbol used to align multiple layers, or separations, of photos or illustrations. Registration marks ensure that colors will appear in the proper places when the overlays are printed. (See *Crop marks* and *Separations*.)

Replace — A command in most word processing and many page layout programs that lets you search for text or formatting commands, and automatically replace them with others. For example, you can quickly replace underlined type with italicized type or abbreviations with spelled-out words, or you can substitute single spaces for double spaces at the ends of sentences. (See *Search*.)

Resident font — Typeface built into a printer. Times Roman and Helvetica are resident in most PostScript printers. Courier, a typewriter-like font, is often found in non-PostScript laser printers.

Resizing — Increasing or decreasing the size of a graphics file. Proportional resizing maintains the proportions of the original file.

Resolution — The level of clarity and definition that an output device can provide. Laser printers, for example, are capable of 300-dot-per-inch resolution. In photography, *resolution* refers to lines per inch in an electronically reproduced photograph.

Reverse — Text and graphics printed in white against a background of black or a dark color.

Rotation — Text rotated for special effects, such as text set at a 45-degree angle at the upper right-hand corner of the cover page.

Rule — Horizontal or vertical lines used in various thicknesses as borders and separators, e.g., to define adjacent columns of text or articles within a column.

S

Saccadic jump — The tendency of the human eye to jump from word cluster to word cluster, rather than process letters one at a time. This perceptual phenomenon has important implications regarding the relationship between type size and line length as well as the limitations of headlines set in uppercase type.

Sans-serif — One of the two primary families of typeface design. Sans-serif type lacks serifs—decorative strokes at the end of letters that provide letter-to-letter transition. (See *Serif.*)

Scaling — Re-sizing photographs or imported graphics to fit your page layout. (See *Constraining.*)

Scalloped column — Page layout with columns of unequal length. Because column lengths don't have to align, pages with scalloped columns are easier to produce. They can look more interesting because of the varying amounts of white space at the bottom of each page.

Scholar's margins — White space added to the outside margins of two-page spreads, or to the left margin of a front cover. The term comes from the wide margins allowed for note-taking in scholarly texts. Scholar's margins are generally less than half the width of adjacent body-copy columns.

Screen — A shade of gray used for text backgrounds or graphics. Black is 100 percent screening; white is 0 percent. Screening is also the process of breaking up a photograph into dots of black or white for easier printing. (See *Continuous-tone photograph* and *Halftone.*)

Screen font — The part of a downloadable typeface that provides an accurate on-screen preview of how a typeface will look when printed.

Script — A typeface style that resembles handwriting. Script typefaces are effective in nameplates or headings where readers are already familiar with the newsletter.

Search — A function available on many word processing and page layout programs that automatically searches the text for specific words or typographic formatting commands and, with the Replace command, automatically modifies or deletes them. (See *Replace*.)

Separations — Individual layers of a multicolor image, each layer containing the amount of each primary color needed to produce a four-color image when layers are superimposed on each other.

Serifs — Tiny feet that project from the main strokes of typeface characters. Serifs make a block of text easier to read by providing letter-to-letter transition. (See *Sans-serif*.)

Service bureau — A business, often associated with a commercial printer, that can process electronic text files on high-resolution phototypesetting equipment.

Shadow box — See *Drop shadow*.

Sidebar — A short article within an article, usually set off by a box or a screened background.

Silhouetting — Eliminating the background from all or part of a photograph. Silhouetting changes the shape of a photograph.

Sink — A consistent amount of white space between the top of a page and the start of each column of text. (See also *Drop*.)

Small caps — Uppercase letters, set approximately 20 percent smaller than normal, used for emphasis in a headline or text to avoid darkening a page with boldface type.

Smart quote — See *Curly quote*.

Soft font — Typeface stored on your hard disk that can be downloaded to a printer as needed. (See *Bit-mapped font* and *Outline font*.)

Spot color — Color applied to graphic accents, such as bars or vertical downrules, or to individual text blocks, headlines or pull-quotes.

Spread — Facing left- and right-hand pages.

Standing head — Distinctive headline that introduces a department or feature repeated in every issue.

Stress — The proportional variation between the thick and thin strokes of a letter. Some typefaces have little or no stress; others are characterized by extreme stress.

Stroke — The thickness of the letters. Some typefaces are available with variations in stroke thickness, ranging from Light (thin) to Black or

Heavy (thick). Stroke thickness can also vary within individual letters. (See *Stress.*)

Style — Manipulated typeface weight and angle, used to emphasize key words. Boldface, italics and bold italics are common type styles.

Style — Electronic file that stores typeface, size, style, letter spacing, alignment, indent and other information. Styles help you maintain consistency and quickly format or reformat your document.

Subtitle — A sentence or two placed above or below a headline that summarizes the subject of the article. (See *Blurb.*)

Symbol — Typeface character used as a graphic accent, such as ballot boxes, bullets, or copyright symbols. (See *Extended character set.*)

T

Table — Information, often numerical, displayed in rows and columns within a ruled box. Tables communicate a lot of information at a glance, but require careful alignment of characters.

Table of contents — A listing of articles and features in a newsletter and the page number where each begins. Newsletters of eight or more pages should contain a front-page table of contents that directs readers' attention to articles inside.

Tag — Style, or file, containing formatting information that Ventura Publisher applies to word processing files.

Teaser — A short phrase or tantalizing description on a newsletter's front cover, designed to interest people in reading articles that begin on inside pages.

Template — An empty page layout file containing formatting instructions for newsletter copy. Templates can contain a previously created and precisely positioned nameplate and masthead, as well as defined positions for columns of text.

Text mode — A view of a word-processed file that displays all text in the same size and typeface. Text mode makes editing easy, because your eye isn't distracted by different-sized type.

Text monitor — A monitor that displays all letters and numbers in characters of equal size on the computer screen. A text monitor isn't as suitable for desktop publishing applications as is a graphics monitor, since it can't show different typefaces, sizes or graphic elements. Nor can it preview the appearance of finished pages. (See *Graphics monitor.*)

Text offset — The amount of white space a software program automatically adds between text and adjacent graphics. *Text offset* also refers to how closely text wraps around an irregularly shaped scanned photograph or illustration. (See *Wraparound.*)

Textured screen — Includes lines at varying angles or exaggerated dot patterns that can convert a commonplace photo into an interesting graphic resembling a hand-drawn illustration. Many desktop publishing and photo enhancement software programs let you enhance a scanned photographic image by adding a textured screen.

Thumbnail — A small, hand-drawn sketch of a newsletter page. Thumbnails can also be created with PostScript laser printers; you can preview up to 16 pages of a newsletter at reduced size on a single 8 1/2- by 11-inch page.

TIFF — (Tagged Image File Format) A file format used to describe scanned photographs containing multiple layers of gray.

Tiling — Lets PostScript laser printers print pages larger than 8 1/2 by 11 inches. An 11- by 17-inch tabloid page, for example, can be created from four 8 1/2- by 11-inch pages, "pasted" together after emerging from the printer.

Tilting capitals — Alternative versions of some Adobe typefaces, specially designed to be used at large sizes for such elements as nameplates.

Tint — Shade of gray used as a background for text or graphics that need emphasis.

Tombstone headline — Headline in adjacent column that creates unwanted parallelism in page design and confuses readers by causing them to read across, instead of down, a column of text.

Tracking — Uniformly increasing or reducing spacing between all characters in a headline or text block. Tightening up letter spacing increases word density; opening up letter spacing improves readability. (See *Kerning.*)

Trapped white space — Accidentally formed pools of white space between text and graphic elements that distract the reader rather than perform a useful function.

Trim size — The final size of a printed newsletter page. If the newsletter contains bleeds, the trim size will be smaller than the paper the newsletter was originally printed on, allowing space to trim off the gripper area of the printing press. (See *Bleed* and *Live area.*)

U

Undo — A command in many word processing and desktop publishing programs that lets you restore recently deleted text or eliminate recent formatting changes.

UPS — (Uninterruptible Power Supply) An accessory for your word processing or desktop publishing system that protects against power surges and includes an automatic battery backup, in case power to your computer is reduced or interrupted.

V

Vertical justification — Aligning the bottom of adjacent columns of text by adding small amounts of white space between lines of text (see *Feathering*) or by adding extra space between paragraphs and/or between text and adjacent headlines, subheads or photos.

VGA — (Video Graphics Array) The highest-quality graphics monitor for MS-DOS computers. It provides the most accurate on-screen previews of how pages will look when printed. (See *CGA* and *EGA.*)

W

Weight — A typeface's degree of thickness. Heavy, or black, versions of a typeface have thick horizontal and vertical strokes. Light weights have thinner strokes than medium—the weight normally used for text.

Widow — A portion of a word, or a single word on a line by itself at the end of a page or column of type. (See also *Orphan.*)

Word shape — The distinctive outline created by the interplay of x-height, ascenders and descenders, which helps readers identify words. Uppercase shapes are harder to identify, since they tend to form uniform rectangles lacking variety in letter height. (See *Ascender, Descender, X-height.*)

Wraparound — Lines of varying length that flow around an illustration or silhouetted photograph.

WYSIWYG — A slightly overworked acronym for "What You See Is What You Get." It refers to the ability to see text and graphics on your computer screen the same way they'll appear when the page is printed.

X

X-height — The distance between the baseline of a line of type and the height of lowercase letters like a, e, i, o and u, which don't have ascenders. (See *Ascender*; see also *Baseline.*)

Z

Zooming — A feature of many paint-type and image enhancement programs that lets you focus on part of an image at greatly magnified size, permitting work on tiny details that would otherwise be lost. Often, a small window shows you how the changes you're making affect the overall image.

BIBLIOGRAPHY

BOOKS

American Press Institute. **Newspaper Design: 2000 and Beyond.**
Reston, VA: American Press Institute, 1989.

A fascinating, thought-provoking look at the ways newspapers are
changing in order to survive and compete in the television age. Each
two-page spread features a redesigned newspaper, with a colored grid
showing how the article modules were successfully put together.

Bauermeister, Benjamin. **A Manual of Comparative Typography:
The PANOSE System.** New York: Van Nostrand Reinhold, 1987.

A valuable guide to evaluating and selecting typefaces, using letters of
the alphabet (uppercase P, A, N, O, S and E) to clearly demonstrate
individual typeface characteristics and variations in design.

Beach, Mark. **Editing Your Newsletter: How to Produce an
Effective Publication Using Traditional Tools and Computers.** Portland, OR: Coast to Coast Books, 1988.

A perennial classic that belongs in every newsletter editor's library.
Covers all aspects of newsletter planning and writing, establishing a
production cycle and learning how to delegate responsibility.

Beach, Mark, and Pattison, Polly. **Outstanding Newsletter Designs.** Portland, OR: Coast to Coast Publishing, 1990.

An inspirational potpourri showing the latest and best newsletter designs. Useful for newsletter design and redesign, with large illustrations interpreted by two of the leading designers/lecturers/writers in the field.

Beach, Mark, and Russon, Ken. **Papers for Printing: How to Choose the Right Paper at the Right Price for Any Printing Job.** Portland, OR: Coast to Coast Books, 1989.

A thorough and excellent treatment of the subject of choosing the right paper. Numerous samples show how the paper affects the appearance of text and illustrations.

Beach, Mark, Shepro, Steve, and Russon, Ken. **Getting It Printed: How to Work with Printers and Graphic Arts Services to Assure Quality, Stay on Schedule, and Control Costs.** Portland, OR: Coast to Coast Books, 1986.

Shows how to choose the right printing firm and provide them with artwork they need. Contains dozens of time- and money-saving tips. A necessary addition to any desktop publisher's library.

Beale, Stephen, and Cavuoto, James. **The Scanner Book: A Complete Guide to the Use and Applications of Desktop Scanners.** Torrance, CA: Micro Publishing Press, 1989.

Describes important hardware and software features to look for before you buy, and time-saving tips and techniques that will help you make the most of your scanner.

Bigelow, Charles, Duensing, Paul Hayden, and Gentry, Linnea. **Fine Print on Type: The Best of Fine Print Magazine on Type and Typography.** San Francisco: Bedford Arts Publications, 1988.

Provides a perspective on the evolution, history and future directions of fine typography. If your newsletter editing experiences have aroused your interest in learning more about the centuries-old tradition of fine arts typography, this book is for you.

Binns, Betty. **Better Type. Learn to see subtle distinctions in the faces and the spaces of text type....** New York: Watson-Guptill, 1989.

Combines concise text with generous illustrations showing how legibility and readership are influenced by even the subtlest changes in letter, line and word spacing.

Bly, Robert W. **The Copywriter's Handbook: A step-by-step guide to writing copy that sells.** New York: Dodd, Mead, 1985.

Excellent advice to help you write more effective copy for newsletters, brochures and direct-mail solicitations.

Brady, Philip. **Using Type Right: 121 Basic No-Nonsense Rules for Working with Type.** Cincinnati: North Light Books, 1988.

An entertaining book of tips and techniques to help you make better use of your desktop publishing or page layout program. Combines concise descriptions of design principles with graphic examples in an oversized format that's a joy to read.

Brownstone, David M., and Franck, Irene M. **The Self-Publishing Handbook: A step-by-step guide to the publishing process for those who want to produce their own books.** New York: New American Library, 1985.

The more you know about the publishing process, the better you'll be at producing your newsletter or transferring your editing skills to your own publishing projects.

Burke, Clifford. **Type from the Desktop: Designing with Type and Your Computer**. Chapel Hill, NC: Ventana Press, 1990.

A thought-provoking exploration into the world of typography and design. Filled with type examples, this book explores the functions and aesthetics of type.

Cook, Alton, ed. **Type and Color: A Handbook of Creative Combinations**. Rockport, MA: Rockport Publications, 1989.

Previews more than 800,000 possible type/background combinations. Contains more than 100 pages of color samples and removable acetate overlays to let you experiment with black, colored or reversed type on a variety of background colors. Also contains essays addressing the many ways your editorial message can be reinforced through effective use of typography and color.

Dair, Carl. **Design with Type.** Toronto, Canada: University of Toronto Press, 1982.

A reprint of the original written in the 1960s. This slim volume contains unforgettable lessons that extend far beyond page design and typography into the writer/designer/reader relationship.

Fenton, Erfert. **The Macintosh Font Book: Typographic Tips, Techniques and Resources.** Berkeley, CA: Peachpit Press, 1989.

Lists numerous resources, features and shortcuts to help you make the most of your software program's typographic capabilities, including manipulating and editing typefaces.

Gosney, Michael, and Dayton, Linnea. **Making Art on the Macintosh II**. Glenview, IL: Scott, Foresman, 1988.

Provides valuable ideas for creating state-of-the-art computer graphics with Mac II computers, as well as MS-DOS and Macintosh SE computers. Offers tips, techniques, program comparisons and examples of computer art that rival effects achieved with traditional painting and photography.

Hudson, Howard Penn. **Publishing Newsletters: A Complete Guide to Markets, Editorial Content, Design, Printing, Subscriptions, Management, and Much More...**, Revised Edition. New York: Charles Scribner's Sons, 1988.

Comprehensive coverage of all aspects of newsletter publishing, by a well-informed observer of the newsletter scene and publisher of the influential *Newsletter on Newsletters*.

Kelly, Kevin. **Signal: Access to Communication Tools and Information Frontiers** (Whole Earth Catalog Series). New York: Random House, 1989.

A valuable resource, in the *Whole Earth Catalog* tradition, that can help you locate even the most arcane books, tapes and sources relating to all aspects of broadcast, personal and print communication.

Lubow, Martha, and Pattison, Polly. **Style Sheets for Newsletters: A Guide to Advanced Designs for Xerox Ventura Publisher.** Thousand Oaks, CA: New Riders Publishing, 1988.

For Ventura Publisher users, style sheets (or templates) that illustrate the basic principles of newsletter design.

McClelland, Deke. **Painting on the Macintosh: A non-artist's drawing guide to MacPaint, SuperPaint, PixelPaint, Hyper-Card, and many others.** Homewood, Il: Dow Jones-Irwin, 1989.

Helpful information on choosing the best paint-type program and using it effectively to produce better-looking newsletters. Contains a strong section on enhancing clip art with paint-type programs.

Mitchell, Joan P. **The New Writer: Techniques for Writing Well with a Computer.** Redmond, WA: Microsoft Press, 1987.

Shows you how to prepare better newsletters by making the most of the computer's ability to help you quickly organize, edit and rewrite.

Moen, Daryl R. **Newspaper Layout and Design.** Second Edition. Ames, IA: Iowa State University Press, 1989.

Includes numerous examples of newspaper design tools that can be effectively adapted to newsletters, especially tabloids.

Nace, Ted, and Gardner, Michael. **LaserJet Unlimited: Edition II.** Berkeley, CA: Peachpit Press, 1988.

A comprehensive guide for editors using Hewlett-Packard LaserJet printers. Compares the performance of the various LaserJet models; suggests ways to maximize performance of both popular and hard-to-find software programs with the LaserJet; describes how to upgrade your LaserJet; and surveys available LaserJet font resources.

Naiman, Arthur, editor. **The Macintosh Bible: thousands of tips, tricks & shortcuts logically organized and fully indexed**, Second Edition. Berkeley, CA: Goldstein & Blair, 1988.

Provides clear, concise descriptions and informed opinions of the major hardware and software options in the fast-moving Macintosh environment. Contains software-specific tips and techniques for the most popular programs, as well as software utilities you'd be unlikely to find in a computer store.

O'Dell, Peter. **The Computer Networking Book.** Chapel Hill, NC: Ventana Press, 1989.

A friendly but comprehensive plain-English guide to linking computers—including PC and Macintosh systems—to share information and increase their capabilities.

Pattison, Polly. **How to Design a Nameplate: A guide for art directors and editors.** Chicago: Ragan Communications, Inc., 1982.

A source of inspiration for anyone looking for additional ways to design—or redesign—a newsletter's title and subtitle.

Perfect, Christopher, and Rookledge, Gordon. **Rookledge's International Type-Finder: The Essential Handbook of Typeface Recognition & Selection.** Savannah, GA: Frederic C. Beil Publications, Inc., 1986.

A valuable resource to help you recognize and identify type characteristics that will enhance your newsletter's specific communications goal. Similar typefaces are compared letter for letter, emphasizing how an emotional response to a typeface results from the interaction of many small details.

Poynter, Dan. **The Self-Publishing Manual: How to write, print & sell your own book,** Fifth Edition. Santa Barbara, CA: Para Publishing, 1989.

Offers valuable advice on transferring from newsletter publishing to book publishing. Contains sample forms and worksheets to help you evaluate the feasibility of your new publishing venture.

Quark, Inc. **Quark XPress Tips.** Denver, CO: Quark, Inc., 1989.

Required reading for Quark XPress users who want to make the most of their program's power. Contains numerous illustrated suggestions showing how to achieve sophisticated effects in newsletter, newspaper and magazine design.

Rehe, Rolf F. **Typography: how to make it most legible.** Camel, IN: Digital Research International, 1984.

A slim, reader-friendly volume showing the importance of making typography functional, attractive and easy to read. Numerous illustrations show the effects achieved by changing type size, line length, line spacing and other typographic attributes.

Robey, Adele, and Weiss, Clifford. **Typography for Newsletters.** Arlington, VA: National Composition Association, 1988.

A combination text/workbook covering various newsletter layouts—from simple to complex—with alternative type arrangements, accompanied by a running commentary describing the principles at work.

Romano, Frank J. **Desktop Typography with Quark XPress.** Blue Ridge Summit, PA: Windcrest Books (Tab Books), 1988.

An indispensable guide for newsletter editors using Quark XPress, relating the tools of typographic manipulation to the specific Quark commands used to implement them. Users of other software programs will also benefit from this book, because many other programs offer similar commands.

Romano, Frank J. **The TypEncyclopedia: A User's Guide to Better Typography.** New York: R.R. Bowker, 1984.

A treasure trove of ideas presented in an easy-to-read oversized format. Organized alphabetically, it's valuable as both a quick reference source and a well-integrated, cover-to-cover read.

Ross, Tom, and Ross, Marilyn. **The Complete Guide to Self-Publishing: Everything you need to know to write, publish, promote and sell your own book.** Cincinnati, OH: Writers Digest Books, 1989.

Describes the next logical step after your subscription newsletter is a phenomenal success—turn it into a book! Lives up to its title by describing in detail all the steps necessary for success.

Sitarz, Daniel. **The Desktop Publisher's Legal Handbook: A Comprehensive Guide to Computer Publishing Law.** Carbondale, IL: Nova Publishing, 1989.

Explores legal issues involved in establishing a desktop publishing service business, to help you avoid libel and defamation problems. Contains sample client contracts and copyright registration forms.

Strunk, William, Jr., and White, E.B. **The Elements of Style**, Third Edition. New York: Macmillan, 1979.

Short, entertaining and extremely focused, this classic deserves its "indispensable" reputation earned over three-quarters of a century.

White, Alex. **How to Spec Type.** New York: Watson-Guptill, 1987.

A literate, lean text with striking visual examples distinguishes this guide to effective typography. Includes a strong section on designing initial caps.

White, Alex. **Type in Use.** New York: Design Press, 1990.

Further explores the seemingly infinite number of ways type can be placed and manipulated on a page. Contains hundreds of thought-provoking samples that will provide inspiration for newsletter editors.

White, Jan V. **Editing by design: A guide to effective word-and-picture communication for editors and designers**, Second Edition. New York: R.R. Bowker, 1982.

Still one of the most valuable resources available to desktop publishers on using graphic design as a tool of communication rather than adornment or decoration. Highly readable; full of interesting examples.

Zinsser, William. **On Writing Well.** New York: Harper & Row, 1987.

An excellent contemporary guide to effective writing. Will help newsletter editors develop their inherent abilities and learn to write as clearly and concisely as possible.

Zinsser, William. **Writing to Learn: How to Write—and Think—Clearly About Any Subject at All.** New York: Harper & Row, 1989.

Advice on how to build upon your newsletter editing skills and move into new territory.

Zinsser, William. **Writing with a Word Processor.** New York: Harper & Row, 1983.

Required reading for any typewriter-oriented newsletter editor who needs help making the transition to preparing copy with a word processor. Warm, friendly and useful.

PUBLICATIONS

Aldus Magazine, Aldus Corp., 411 First Ave. South, Ste. 200, Seattle, WA 98104. *Bimonthly.*

Provides inspiration to newsletter editors by showcasing documents produced with PageMaker and Freehand and describing how they were created using the latest design techniques and applications ideas.

Before & After: How to Design Cool Stuff on Your Computer, PageLab, Sacramento, CA.

A testament to the vision and talents of John McWade, one of the country's first—and, still, most influential—desktop designers. The emphasis is on design excellence, with an informative how-you-can-achieve-these-results tutorial approach.

EXpressions: The Newsletter from Quark, Quark, Inc., 300 S. Jackson St., Ste. 100, Denver, CO 80209. *Monthly.*

Presents news about the latest Quark XPress upgrades; Quark-specific tips and techniques; and third-party software that can help Quark users make the most of their program.

Font & Function: The Adobe Type Catalog, Adobe Systems, Inc., P.O. Box 7900, Mountain View, CA 94039-7900. *Thrice yearly.*

A quarterly publication describing the latest Adobe fonts and reviewing old favorites; also presents interviews with typeface users and typeface designers. If you use a PostScript laser printer, you owe it to yourself to request a free subscription to **Font & Function**.

In-House Graphics, United Communications, 4550 Montgomery Ave., Ste. 700N, Bethesda, MD 20814. *Monthly.*

An advertising-free publication containing a healthy and pragmatic mix of newsletter design and content articles that extend beyond the desktop to the commercial printing environment.

ITC Desktop, International Typeface Corp., 2 Hammarskjold Plaza, New York, NY 10017. *Bimonthly.*

Approaches desktop publishing from a design more than a hardware/software applications standpoint.

MacWeek, Coastal Associates Publishing, One Park Ave., New York, NY 10016. *Weekly (with few exceptions).*

Well-balanced reporting on the latest hardware and software issues, for newsletter editors using Macintosh systems.

Metropolis, Bellerphon Publications, New York. *Ten issues per year.*

In-depth coverage of all aspects of contemporary design—architecture, city planning (or lack thereof) and furnishings included—for the newsletter editor whose thirst for design excellence extends beyond the printed page.

Newsletter Design, The Newsletter Clearinghouse, 44 West Market St., P.O. Box 311, Rhinebeck, NY 12572. *Bimonthly.*

A great source of design inspiration; shows sample pages of all types of newsletters with commentary on what makes them succeed, along with suggestions for improvement.

Newsletter on Newsletters, The Newsletter Clearinghouse, 44 West Market St., P.O. Box 311, Rhinebeck, NY 12572. *Biweekly.*

Good advice on all aspects of newsletter publishing, including editorial, financial and graphic; updates on postal regulations and promotional ideas; opportunity to enter a yearly design competition.

PC Publishing, Hunter Publishing Co., Inc., 950 Lee St., Des Plaines, IL 60016. *Monthly.*

Trouble-shooting advice for newsletter editors who operate in the MS-DOS environment, plus news about the latest hardware and software advances.

Personal Publishing, Hitchcock Publishing Co., 25W550 Geneva Rd., Wheaton, IL 60188. *Monthly.*

Balanced treatment of both Macintosh and MS-DOS desktop publishing issues. The monthly software "Updates" feature alone is worth the price of a subscription.

Print: America's Graphic Design Magazine, RC Publications, Inc., 6400 Goldsboro Rd., Bethesda, MD 20817. *Bimonthly.*

Covers the techniques and economics of professional graphic design, keeping an eye on advances in desktop publishing. Its yearly Regional

Design and Advertising Design issues, as well as its book club selections, make it well worth the subscription price.

Publish! PCW Communications, Inc., 501 Second St., San Francisco, CA 94107. *Monthly.*

Combines in-depth treatment of the latest hardware and software issues with helpful design- and technique-oriented articles. Of special interest is its monthly typography column.

Step-by-Step Electronic Design: The How-To Newsletter for Desktop Designers. Dynamic Graphics, 6000 North Forest Park Dr., P.O. Box 1901, Peoria, IL 61656. *Monthly.*

This advertising-free, technique-oriented publication is geared to helping advanced desktop publishers and others who aspire to greater proficiency in layout and design.

The Page, Box 14493, Chicago, IL 60614. *Monthly.*

An example of newsletter publishing at its very best. Focused on the practical needs of Macintosh desktop publishers, it's impartial, informed, engaging and reader-friendly.

The Weigand Report: The Working Newsletter for Desktop Publishers, Rae Productions International, P.O. Box 647, Gales Ferry, CT 06335. *Eight issues per year.*

The subtitle accurately describes its function: unbiased reporting and analysis on the ever-changing hardware/software, image-scanning and commercial printing scenes, among other timely issues.

TypeWorld, Gama Publishing, Salem, NH. *Biweekly.*

Approaches desktop publishing from an advanced typesetter's perspective; forthright, unblinking comment on new hardware and software offerings months before you read about them elsewhere.

U&lc, International Typeface Corp., 2 Hammarskjold Plaza, New York, NY 10017. *Bimonthly.*

An inspiring large-format tabloid, containing features by many of the world's leading designers; balances a historical, intellectual perspective with down-to-earth treatment of contemporary issues.

Ventura Professional, Ventura Users Group, Morgan Park, CA. *Monthly*.

A one-stop source for tips and techniques to help newsletter editors who use Ventura Publisher get the most out of Ventura Professional—by itself, and in combination with other software programs.

WordPerfect: The Magazine, WordPerfect Publishing Corp., 1555 North Technology Way, Orem, UT 84057. *Monthly*.

Useful tips, techniques and features for newsletter editors using Word-Perfect as a page layout program, including reviews of basic Word-Perfect formatting commands and features that describe how to integrate WordPerfect with other software programs.

ASSOCIATIONS, USER GROUPS AND WORKSHOPS

Dynamic Graphics & Education Foundation
6000 North Forest Park Dr.
P.O. Box 1901
Peoria, IL 61656-1901

Workshops on Designing for Desktop Publishing, Basic Layout and Pasteup, Typography in Design, Publication Design, and more.

Electronic Directions
21 East Fourth St.
New York, NY 10003

Software-specific courses and seminars on Ventura Publisher, PC Pagemaker, Using Ready, Set, Go!, Using Quark Xpress, Using Adobe Illustrator, PostScript for Designers and more.

National Association of Desktop Publishers
P.O. Box 508, Kenmore Station
Boston, MA 02215

Sponsors seminars, publishes newsletter and quarterly.
Works toward establishing standards for desktop publishers.

Newsletter Association
1401 Wilson Blvd., Ste. 403
Arlington, VA 22209

Sponsors seminars and periodicals for newsletter editors and publishers.

Performance Seminar Group
204 Strawberry Hill Ave.
Norwalk, CT 06851

Seminars on Designing Effective Newsletters, How to Write and Design Sales Literature and more.

Promotional Perspectives
1955 Pauline Blvd., Ste. 100A
Ann Arbor, MI 48103

Seminars on Newsletter Editing, Design and Production and Fundamentals of Design for Desktop Publishing. Participants receive an unusually complete set of working tools and hand-out materials.

The Newsletter Clearinghouse
44 West Market St.
Rhinebeck, NY 12572

Publishes books and newsletters, membership listings and special studies. Sponsors seminars and design competitions.

RESOURCE GUIDE

It would be impossible to list all available desktop publishing hardware and software resources, since the industry is growing and changing constantly. Therefore, the listings that follow will serve only to get you started in your search for the perfect desktop publishing system.

To supplement the names given here, you'll find valuable information in the publications listed in the bibliography. And a great deal of help can come from computer users' groups, comparing notes with other newsletter editors, and taking advantage of vendors' toll-free phone numbers, trial diskettes and low-cost videotapes.

Abaton
48431 Milmont Dr.
Fremont, CA 94538
800-444-5321

Grayscale scanners and software for use with Macintosh or MS-DOS computers.

Adobe Systems
1585 Charleston Rd.
Mountain View, CA 94039
800-83-FONTS

Products for PostScript printers and high-resolution typesetters (Mac and DOS): printer hard disks; screen-font quality enhancers; typeface combination packs; drawing programs; clip-art packages.

Agfa Compugraphic
200 Ballardvale St.
Wilmington, MA 01887
800-622-8973

Font cartridges and downloadable typefaces for Hewlett-Packard (H-P) LaserJet printers; image scanners and high-resolution Post-Script-compatible phototypesetters.

Aldus
411 First Ave. So., Ste. 200
Seattle, WA 98104
206-628-6600

Freehand drawing program for the Mac; Snapshot image-grabber for DOS; PageMaker template packages for Mac and DOS.

Alsoft
P.O. Box 927
Spring, TX 77383
713-353-1510

Font Juggler—a font identification and font management program—for Mac environments.

Altsys Corp.
720 Avenue F, Ste. 109
Plano, TX 75074
214-424-4888

The Fontographer, for custom-designing typefaces for headlines, logos, nameplates, etc.

Apple Computer
20525 Mariani Ave.
Cupertino, CA 95041
408-996-1010

Macintosh computers; image scanners; PostScript and other printers; big-screen monitors.

Astral Development
Londonderry Square, Ste. 112
Londonderry, NH 03053
603-432-6800

Picture Publisher, the first, and still leading, photo image editor in the MS-DOS environment.

Berkeley Systems
1700 Shattuck Ave.
Berkeley, CA 94709
415-540-5535

Stepping Out II, a Macintosh utility providing enhanced small-screen monitoring.

Bitstream
Athenaeum House
214 First St.
Cambridge, MA. 02142
800-522-FONT

Large typeface library, compatible with Macintosh, MS-DOS and LaserJet or PostScript printers.

Casady & Greene
26080 Carmel Rancho Blvd., Ste. 202
Carmel, CA 93923
800-331-4321 (CA: 800-851-1986)

A variety of quality typefaces for Mac computers and PostScript printers.

Claris
5210 Patrick Henry Dr.
Santa Clara, CA 95052
408-987-7000

MacDraw, MacPaint and MacWrite—staples of the Macintosh environment since the earliest days of desktop publishing.

Computer Associates
10505 Sorrento Valley Rd.
San Diego, CA 92121
800-531-5236

Cricket Draw, Cricket Paint and Pict-o-graph programs for the Macintosh computer.

Computer Support
15926 Midway Rd.
Dallas, TX 75244
214-661-8960

Arts and Letters, a powerful MS-DOS drawing program; extensive collections of fonts and clip art.

Corel Systems
1600 Carling Ave.
Ottawa, Ontario, Canada K1Z 8R7
613-728-8200
Corel Draw, a popular drawing program for MS-DOS Windows.

Custom Applications
900 Technology Park Dr., Bldg. 8
Billerica, MA 01821
800-873-4367
Freedom of the Press, a software program for Mac and DOS computers; lets non-PostScript printers process PostScript files.

DataViz
35 Corporate Dr.
Trumbull, CT 06611
203-268-0030
MacLink Plus software and cable for file transfer between Mac and DOS computers.

Dayna Communications
50 South Main St., Ste. 530
St. Lake City, UT 84144
800-531-0600
External disk drives for the Mac, to permit reading and writing both 3 1/2- and 5 1/4-inch DOS diskettes.

Dynamic Graphics
5000 North Forest Park Dr.
Peoria, IL 61614
800-258-8800
Clip art for Mac and DOS environments.

Edco Services
12410 North Dale Mabry
Tampa, FL 33618
800-523-8973
LetraTuck, a Macintosh software program that lets you modify letter spacing.

Fifth Generation Systems
11200 Industriplex Blvd.
Baton Rouge, LA 70809
800-87-FIFTH
Suitcase II, a Mac desk accessory for font identification and preview of typeface choices.

Hewlett-Packard
19310 Pruneridge Ave.
Cupertino, CA 95014
800-,52-0900
Laser and inkjet printers and image scanners for both Mac and DOS environments; classic-design downloadable fonts and font cartridges; the PaintJet color printer for previewing two-color newsletters.

Intel
P.O. Box 14070
Portland, OR 97214
800-538-3373
Visual Edge increases resolution and grayscale range, and significantly reduces printing time.

IQ Engineering
P.O. Box 60955
Sunnyvale, CA 94086
408-733-1161
SuperCartridge, offering 55 fonts in one convenient H-P font cartridge.

Laser Connection
7852 Schillinger Pk. W.
Mobile, AL 36608
800-233-6687
QMS direct marketing division and major PostScript laser printer manufacturer, offering LaserJet font cartridges and PostScript adapter boards.

LaserMaster
7156 Shady Oak Rd.
Eden Prairie, MN 55344
612-USA-TYPE
Increased resolution for H-P LaserJet printers; on-the-fly font scaling for Bitstream outlines; special effects font manipulation programs; 19-inch monitor with accurate font displays.

Letraset USA
40 Eisenhower Dr.
Paramus, NJ 07653
800-343-TYPE
Advanced Mac page layout, image manipulation and font editing software programs.

Linotype Co.
425 Oser Ave.
Happauge, NY 11788
800-645-5764

Linotronic, the original high-resolution PostScript phototypesetter, has been upgraded, offers a full line of Mac typefaces.

Marketing Graphics
4401 Dominion Blvd., Ste. 210
Glen Allen, VA 23060-3379
800--368-3773

Business and government-oriented clip-art images for Mac and DOS.

Metro Imagebase
18623 Ventura Blvd., Ste. 210
Tarzana, CA 91356
800-525-1552

Functional clip art—exercise and fitness, food, sports and travel motifs—for Mac and DOS computers.

Micrografx
1303 Arapaho
Richardson, TX 75080
800-272-3729

Micrografx Designer popular drawing program; other charting and graphing programs; extensive clip-art collections.

Microsoft Corp.
16011 NE 36th Way
Redmond, WA 98052
800-426-9400

Powerful word processing, page layout, drawing, charting and graphing programs.

Microtek
680 Knox St.
Torrance, CA 90502
800-654-4160

Mac and DOS image scanners with advanced features.

Moniterm Corp.
5470 Green Circle Dr.
Minnetonka, MN 55343
612-935-4151

Big-screen Viking monitors, including grayscale models, to enhance MS-DOS newsletter publishing systems.

Monotype
2500 Brickvale Dr.
Elk Grove, IL 60007
800-MONOTYP
High-quality PostScript fonts for the Mac.

North Edge Software Corp.
239 Western Ave.
Essex, MA 01929
508-768-7490
Timeslips, a time-and-billing software program helpful to freelance newsletter designers and useful in accounting for time and money spent on revisions.

Pacific Data Products
6404 Nancy Ridge Dr.
San Diego, CA 92121
619-552-0880
Simple, plug-in PostScript board for H-P LaserJet printers.

Princeton Publishing Labs
198 Wall St.
Princeton, NJ 08540
609-924-1153
Fast PostScript upgrade boards for LaserJet printers, as well as high-resolution MS-DOS big-screen monitors and graphics adapter boards.

Quark
300 South Jackson, Ste. 100
Denver, CO 80209
800-356-9363
Quark XPress, a Macintosh page layout program with unparalleled typographic power; QuarkStyle, a less expensive version with several publication templates.

Radius
1710 Fortune Dr.
San Jose, CA 95131
800-527-1950
Monitors for Mac and DOS environments, including black-and-white, color and grayscale versions.

Reference Software
330 Townsend, Ste. 123
San Francisco, CA 94107
800-872-9933

Grammatik III, a DOS-based grammar checker for improper sentence structure and other embarrassing errors.

RightSoft
4545 Samuel St.
Sarasota, FL 34233
800-992-0244

RightWriter, a grammar checker for DOS computers.

Silicon Beach Software
9770 Carroll Center Rd.
San Diego, CA 92126
619-695-6956

Digital Darkroom, a pioneering image-manipulation program for Macs; page layout and advanced drawing programs.

Softcraft, Inc.
16 N. Carroll St., Ste. 500
Madison, WI 53703
800-351-0500

Font Solution Pack font editing and font manipulation programs, including special effects like shading and rotating type.

Software Publishing
1901 Landings Dr.
Mountain View, CA 94039-7210
800-255-5550

PFS:First Publisher, a powerful, low-cost DOS page layout program; clip-art and font collections; Harvard Graphics advanced charting and graphing program.

Solutions International
30 Commerce St.
Williston, VT 05495
802-658-5506

Curator manages Mac clip-art collections; Smartscrap saves and retrieves multiple graphic images.

T/Maker
1390 Villa St.
Mountain View, CA 94041
415-962-0195
Clip art for Mac and DOS—holiday, Christian and business themes.

Tops
950 Marina Village Pkwy.
Alameda, CA 94501
800-445-TOPS
TOPS system permits easy file-sharing between Mac computers, using the AppleTalk system.

Varityper
11 Mount Pleasant Ave.
East Hanover, NJ 07936
201-887-8000
High-resolution PostScript phototypesetters.

WordPerfect
1500 North Technology Way
Orem, UT 84057
Powerful page layout and word processing for Mac and MS-DOS, plus new MS-DOS DrawPerfect.

Xerox
Desktop Software Div.
9745 Business Park Ave.
San Diego, CA 98104
800-822-8221
Ventura Publisher, one of the most popular DOS page layout programs, soon available for the Mac.

Zsoft
540 Franklin Rd., Ste. 100
Marietta, GA 30067
404-428-0008
Publisher of Paintbrush IV, the latest version of the popular DOS paint-type program with extensive image-enhancement capabilities.

CREDITS

The following publications are reproduced in this book through the courtesy of their respective publishers:

Change, Glaxo, Inc., Research Triangle Park, NC

Channelmarker, Merrin Information Services, Inc., Palo Alto, CA

SAE Technical Paper Series, Society of Automotive Engineers, Warrendale, PA

Cram Notes, The George F. Cram Co., La Grange, TX

Ford Products, *The Power Report*, Agoura Hills, CA

Gramophone report, Gramophone ltd., Lutherville, MD

Harbor Light, The Salvation Army, Cleveland, OH

Infidelity, Keith Yates Audio, Sacramento, CA

In House Graphics, United Communications Group, Bethesda, MD

Issues Bulletin, The Food Marketing Institute, Washington, DC

LabLines, IBM, Cary, NC

Magnolia Hi-Fi & Video, Seattle, WA

MIT Club, MIT Club of Northern California, Cupertino, CA

Newsletter on Newsletters, Newsletter Clearinghouse, Rhinebeck, NY

Nucleus, Union of Concerned Scientists, Cambridge, MA
Designer is Herb Rich III.

Practical Supervision, Professional Training Associates, Inc., Round Rock, TX

Professional Telephone Selling, Bureau of Business Practice, Prentice Hall, Waterford, CT

Profiles, Don Richard Associates, Washington, DC

Providence Today, Providence Medical Center, Seattle, WA

Second Wind, Second Wind Advertising Services, Wyomissing, PA

Service Bureau Newsletter, Technology Database Associates, Westport, CT

Small Business Source, Upstart Publishing Co., Dover, NH

String Instrument Craftsman, Pen/Lens Productions, Milpitas, CA

The Consultant, Northern California Independent Computer Consulting Association, Walnut Creek, CA

The Network News, State of Washington Department of Social and Health Services, Olympia, WA

The Works, The Works Athletic Club, Somersworth, NH

The Weigand Report, P.O. Box 647, Gales Ferry, CT 06335

Future Views, Future Computing, Inc., Dallas, TX

Weekly Hardwood Review, Charlotte, NC

The following desktop graphic designers created original illustrations:

Cassell Design
Keith Cassell
3325 Chapel Hill Blvd.
Durham, NC 27707

Jo Northrup
1433 Nottingham Rd.
Raleigh, NC 27607

Creative Endeavors
Susan S. Worsley
Route 4, Box 371
Pittsboro, NC 27312

Jay Parsons
104-22 Melville Loop
Chapel Hill, NC 27514

INDEX

the
Ventana Press

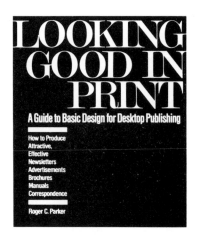

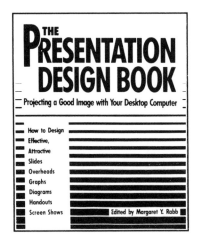

Desktop Design Series

Available from bookstores or Ventana Press. Immediate shipment guaranteed. Your money returned if not satisfied. To order or for more information contact:

Ventana Press, P.O. Box 2468, Chapel Hill, NC 27515
919/942-0220   FAX 919/942-1140

Looking Good in Print
(100,000 in print!)
$23.95
230 pages, Illustrated
ISBN: 0-940087-05-7

The most widely used reference book for desktop design offers dozens of tips and tricks that help you add style and appeal to your documents. For use with any hardware and software.

The Presentation Design Book
$24.95
280 pages, Illustrated
ISBN: 0-940087-37-5

How to design effective, attractive slides, overheads, graphs, diagrams, handouts and screen shows with your desktop computer.

The Makeover Book: 101 Design Solutions for Desktop Publishing
$17.95
245 pages, Illustrated
ISBN: 0-940087-20-0

"Before-and-after" desktop publishing examples demonstrate how basic design revisions can dramatically improve a document.

Type from the Desktop
$23.95
290 pages, Illustrated
ISBN: 0-940087-45-6

Learn the basics of designing with type from a desktop publisher's perspective.

Desktop Publishing with WordPerfect
$21.95
350 pages, Illustrated
ISBN: 0-940087-15-4

WordPerfect offers graphics capabilities that can save users thousands of dollars in design and typesetting costs. Includes invaluable information on creating style sheets for consistency and speed.

TO ORDER ADDITIONAL COPIES OF
NEWSLETTERS FROM THE DESKTOP

Please send me _____ additional copies of *Newsletters from the Desktop* at $23.95 per book. Add $3.60 per book for normal UPS shipping ($1 per book, thereafter); $5 for UPS "two-day" air. North Carolina residents add 5% sales tax. Immediate shipment guaranteed.

Note: 15% discount for purchases of 5-9 books. 20% discount for purchases of 10 or more books. Resellers please call for wholesale discount information.

Name _____ Co. _____

Address (no P.O. Box) _____

City _____ State _____ Zip _____

Daytime telephone _____

_____ Payment enclosed (check or money order; no cash please)

_____ Charge my VISA/MC Acc't # _____

Exp. Date _____ Interbank # _____

Signature _____

Ventana Press ■ P.O. Box 2468 ■ Chapel Hill, NC 27515 ■ 919/942-0220
FAX 919/942-1140 (Please don't duplicate your fax orders by mail.)

Please send me _____ additional copies of *Newsletters from the Desktop* at $23.95 per book. Add $3.60 per book for normal UPS shipping ($1 per book, thereafter); $5 for UPS "two-day" air. North Carolina residents add 5% sales tax. Immediate shipment guaranteed.

Note: 15% discount for purchases of 5-9 books. 20% discount for purchases of 10 or more books. Resellers please call for wholesale discount information.

Name _____ Co. _____

Address (no P.O. Box) _____

City _____ State _____ Zip _____

Daytime telephone _____

_____ Payment enclosed (check or money order; no cash please)

_____ Charge my VISA/MC Acc't # _____

Exp. Date _____ Interbank # _____

Signature _____

Ventana Press ■ P.O. Box 2468 ■ Chapel Hill, NC 27515 ■ 919/942-0220
FAX 919/942-1140 (Please don't duplicate your fax orders by mail.)

BUSINESS REPLY MAIL

FIRST CLASS PERMIT #495 CHAPEL HILL, NC

POSTAGE WILL BE PAID BY ADDRESSEE

Ventana Press

P.O. Box 2468

Chapel Hill, NC 27515

BUSINESS REPLY MAIL

FIRST CLASS PERMIT #495 CHAPEL HILL, NC

POSTAGE WILL BE PAID BY ADDRESSEE

Ventana Press

P.O. Box 2468

Chapel Hill, NC 27515

TO ORDER ADDITIONAL COPIES OF
NEWSLETTERS FROM THE DESKTOP

Please send me _____ additional copies of *Newsletters from the Desktop* at $23.95 per book. Add $3.60 per book for normal UPS shipping ($1 per book, thereafter); $5 for UPS "two-day" air. North Carolina residents add 5% sales tax. Immediate shipment guaranteed.

Note: 15% discount for purchases of 5-9 books. 20% discount for purchases of 10 or more books. Resellers please call for wholesale discount information.

Name _____ Co. _____

Address (no P.O. Box) _____

City _____ State _____ Zip_____

Daytime telephone _____

_____ Payment enclosed (check or money order; no cash please)

_____ Charge my VISA/MC Acc't # _____

Exp. Date _____ Interbank # _____

Signature _____

**Ventana Press ■ P.O. Box 2468 ■ Chapel Hill, NC 27515 ■ 919/942-0220
FAX 919/942-1140 (Please don't duplicate your fax orders by mail.)**

Please send me _____ additional copies of *Newsletters from the Desktop* at $23.95 per book. Add $3.60 per book for normal UPS shipping ($1 per book, thereafter); $5 for UPS "two-day" air. North Carolina residents add 5% sales tax. Immediate shipment guaranteed.

Note: 15% discount for purchases of 5-9 books. 20% discount for purchases of 10 or more books. Resellers please call for wholesale discount information.

Name _____ Co. _____

Address (no P.O. Box) _____

City _____ State _____ Zip_____

Daytime telephone _____

_____ Payment enclosed (check or money order; no cash please)

_____ Charge my VISA/MC Acc't # _____

Exp. Date _____ Interbank # _____

Signature _____

**Ventana Press ■ P.O. Box 2468 ■ Chapel Hill, NC 27515 ■ 919/942-0220
FAX 919/942-1140 (Please don't duplicate your fax orders by mail.)**

BUSINESS REPLY MAIL
FIRST CLASS PERMIT #495 CHAPEL HILL, NC

POSTAGE WILL BE PAID BY ADDRESSEE

Ventana Press

P.O. Box 2468

Chapel Hill, NC 27515

BUSINESS REPLY MAIL
FIRST CLASS PERMIT #495 CHAPEL HILL, NC

POSTAGE WILL BE PAID BY ADDRESSEE

Ventana Press

P.O. Box 2468

Chapel Hill, NC 27515

TO ORDER ADDITIONAL COPIES OF
NEWSLETTERS FROM THE DESKTOP

Please send me _____ additional copies of *Newsletters from the Desktop* at $23.95 per book. Add $3.60 per book for normal UPS shipping ($1 per book, thereafter); $5 for UPS "two-day" air. North Carolina residents add 5% sales tax. Immediate shipment guaranteed.

Note: 15% discount for purchases of 5-9 books. 20% discount for purchases of 10 or more books. Resellers please call for wholesale discount information.

Name _____ Co. _____

Address (no P.O. Box) _____

City _____ State _____ Zip _____

Daytime telephone _____

_____ Payment enclosed (check or money order; no cash please)

_____ Charge my VISA/MC Acc't # _____

Exp. Date _____ Interbank # _____

Signature _____

Ventana Press ■ P.O. Box 2468 ■ Chapel Hill, NC 27515 ■ 919/942-0220 FAX 919/942-1140 (Please don't duplicate your fax orders by mail.)

Please send me _____ additional copies of *Newsletters from the Desktop* at $23.95 per book. Add $3.60 per book for normal UPS shipping ($1 per book, thereafter); $5 for UPS "two-day" air. North Carolina residents add 5% sales tax. Immediate shipment guaranteed.

Note: 15% discount for purchases of 5-9 books. 20% discount for purchases of 10 or more books. Resellers please call for wholesale discount information.

Name _____ Co. _____

Address (no P.O. Box) _____

City _____ State _____ Zip _____

Daytime telephone _____

_____ Payment enclosed (check or money order; no cash please)

_____ Charge my VISA/MC Acc't # _____

Exp. Date _____ Interbank # _____

Signature _____

Ventana Press ■ P.O. Box 2468 ■ Chapel Hill, NC 27515 ■ 919/942-0220 FAX 919/942-1140 (Please don't duplicate your fax orders by mail.)

BUSINESS REPLY MAIL

FIRST CLASS PERMIT #495 CHAPEL HILL, NC

POSTAGE WILL BE PAID BY ADDRESSEE

Ventana Press

P.O. Box 2468

Chapel Hill, NC 27515

BUSINESS REPLY MAIL

FIRST CLASS PERMIT #495 CHAPEL HILL, NC

POSTAGE WILL BE PAID BY ADDRESSEE

Ventana Press

P.O. Box 2468

Chapel Hill, NC 27515